JEAN VIGO

P. E. Salles Gomes

D0815403

UNIVERSITY OF CALIFORNIA PRESS
Berkeley and Los Angeles

University of California Press
Berkeley and Los Angeles

© 1971 by The Regents of the University
of California

Library of Congress Catalog Card Number: 72–104102

ISBN: 0–520–01676–9

Note: The original French edition, *Jean Vigo*, was
published in the "Cinémathèque" series by Editions
du Seuil, 1957. Translated by permission. The
author's name is correctly given in this edition;
it was rendered as "Salès Gomès" in the original.

Printed in Great Britain by Jarrold and Sons Ltd, Norwich

Contents

To Henri Langlois, Ernest Lindgren
and Plinio Sussekind Rocha

Author's Note

This book was possible thanks to the cooperation of M. Claude Aveline who very kindly gave me free access to the film records in the Jean Vigo archives. Some personal material was kindly made available to me by Mme. Luce Vigo when I was in the process of writing the final draft.

The following persons were of great assistance, either by giving me personal information or by making certain documents available: Mlle. Antoinette Aubès, Messrs. Henri Storck, Pierre de Saint-Prix, Gilles Margaritis, Maurice Nicolas, Jean Colin, Jacques Bruel, Georges Caussat, Pierre Merle, Francis Jourdain, Jacques-Louis Nounez, Louis Chavance, Henri Beauvais, Charles Goldblatt, and Albert Riéra.

P.E.S.G.

Editor's Note

We are deeply indebted to Mme. Luce Vigo for her invaluable cooperation in providing the stills of Miguel Almereyda, Emily Cléro and the young Jean Vigo which appear in this volume. We are also grateful to M. Rui Nogueira, Mr. Brian Mills, and the National Film Archive for their kind help in obtaining stills.

1. Miguel Almereyda

Miguel Almereyda

Eugène Bonaventure de Vigo was the son of Eugène and the grandson of Bonaventure de Vigo, the magistrate and military chief of Andorra in 1882. Bonaventure de Vigo, proud of his descent from a line of petty provincial nobility[1] never accepted his son's liaison with Aimée Salles for, even though renowned for her beauty in the whole Perpignan region, she was a commoner. The birth of a grandson in 1883 did not make him change his mind. Eugène, who was tubercular, died at la Tour de Carol when he was twenty. Aimée Salles returned with her child to her parents' home in Perpignan. There a year later she met Gabriel Aubès, a young photographer from Sète who married her as soon as he had become established in business. The child stayed with Aimée's parents when the household left for the Dordogne before migrating to Paris. Aimée was irritable and unstable, so much so that the couple were not happy. When Eugène Bonaventure joined them at fifteen, the household's oppressive atmosphere and Aimée's irritability did not make understanding between him and those he addressed as "aunt" and "uncle" easy. Aubès helped him become an apprentice photographer, and the adolescent began living by himself in Paris.

He experienced unemployment, hunger, and loneliness, the latter somewhat mitigated by his association with anarchist circles, and his name was added to the files of Fouquet, head of the 3rd Brigade of Investigations, known as the Anarchist Brigade. Among the libertarians he made a great friend, Fernand Desprès, who was a little older than he.

After a long period of unemployment, Vigo joined the Manhès Company in the rue du Faubourg Saint-Honoré as a photographer. He had arranged to be paid each Saturday, but had started his first day without a penny. During lunch-time he would walk in the Tuileries Gardens and watch the birds eat. Before he had completed his first week, his landlord threatened to withhold his key if he did not pay his back rent. Manhès' thirteen-year-old son found him in the shop in tears, and Vigo confessed his misfortune. The boy found a solution: he took twenty francs from his father's cashbox. All that remained now was to wait until Saturday and replace the money. Unfortunately, Mme. Manhès checked the cashbox, questioned her son, and pressed charges. The charges were withdrawn after Vigo's explanation, but he had to look for another job. One day, towards the end of May 1900, he was arrested: the public prosecutor had taken official action against him as an accessory in the receipt of stolen goods. This step was taken because of the file on him as an anarchist, and Vigo was sentenced to two months in prison, a sentence he served at la Petite Roquette. His reaction was one of defiance, and he replaced the name Vigo with one in which "there is shit" [y a (de) la merde]: Almereyda. The choice of this anagram is explained by the belief of certain libertarian circles in the revolutionary virtues of "obscenities." The result, Miguel Almereyda, sounded Spanish and anarchist.

Once out of prison, Vigo-Almereyda found work with M. Gallay, a photographer on the Boulevard Saint-Denis; he made a bomb with which to take his revenge; and he published his first article in *Le Libertaire*,[2] about the gesture he was preparing. He bided his time, awaiting public reaction, which in this case took the form of advice to be prudent liberally showered on him by his mother and Gabriel Aubès. This advice exasperated him and resulted in a second article, "Du Calme,"[3] dedicated "to my Aunt" (his mother) and "to M. Aubès," whom he no longer wanted to call "uncle". The seventeen-year-old pamphleteer reveals himself as something of a cad: he reminds his mother and Aubès of their youthful adventures, and concludes by praising "the pride of the individual, brutally and haughtily asserting itself."

He manufactured his bomb: a small amount of magnesium powder, with sulphur to set off the explosion, all in a small shoe-polish can, bound with wire and with a hole punched in it into which he placed a tinder fuse.

The judge who had sent him to jail was the chosen victim, but afraid of harming innocent bystanders, Almereyda, after having lit the fuse, left this bomb in a *pissoir* near the Place Voltaire and stood watch some sixty feet away. It failed even to explode and the young anarchist left, much annoyed.

One day Fouquet summoned him for questioning about a friend arrested for possession of explosives. At random, the inspector asked him about a collection of bombs which he had in a cupboard. When he brought out the small tin can, the police officer's trained eye noticed some hesitation on Almereyda's part and he threatened him until he finally confessed.

In court, on June 26, 1901, an official police chemist, M. Girard, stated that the explosive in the box was of an unknown substance and of remarkable power. Almereyda, speechless with emotion and bursting with pride, said nothing, explained nothing, and found himself sentenced to a year in prison, which he served almost entirely in solitary confinement in semidarkness and silence. Almereyda was never to forget the warders who would pretend to walk away so as to catch the boys trying to speak to each other and then beat them with the huge bunches of keys they carried and used as brass knuckles. A guard named Cornua used to walk silently by the open peepholes in the cell doors and spit through them into the face of any boy who came close enough.

Up until then, Almereyda's mother and Gabriel Aubès had tried, clumsily perhaps, to help the young rebel, but now even this slim support had vanished. Aimée had gone insane and been committed to an institution. Aubès had left for Sète, where he again took up his profession.

Almereyda's imprisonment had not gone unnoticed. Laurent Tailhade had written about it in an article. Fernand Desprès had sought the help of a young anarchist painter, Francis Jourdain, who in turn had alerted Séverine, widow of Jules Vallès, and together they launched a campaign urging a pardon for Almereyda. They succeeded only a month before his sentence was up and went to the prison to collect the young man, who struck them as a "poor and generous little rebel, intelligent, courageous and full of good will."[4] However, Jourdain also noted: "After we had paced up and down in front of the prison, Fernand [Desprès] and I finally saw a gaunt, sad-looking boy come out. His face was as pale as the dawn which watched over us. . . . When we finally arrived in Montmartre, reassured by the steadiness of his step we let him accompany us to a friend's whom we were helping to move; Miguel, in the grip of some sort of fainting spell, collapsed under the weight of a wardrobe. When he finally came to, it was to find Fargue, his usual witty self, seated behind a cup of coffee and gravely focusing on him the Kodak he always carried with him but never loaded with any film."[5]

Séverine took Almereyda to the country; he returned a month later in fine fettle. He found a job with the photographer Gershell, Boulevard des Capucines, and his name soon appeared again in *Le Libertaire*, this time at the end of an antimilitarist manifesto, together with the names of Sébastien Faure, Pierre Monatte, Fernand Desprès, Victor Méric, Francis Jourdain, and a few others.[6]

At the beginning of October Almereyda saw some angry men assault a child who had been caught stealing some pieces of wood. His nerves still frayed by his recent experience of the power of the adult world, he intervened violently and the same spontaneous impulse induced him to write a short article which Matha, the editor of *Le Libertaire*, liked. From then on Almereyda wrote regularly for the paper, and by the beginning of 1903 had become one of the anarchist organ's most active collaborators. In March he quit Gershell's and photography to dedicate himself entirely to political agitation and journalism.

Then came the blackest period in his life. One day, while trying to organize a meeting at the Sociétés Savantes, he fainted from hunger in the Labour

Exchange, although he had for several days been carrying the money required to rent the hall in his pocket.

In the spring of 1903 Almereyda, now twenty years old, had his first encounter with love; he met Emily Cléro, a young militant slightly older than he. To be with him she left her companion Philippe Auguste, a wood sculptor. She had had several children by Auguste, but nearly all of them had died at an early age. One of the survivors had been the victim of a horrible accident; she had let the child fall from a window. Francis Jourdain remembers Emily as a very reserved woman of rare stamina and probably not very sensitive, with the faint suggestion of a smile as her only affectation—hiding her bad, tiny, underdeveloped teeth, barely protruding above her gums. Emily had for both Almereyda and their cause a discreet devotion, never spectacular, but always constant.

At the time Almereyda was strongly attracted to anarcho-individualist views. The thinking of Julien Grave, even of Kropotkin, struck him as largely academic. He did not long restrict himself to ideological arguments, and soon antimilitarist action became his exclusive concern. In June 1904 the Dutch anarchist Domela Nieuwenhuis organized an international antimilitarist congress in Amsterdam. Thanks to public subscription[7] a large French delegation including Almereyda, who was to become one of the leading figures of the congress, was able to go to Holland. One of his proposals served as the basis for the proclamation of a new Association Internationale Antimilitariste or A. I. A.

Almereyda thought that he had found an instrument for revolution in that organization, and he was the moving spirit of the French section of the A. I. A. It was mainly composed of anarchists and syndicalists, whose positions were then ideologically very close, but it also included writers with libertarian attitudes and a few socialists. A first national congress was to take place in the near future in Saint-Etienne.

One April evening after one of his innumerable meetings in support of the congress, Almereyda and several of his friends, including Francis Jourdain, had lingered to talk, and they continued as they accompanied Almereyda to the door of his home. "Are you coming up to see my latest addition?" Almereyda asked his friends. "Another one?" they said in tones of reproachful amusement. Almereyda had a mania for cats. He had already littered his single attic room with a number of foul-smelling, famished alley cats. Francis Jourdain had often reproached him for fouling the tiny room with his animals and most of all for sacrificing part of the meagre rations he had for Emily and himself. Raging at Almereyda, everyone nevertheless went up with him to see the new boarder. They were stunned when they found that a slightly pale-looking Emily had a child in her arms. The evening before she had gone out with them. As usual, she had gone home only after the inevitable prolonged café arguments. The child had been born a few hours later without a sound from the mother to disturb the neighbours. No one in the building knew, any more than her friends had, that Emily was pregnant. Once over the initial surprise, the incident seemed so funny that everyone burst out laughing.

Miguel Almereyda

The discreet arrival into the world of Jean Vigo on April 26, 1905, in the rue Polonceau in Paris, the son of undernourished parents, in a dirty little attic room full of scrawny cats, was greeted as a "miracle of comedy."[8]

Almereyda was happy to be a father. Emily was as determined as ever to accompany Almereyda everywhere. During his trips in preparation for the congress, Emily resigned herself to staying at home with the newborn child.

The child had been nicknamed Nono, after the hero in one of Jean Grave's children's stories. In Janine Champol, a revolutionary full of memories of the Paris Commune, and an admirer of Almereyda, they found a tender nursemaid. Mme. Blanc, a concierge and midwife, married to a syndicalist militant, also took care of Jean. However, neither she nor Janine was always available, and not being able to leave the child alone in the house with the cats the Almereydas had to take him around with them everywhere they went. "Often, at meetings," Francis Jourdain recalls, "one could hear the squealings of the famished baby. While he continued with his analysis of the political situation or his refutation of an adversary's arguments, Miguel, at the speaker's stand, would take a bottle from his pocket and hold it out to a comrade, who would pass it to the interested party. . . .

"On other evenings poor Jean slept amid the conscientiously maintained smoke of the noisy propagandists at the rue Polonceau. When the clamour of our voices woke him, his father, without ever ceasing to gesticulate, would lean over the crib and rock his son to and fro until the kid went back to sleep. By midnight we would all get very thirsty and go for a beer at the Pioch, a bar on the Boulevard Barbès. Rain or snow, Nono was taken out of his crib, wrapped in a blanket and carried in his mother's arms. She was extremely tired and yet never complained, patiently waiting until we had solved the social problem."[9]

At the Saint-Etienne congress, which took place in July 1905, Almereyda became acquainted with Gustave Hervé, a young history teacher from a lycée in Sens, and an ardent antimilitarist activist. Three months later they stuck "the red poster", signed by the members of the A.I.A. coordinating committee elected at Saint-Etienne, on walls all over Paris. In it they exhorted future soldiers to respond by insurrection to any attempt to mobilize them. Brought before a criminal court, they were found guilty on December 30. When compared with the socialist-revolutionary speech made by Hervé at the trial, an extremely courageous statement made by Almereyda nonetheless reveals a very definite confusion and ideological impoverishment. Leaderless, the A.I.A. was on the verge of collapse. Certain militants attributed this deterioration to the fact that the anarchists in the A.I.A. organization had become corrupted by their contact with the collectivists in the same organization.

At Clairvaux Prison, Almereyda, the anarchist, and Hervé, the collectivist, were getting along better and better. Hervé's knowledge of history opened up new horizons for Almereyda. Hervé, for his part, found a revolutionary fervour in Almereyda which he felt was terribly lacking in the socialist party.

Everyone was freed by an amnesty on July 14, 1906, and at the end of that same year Almereyda and his friend, Eugène Merle, founded the weekly *La Guerre Sociale*. At their request, Gustave Hervé became a sort of editor-in-chief. The other staff writers were a judicious mixture of anarchists, socialists, and syndicalists.

This is not the place to recount in detail the rich history of *La Guerre Sociale*. At the time, the Clemenceau government was the *bête noire* of the revolutionaries. Because of the intensity of their hatred for the government, *La Guerre Sociale* even went so far as to print an issue with an enormous headline: "Down With The Republic! If the old monarchist parties had any guts at all they would sweep the republican gang out of office and not one of us would lift a finger in its defence."[10]

Maurras, Pujo, and their friends pricked up their ears. The staff of *L'Action Française* and *La Guerre Sociale* were soon to become better acquainted at La Santé prison.

The constant calls to revolt directed at soldiers resulted in a shower of prison sentences for *La Guerre Sociale*. Almereyda's share was a two-year sentence awarded in April 1908 for having praised the mutiny of the Seventeenth Battalion at Narbonne, plus another year for an article criticizing the Moroccan Expedition. While in prison, he collected several additional weeks for insults against Clemenceau.

The prisoners, who never ceased to insist that the authorities treat them in a way appropriate to their status as political prisoners, were now claiming the right to be alone in their cells with relatives and friends during visiting hours. After much insistence, and numerous letters from Almereyda, all of which the administration forwarded, Clemenceau finally agreed to grant permission for mother, father, and legal wife. He specified "legal" wife, fully understanding what that entailed. The effect was devastating since no one was legally married. Almereyda again wrote a long letter to Clemenceau pointing out that in revolutionary circles no importance was attached to legal ceremonies, and cited his own case—that he had lived for a long time with his mistress, who had borne his child—as an example. In addition, he could not resist including in his letter all the anarchist arguments in favour of "free love." It seems that the head of the government when confronted with the letter exploded, "What's this! They're making a fool of me!" But he finally relented—with one restriction: "All right, let them receive their women. But careful! I insist that they must always be the same ones!" Almereyda was overjoyed, and not only did he sometimes pursue conjugal life in his prison cell, but also an intimate family life. He celebrated Christmas with Emily and Nono, who was now over three and received his gifts there.

Clemenceau was also at odds with the Royalists, whose activities increased daily. During a certain period all those closest to Maurras and Daudet—Pujo, Real del Sarte, and Plateau—were imprisoned in La Santé. They made good companions for the revolutionaries, and together they envisioned the possibility of an alliance between the extreme right and the extreme left in a common fight against the republican government.

Miguel Almereyda remained in prison until August 1909. His health had deteriorated, but as soon as he was freed he threw himself into a campaign in support of Francisco Ferrer, the educator who had been condemned to death in Barcelona. For a few days *La Guerre Sociale* became a daily, and Almereyda played an important part in the demonstrations which culminated in the organization of a gigantic march of 500,000 people, led by Jaurès.

Realizing to what degree the different revolutionary groups had been superseded by the course of events, the need for a central revolutionary organization became very apparent to Hervé and Almereyda. Ideologically they had already gone beyond antimilitarism to revolutionary militarism. Both thought that soldiers should not merely be made to reject their profession, but rather that they should be won over to revolutionary ideas.

For months Almereyda worked with the different groups with the idea of creating a Revolutionary Party. Then he plunged into the "Liabeuf affair,"* for which he was primarily responsible. On the day the young cobbler was guillotined, a crowd consisting of several tens of thousands, led by Almereyda, crowded around the barricades built near the Saint-Jacques intersection at two in the morning chanting, "Murderers! Murderers!" Revolver shots rang out and a detective from the Anarchist Brigade was killed. A comrade of

---

* Unjustly accused of being a pimp, Liabeuf had killed an officer of the vice squad.

Russian origin named Kibaltchiche, later known as Victor Serge, was at Almereyda's side.

An article defending Liabeuf resulted in a long sentence for Hervé, and Almereyda found himself in sole charge of the paper. With more on his hands than he could handle, he sent Nono for a short stay with Gabriel Aubès, who had set up a photography studio in Montpellier. Aubès had taken a niece as a partner and she became very attached to Jean. Subsequently, Mlle. Aubès often asked whether the child, for whom these visits to the south were real periods of recuperation, could come to stay. The frenetic pace of Almereyda and Emily's lives was undermining their health as well as their son's.

The railroad strike in October 1910 offered the group associated with *La Guerre Sociale* great opportunities, and they created a combat group to coordinate sabotage. Almereyda and Merle soon rejoined Hervé in the political section of La Santé prison. There they continued to rethink their ideology and realized that the activities of the nationalist right had become menacing.

Freed in March 1911, Almereyda established the "Jeunes Gardes Révolutionnaires." The police soon became acquainted with their courage, and thirty years later Lépine in his memoirs still remembered them.

Having quite definitely got over their libertarian optimism, Almereyda and his friends now wanted to organize everything, and they wanted to undertake, in a coherent and consistent manner, a counterespionage operation. The "Organization for Revolutionary Security" was in charge. They started by exposing one of the directors of *Le Libertaire* as a police agent, and they then discovered that a syndicalist militant, Lucien Métivier, was a police informer. They summoned him, and a few hours later, in the presence of representatives from several newspapers, the staff of *La Guerre Sociale* constituted themselves a revolutionary tribunal and passed judgment on the informer. He confessed and they were astounded to learn that he had been personally recruited by Clemenceau.

The next day the entire press criticized the underhand way in which each of the successive French governments, from Clemenceau to Caillaux, the most recent, had confronted the working-class movement. Caillaux retaliated by having *La Guerre Sociale* raided, but Almereyda and Merle left for Belgium where their friend Victor Serge, still known as Kibaltchiche, welcomed them. Both Almereyda and Kibaltchiche had changed a great deal since their last meeting. Almereyda, who felt that he was becoming more and more "realistic," found Victor full of Tolstoyan whimsy and quite openly made fun of him. Kibaltchiche calmly replied: "You will never be more than an '*arriviste*,' you started off wrong." To which Almereyda, exasperated, answered: "You don't understand what's going on in Paris, my friend. Forget about Russian novels. In Paris, the revolution needs money."[11]

During the trial for sequestration and breach of privacy which Almereyda had to face in August, he proved that Métivier was an "agent provocateur" who had thrown a bomb at the home of a journalist from *La Patrie*, and the whole group associated with *La Guerre Sociale* was acquitted with the jury's congratulations.

Almereyda continued his tireless campaign to unite all revolutionaries (Communists, libertarians, disciples of Jules Guesde, disciples of Jaurès). At the same time disagreement between *La Guerre Sociale* and the revolutionary syndicalists blossomed.

At the end of 1911, in a brawl with the police, Almereyda was struck on the head by a sabre and was forced to spend a week in bed. Just as he recovered, an attack of nephritis returned him to bed. He got up to prepare a special eight-page issue of *La Guerre Sociale* filled with letters from celebrities to Gustave Hervé, still in prison. The scope of *La Guerre Sociale*'s sympathies had greatly broadened. They now went from anarchism, syndicalism, and extreme left-wing socialism represented by Vincent Auriol, to the right-wing socialism of Marcel Sembat by way of Guesde and Jaurès. They had almost attained a position closer to liberalism than to a truly revolutionary one.

La Guerre Sociale was still continuing its campaign for alliance between revolutionary groups, but at the same time it gave more and more emphasis to the republican ideal. As is common in France, a leftist organization fostering social struggle was evolving into a leftist political party.

The break between *La Guerre Sociale* and most of the anarchists occurred in October 1912, and in December Almereyda joined the Socialist Party. His friends, Merle and Emile Dulac, and the "young guards" followed in his footsteps.

In the opening months of 1913 Almereyda led his Jeunes Gardes in a series of raids that swept the royalist toughs out of the Latin Quarter. Radical and socialist professors and politicians were quite pleased at now being able to deliver their speeches and lectures in the Latin Quarter in peace. Almereyda recovered among the liberal bourgeoisie of the capital the prestige he had lost in anarchist and syndicalist circles. The feat which *La Guerre Sociale*'s staff had accomplished by increasing its circulation from 15,000 in 1908 to 50,000 in 1913 had created quite a stir; Almereyda was considered one of the best desk editors in Paris, and this reputation resulted in both Merle and him being invited to collaborate on the weekly *Courrier Européen*, a journal of international politics which Charles Paix-Séailles was preparing to publish in a new series. In March 1913 Hervé made an emotional announcement of his departure with Almereyda and Merle from *La Guerre Sociale*.

The two friends made new contacts and prepared to realize an old project of theirs, a satirical weekly. Paix-Séailles gave them the means with which to start *Le Bonnet Rouge* in November 1913. He encouraged them to turn it into a daily, which they did on March 24, 1914. Almereyda became editor-in-chief, and Merle became general editor. The staff was rounded out by a group of young people, almost all of whom were already old comrades: Victor Méric, Goldsky, Dolié, Maurice Fournier, Fanny Clar, and Raphaël Diligent. By the first issue the money had been swallowed up and, as Fournier says, it was thanks to "the exceptional devotion of friends and collaborators that the paper was able to continue to appear."[12] It was also thanks to the radical leader Joseph Caillaux, who supported the paper because it had defended his wife when she appeared in criminal court charged with having killed the director of *Le Figaro*.

When confronted with the European crisis before the outbreak of war, Almereyda, short on ideology, simply reproduced Hervé's editorials. On July 31, *Le Bonnet Rouge* reproduced an article titled "Revolutionary Militarism" in which their previous formulation took on a new meaning. "And today, as in 1793, today, as in the days of *total war* waged by the Commune, our revolutionary patriotism, should it prove necessary, will be the last great resort and ultimate safeguard of our endangered country."

Le Bonnet Rouge, like *La Guerre Sociale*, joined with the rest of the syndicalist and socialist press in accepting the war. The ease with which the whole progressive press had been conned, as exemplified by the French papers, revealed the general collapse of the European working-class movement brought on by the outbreak of war.

Almereyda was at the Café Croissant with Nono, who was playing with the owner's son, when Jaurès was assassinated. Almereyda's articles at the outbreak of hostilities were barely distinguishable from the rest of the French press. After war had been declared, Almereyda had persuaded Malvy, the Minister of the Interior, not to implement Plan B, that famous list of suspects who were to have been arrested automatically should mobilization occur. A link had been established between them, perhaps even a certain friendship. The circulation of *Le Bonnet Rouge* had fallen drastically. Malvy gave Almereyda a subsidy from the Ministry of the Interior's secret funds.

After the battle of the Marne there was a sudden change of tone in Almereyda's articles. He had visited the battlefields, and in the articles recording his impressions he did not talk of Krauts, barbarians, or the heroism of French soldiers. He spoke only of young men's dead bodies and of the horrors of the war. On January 1, 1915, while drawing up the balance sheet of the events of the previous year, Almereyda wrote: "You have roused our atavistic instincts and you have stirred up the monster in each of us."

At the same time, it became clear that the Union Sacrée was no longer relevant, and that the question was whether the war would be waged from a rightist perspective or a leftist one. The government in power was on the whole leftist in orientation, but the nationalist, Church, and militarist forces did not want to waste a good opportunity. *Le Bonnet Rouge* adopted a line in "defence of the Republic"; praising the legislative body, the government and "non-Jesuit" generals like Sarrail, an old Dreyfus supporter; fighting against the clergy's influence; and criticizing Barrès and *L'Echo de Paris* as well as *L'Action Française*. Many members of the legislature started to contribute to *Le Bonnet Rouge*. They ranged from leftist elements in the Radical Party such as Ferdinand Buisson and Edouard Herriot to the right and centre elements in the Socialist Party, Marcel Cachin and Jean Longuet, who was Marx's grandson.

When, in August 1915, Sarrail was appointed Commander of the Army in the East, headquartered in Salonika, Almereyda gave a good deal of coverage

Jean Vigo

to the appointment. For the purpose of starting a press campaign, *Le Bonnet Rouge*, through Paix-Séailles, received secret documents on the military situation in the East. In the future, Almereyda was to receive confidential documents more than once, again for the purpose of fostering press campaigns. Whether used or not, he locked them up in the newspaper safe.

Le Bonnet Rouge had started to attack certain members of the government such as Millerand, and its anticlerical tone got more vehement each day. It is difficult to discern a coherent political line in Almereyda's paper at that time. His articles had become very short, and there were long periods in which he wrote nothing at all. He was busy with other things. To provide for the paper's financial needs and for his own by now quite substantial ones, Almereyda had to become involved in all sorts of business deals.

One of the first campaigns undertaken by *Le Bonnet Rouge* had been against alcoholism; now the paper was defending the use of absinthe which was threatened by the possible implementation of a law against it. The paper had started to receive subsidies from the Pernod firm and from a syndicate of liquor wholesalers, money which was passed on through Marion, an advertising agent who sometimes gave Almereyda quite substantial advances.

A good portion of these subsidies was used by Almereyda for his personal needs. In effect, since he had become the head of a newspaper with contacts among the politicians and businessmen of the radical bourgeoisie (the circle of "depraved pleasure-seekers whose morality recalls the morality of the Directoire," as the sober Hervé once lamented[13]), Almereyda's private life had gone through even deeper changes than his political life. It is possible by examining documents to trace the different stages of the latter evolution. Library research, most of the time, will not furnish us with any information about his private life not derived from the distortions of political polemics, and evaluating the results demands a sifting out of the most careful sort. To mention only the three topics recurring most constantly in his adversaries' articles—automobiles, houses, and mistresses—their number and their nature always vary. Monniot tells us of "three expensive mistresses, three residences and three cars."[14] Daudet on his part speaks of two households, a private mansion, and a villa in Saint-Cloud, and of the "five or six automobiles Almereyda owned."[15]

Whatever the facts, in 1915 his old friend Francis Jourdain stopped seeing him. "I quit seeing Miguel, quite bewildered. Editor of a daily paper, he had a car, a mansion, servants, and expensive mistresses."[16] Coming out of prison, Kibaltchiche went to visit him at the *Bonnet Rouge* office and found him in his "Second Empire chocolate-box style editor's office on the Grands Boulevards, more elegant, more Rastignac than ever." Just as nearly all the other revolutionaries had done, he too soon stopped seeing Almereyda who, as the ironical saying went, was "involved in high level politics somewhere in the low sidelines of high finance."[17]

Allowing for some delirious ranting about the number of automobiles and the private mansion, Daudet's statement seems closest to the truth. Following the fashion of the world in which he then revolved, Almereyda had installed his favourite mistress, Emilienne Brévennes, in a Montmartre apartment, and had rented a villa in Saint-Cloud for himself and his family—that is, for Emily and Nono. Emily led her own life; the child hardly ever saw his parents, both of whom were caught up in the frenzy of their lives, and he spent most of his time at home with the servants.

Jean sometimes had the joyous but rare experience of going on short vacations with his father, whom he adored. He often went to the countryside with Fanny Clar, who had become his great friend, and it was to her that he confided his discoveries and impressions of men, nature, and animals, some of which the newspaperwoman used in her column.[18] Usually he spent his summer vacations in the south with the Aubès.

At Saint-Cloud, it was usually only in the evenings on the point of dashing out that Almereyda found time to embrace his son, by that time already in bed. Later, when Jean wanted to describe his father to a friend,[19] he would evoke Almereyda as he was on those evenings, perfumed and impeccably tailored in evening dress. . . .

In his novel, Louis Dumur draws a malicious portrait of Almereyda as he then was, a portrait which nevertheless tallies in some ways with contemporary photographs: "a man still young, thin, almost slender, of somewhat dubious, almost vulgarly overdressed elegance, clad in an expensive otter-skin coat with a soft felt hat worn to one side and slightly on the back of his head, under which appeared a pale oval face, overly pretty with a feverish and debauched expression, a small southern moustache, very fine wavy, curled, silky black hair, and beautiful dark eyes, velvety, captivating, and with hints of depravity in them."[20]

In a story which appeared in *Paris-Télégrammes*, about one of Almereyda's stays in Paramé, we read that "he arrived by car accompanied by a very elegant woman, flanked by a Negro who served as chauffeur, by a Spanish valet, and by two enormous dogs."[21]

These descriptions, fragmentary and subject to caution as they are, nevertheless conjure up an altogether different Almereyda from the one of the days of *Le Libertaire* and *La Guerre Sociale*.

Almereyda was to spend the last of his energy in the renewed struggle against *L'Action Française*. The campaign was launched on June 6, 1915, by the initiation of a page one rubric "Servants of a Foreign Master." Daudet replied the next day with "Vigo the Traitor." A battle of murderous violence began in which no holds were barred. Almereyda used police sources made available to him by Malvy, while Daudet was supported by the military police.

Without ever clarifying what he actually meant, Daudet never stopped insinuating meaningfully that it was not by chance that Vigo hid himself under the name of Almereyda, and that the change of name was the key to many mysteries. In a suit brought against Almereyda by *L'Action Française*, the lawyer for the defendant had to explain: "In fact," Maître de Monzie said in his summation statement, "Miguel Almereyda is indeed a pseudonym, my client's real name is Eugène Bonaventure de Vigo. He is the grandson of

Jean Vigo

the former magistrate and military chief of Andorra."[22] This was the first time that the magistrate's shadow had been invoked in public but that did not prevent Daudet, soon followed by Barrès and others, from flaunting the name "de Vigo" in Almereyda's face, first as a threat, then as an accusation, and finally as an insult.

Meanwhile, Almereyda had started to criticize the government of Viviani and Malvy, who had advised legislators to contribute no longer to *Le Bonnet Rouge*, while they cancelled the government subsidy.

Merle was in the army, and Almereyda's lack of administrative ability, aggravated by the chaos of his personal life and by his increasingly precarious health, was leading *Le Bonnet Rouge* into bankruptcy. Marion, once again, obtained funds, but he also brought with him a man called Duval to manage the paper.

Duval had been a minor employee in the Public Welfare Department and had become a journalist late in life. He was about fifty years old, and his political background was quite different from that of *Le Bonnet Rouge*'s staff. He had been the electoral representative for the nationalist Dausset and editor-in-chief of the *Revue Française*, a rather clerical rightist journal. After the outbreak of the war, with Dausset's help, he had become administrator of a bankrupt company up for liquidation (San Stefano). Representing the interests of the French capitalists, Duval often went to Switzerland, on a regular passport furnished to him by the Ministry of the Interior. He took advantage of his stays there and of the contacts he had established with representatives of German interests in his company, to compile reports on the internal situation in Germany, which he then passed on to the Sûreté Générale. The quite substantial sums at his disposal allowed him to lend *Le Bonnet Rouge* as much as the paper wanted to borrow and even to participate later in the establishment of a new paper. Yet, Duval never stopped leading a modest life—and that too distinguished him in his new environment—with his illiterate wife, a humble washerwoman at the Lariboisière hospital who never gave up her job there. Duval was quite a sophisticated and alert man; in addition to carrying out his duties as an administrator, he was soon to give the full measure of his talent in a new by-line in *Le Bonnet Rouge*, for which he was to be responsible.

Despite the determination of the censors, the pacifist tone of *Le Bonnet Rouge* intensified and the paper published all of Romain Rolland's articles and appeals, a fact which was particularly held against the paper during the 1918 trial. Simultaneously, Almereyda tried to direct the paper to support various ways by which peace might be obtained: Caillaux's ideas of a negotiated peace, and the minority socialists who had separated from the holy union. The defence of "the Zimmerwald and Kienthal groups" which had first been justified as patriotic was henceforth justified in terms of supporting revolutionary internationalism.

Almereyda's bad state of health had become alarming. In order to resist the pain which grew worse day by day, he had recourse to morphine. A first operation brought him some relief without, however, giving him the strength to give up the drug. Around him, people began to foresee the possibility of his death. Duval, whose loans now amounted to more than 150,000 francs, was preparing, together with Marion, to take over the newspaper.

While recovering from a second operation at Marseilles, Almereyda had a sudden burst of energy and left for Paris at the end of 1916, to straighten out *Le Bonnet Rouge*'s financial situation. From Cohen, a banker and business-man, he obtained 200,000 francs, which allowed him to make partial repay-ment to Duval.

Almereyda's views on the issue of peace suddenly became very tenable at the beginning of 1917. Wilson's intervention, asking the belligerents to make their war aims known as a preliminary condition to the peace negotiations, was received with enthusiasm. The Russian revolution in March was re-ceived with even greater enthusiasm, and on May 2, 1917 *Le Bonnet Rouge* divulged the explanations of Lenin (considered by the French press as a whole as an agent of the German General Staff) relative to the conditions under which he had crossed through German territory.

Between the end of April and the end of June the situation at the front lines took a revolutionary turn. Officers were executed, red flags appeared, and soldiers sang the "Internationale." They learned that Indo-Chinese soldiers were shooting women on strike in Paris, and the mutineering soldiers wanted to march on the capital.

These facts were not to become common knowledge until much later. At any rate, there was no organized group in France capable of exploiting the revolutionary crisis and thereby changing the course of events. As for the working class, the nucleus created after the start of the war around Pierre Monatte, Alfred Rosmer and Fernand Desprès, even if its influence had increased, still constituted an insignificant minority. Linked with them, a few socialists like Jean Longuet and Rappoport had also chosen the road to revolution: a handful of men lost among adventurers like Laval, oppor-tunists like Cachin, state corporatists like Thomas, and procrastinators like Renaudel.

On the bourgeois side there was only the conservative lucidity of Joseph Caillaux. He saw that Europe was losing its preponderant position in the world and wanted to stop this development by a negotiated peace with Germany and the creation of a new bourgeois Europe. But Caillaux did not have the means to satisfy this desire and he contented himself with hopes that Sarrail would become commander in chief. Besides, pacifism as it existed in 1917 stemmed from the left, and the military reinforcement of the Germans by troops diverted from the Russian front after the truce there soon made the idea of a revolution unpopular. Pétain's skilful repression and the imminent arrival of the Americans simultaneously subdued the army's revolt and bolstered the country's patriotic morale. The revolutionary crisis was to prove beneficial to the nationalists. The French Republic's successive governments—first Viviani's, Briand's, which had just fallen, Ribot's, which was then in power, Painlevé's, which was to follow—had shown or were to show themselves incapable of really waging war or of effectively making peace. Caillaux thought that he was capable of making peace, Clemenceau, war. The old "Tiger" was getting ready.

In keeping with the needs of the nationalist propaganda fostered by supporters of Poincaré and Clemenceau, the chances and the effectiveness of Caillaux's "peace party," and Almereyda's importance in the movement, have been greatly exaggerated. Caillaux concentrated on establishing contacts and making preliminary overtures in the legislature and the newspapers. The republican league he hoped to establish with the collaboration of Almereyda and other pacifist journalists never got beyond the project stage. By that time, Almereyda was already incapable of any sustained activity. The nationalistic propaganda, however, has left quite durable traces. Thirty years later, Victor Serge, referring to this period which, because he was not in Paris at the time, he would only learn about subsequently, said that Almereyda had become the "condottiere of this party" (of peace) and that had the attempt been successful, "he would have made a popular minister, capable of sincerely and perfidiously manipulating the feelings of the socialist and anarchist masses." In fact, during the first half of 1917, Almereyda was in a state of almost total physical collapse. He could only travel by car and remained on his feet only with the aid of increasing doses of morphine and, later, of heroin.

The fight against *L'Action Française* had not ceased for a single day. Daudet was to realize later that he had been attacked in more than seven hundred issues of the paper.

Daudet's ideas had been considerably enlarged. For the time being, the censors kept him from openly revealing them to the public, and he contented himself with tirelessly exposing them in private to politicians, journalists, and the military. In his eyes, any undesirable event was caused by the skilful combined action of the German General Staff and the Jews. Their efforts had already manifested themselves in Russia during the first half of 1917 with Kerenski's revolution and were being continued by the activities of Lenin and Trotsky. For France these conspirators' plans were very similar. Aside from using their cadres—Malvy and Almereyda, in particular—for effective military espionage, the German General Staff was organizing a revolution in France. The first indications had appeared at the front (the mutinies) and in Paris (a few strikes). The two principal centres for this revolutionary, pro-German activity were the Ministry of the Interior headed by Malvy and *Le Bonnet Rouge*; all of which activity was of course directed by Caillaux. A majority of nationalist politicians, journalists, and military personnel had ended up, often with certain reservations, convinced of the truth of Daudet's accusations. His conclusions were supported by Barrès. A collaboration was established between the two writers. Barrès, who was a member of the Chamber of Deputies, informed Daudet on the Chamber's secret sessions, and received in return Daudet's information from police sources.

The struggle against *L'Action Française* had by now taken on for Almereyda a meaning of its own, and he separated it from the rest of his political perspective. On this particular matter he no longer paid any attention to Caillaux, who for tactical reasons disapproved of continuing the campaign.

By concentrating his attacks on Almereyda and on *Le Bonnet Rouge*, seeking to destroy a dangerous enemy, Daudet nevertheless had his sights on his true objective, a fortress which the censors kept him from attacking directly: Malvy. There is no doubt that even the most optimistic of the nationalists was not prepared for the windfall provided them by the Duval-cheque affair.

Returning on May 15, 1917, from one of his many trips to Switzerland, Duval had been searched at the border by the military police and a cheque drawn on a Paris bank for 100,000 francs was found in his possession. The money was of German origin, and an investigation into commerce with the enemy was initiated against Duval; he was arrested at the beginning of July. In the Chamber of Deputies, Barrès addressed Malvy in the following terms: "When will you arrest that scum from *Le Bonnet Rouge*?" And the affair became political and public. Almereyda vehemently defended himself in *Le Bonnet Rouge*. The president of the Republic would have liked to have had him arrested at once, but faced with the government's procrastination, Poincaré demanded that at the very least the paper be suspended. Ribot, the president of the Council, agreed with this view, and at the meeting of the War Council on May 12, 1917, on the basis of Viviani's report, the indefinite suspension of *Le Bonnet Rouge* was decided on, to take effect that very evening.[23]

Almereyda, summoned as a witness, had given the investigating judge a report on the origin of the funds which both he and the paper had on hand. The money given by Duval constituted only a small portion of the capital Almereyda had managed to amass; and besides, the sum was being repaid, which indicated that it was only a loan.

Nevertheless, the political aspects of the affair had taken the upper hand. Clemenceau judged the moment appropriate for an assault on the government, the weakest point of which was Malvy, whose weakest point in turn was Almereyda.

The "Tiger" prepared for battle. One Sunday in July, with his secretary, Martet, he went for an automobile ride on the outskirts of Paris to visit Claude Monet in Giverny. During the return trip Clemenceau was dozing. Martet writes: "We had been on the road for a quarter of an hour. Suddenly, M. Clemenceau turned to me. He asked me, 'Almereyda? Wasn't he on familiar terms with Malvy?' He had been caught up in the battle again."[24]

He was to give battle victoriously on July 22 in the Senate. That day he crushed Malvy by associating him with Almereyda and opened the way to power for himself. After Clemenceau's speech, "the *Bonnet Rouge* affair" (as the Duval affair was henceforth to be called) had transformed itself in the government's hands into political dynamite. The investigation had proved that Duval had received quite substantial sums of money in Switzerland from a German banker in Mannheim; Viviani hoped to get the matter out of his hands by transferring the investigation over to the military courts, thereby changing the very nature of the offence, and, he thought, enabling them to "really prosecute Almereyda."[25] Yet it was politically indispensable to the government that Almereyda be first arrested by the civil police. They waited their chance.

Malvy had left to rest after Clemenceau's ringing attack, and Viviani now was in charge of both the Ministries of Justice and of the Interior. At the beginning of August he received from *L'Action Française* information according to which certain highly confidential documents were hidden in the wine cellar of Almereyda's house.

Ever since the paper had been suspended, Almereyda, still sick, rarely left his villa in Saint-Cloud. He spent his time there with Jean, Emily, and the few friends who still associated with him. It had been some time since Jean had had the opportunity of spending so much time with his father. He took advantage of the occasion, leaving his father only to go to school or to run errands. One afternoon in early August, he went out to buy some shoelaces for Almereyda. On the way back he admitted the police commissioner who had come to search the house. In his father's company he watched the search, which only resulted in the seizure of some insignificant papers. It was with some anxiety that Jean saw his father leave accompanied by the police commissioner who had asked Almereyda to come with him to the offices of *Le Bonnet Rouge*. He calmed down when his father returned a few hours later.

However, the police investigators had found in the office safe confidential documents on the Sarrail Army which had been given to Almereyda by Paix-Séailles for the paper's campaigns. "When these papers were found," Poincaré wrote, "Vigo got very upset and finally fainted." The judge immediately opened a new investigation. Vigo was tailed. "He will be arrested this evening at home if he gets there before the sun sets, or on the street (which the state of siege allows) anytime he is found there."[26]

Almereyda was only arrested and sent to La Santé prison two days later, on the evening of August 6. The next day the staff of *Le Bonnet Rouge* sent the newspapers a letter in Almereyda's defence,[27] which the censors would not allow to be printed.

Almereyda was not exaggerating when he described his state of almost total physical exhaustion to Judge Drioux. Bail was refused him, but the fact that his physical state required medical attention not available at La Santé prison was acknowledged. Nevertheless, he remained there until the eleventh. His gaoler wrote: "He suffered from an acute intestinal disease, and deprived of morphine he was tortured by pain."[28] Despite the obvious risk of a fatal reaction to his sudden deprivation of the drug, the regulations forbade any injection. He was transferred to Fresnes prison in a paddy wagon; in his state of health this could have killed him.[29]

At Fresnes Almereyda was forced to stay in bed. He asked the doctors to give him morphine and insisted that they take good care of him. He wanted to live and defend himself. On Monday, August 13, he asked to confer with his lawyer. He was to see him the next day.

There is only the slightest shadow of a doubt that Almereyda was murdered on the night of August 13, 1917, in his cell at Fresnes prison. Albert Monniot

Almereyda, Jean and Emily

and barrister Paul Morel's hypotheses on the political motivations behind the murder are inconsistent, but their material reconstruction of the actual events is impeccable.[30] We will not go into their political accusations here. Let us proceed directly to their reconstitution of the actual events. A common criminal named Bernard, who had been put in charge of keeping watch over the sick prisoner that night, supposedly approached Almereyda's bed while he slept, armed with Almereyda's shoelaces. Having knotted the shoelaces together he put them under Almereyda's chin and drew both ends back through the bars and then tied the ends together. Almereyda's neck and the bars of the bed were thus enclosed inside the still slack shoelaces. Bernard then pulled one of the victim's shirts wadded along its length through the laces, using it as a sort of garrotte handle. Bernard had only to twist the wadded shirt energetically, thereby drawing Almereyda's head up against the bars, and hold it there. The victim struggled so little that the secretion characteristic to the hanged dried on his thighs in a small patch not extending beyond the small area of skin moistened by the ejaculation.

That same day an official communiqué released to the press announced that Almereyda had "died of a haemorrhage." One week later, a second official statement announced that Almereyda had hanged himself from the bedstead with his shoelaces.

The autopsy showed that Almereyda was suffering from peritonitis and a ruptured appendix. There was over a litre of pus in his abdomen. His end had been near anyhow.

If one were to ask today who could have given Bernard the order to kill Almereyda, one would have to settle for vague theories, which would prove extremely difficult to verify. In the months immediately following, the theory which found general favour held that Almereyda had been killed by order of Malvy and Caillaux, against whom he supposedly held some terribly compromising secrets. Once Clemenceau was in power, the main outlines of Daudet's theories were taken up again and became official. Against all reason, an attempt was made, notably in the investigation preliminary to Caillaux's trial, to establish these hypotheses as legal fact. Yet it seems that no effort was made to add Almereyda's murder to the extremely tenuous case which had already been drawn up.

As opposed to those who think that the Almereyda case is an "encounter with the most baffling episode in our whole history" (Albert Monniot) or those who assert that "the Almereyda case is the key to an incredible mystery" (Paul Morel), one may wonder whether the drama did not unfold on a rather more banal level.

During the trials of both Malvy and Duval as well as the rest, the police who had testified as witnesses had shown such hatred for Almereyda,* all dating from the period of his most militant battles (held in check and neutralized by Malvy's friendship), that one must add another possible

---

* "A common criminal, a thief, a counterfeiter, a pederast," the policeman Perrette said of Almereyda at the Malvy trial.

explanation—the possibility that the murder was no more than the settling of accounts between Almereyda and the police, venting their rage on a long-standing and now defenceless enemy.

The memoirs published by the celebrities of the time, so rich in details about Almereyda's imprisonment, barely mention his death. Thus Ribot, in his memoirs, passes over the event in silence. Poincaré at the time was visiting the king of Italy. Malvy was on vacation. Viviani never published his memoirs, and when he died in 1925 he had no memories left to write about, for by then he had been insane for years.

The censors had become even more severe in all matters concerning Almereyda, and when he died the newspapers published only the official communiqués. *L'Eveil*, *Le Pays*, and *Le Journal du Peuple* were the only exceptions, the rest were full of insinuations and lies.[31]

If one is to believe the bitter reproaches of Fournier, even Hervé let himself be carried along by the furious outburst of opinion against Almereyda.

Emily, helped by Almereyda's friends, had trouble getting the body turned over to her. She was forced to write several letters to the authorities, as Almereyda's companion, in her own name, but above all "in the name of my son, Jean Vigo."[32] Finally, after a good deal of negotiating, the body was given to her within the walls of the Bagneux Cemetery in Paris. The censors had prohibited the newspapers, under the threat of suspension, from publishing the date of the funeral, and the Prefecture of Police had announced in a special communiqué that the funeral had taken place two days earlier. Some fifty friends nevertheless gathered around Almereyda's grave.

The "Almereyda affair" broke in 1917, the year Poincaré called "the troubled year," a year which could have been the most splendid year in the century. In any case it was a decisive year. In France, one of the war's key expressions, "*il ne faut pas chercher à comprendre*" (*we must not try to understand*), had almost fallen by the wayside. Awareness had been slow in coming but its pace might have suddenly quickened. For a certain period of time this might have benefited the bourgeois common sense and ambitions of Caillaux. However, the real issue of the crisis was expressed by the small group consisting of Pierre Monatte and his friends, heirs of that last great generation of Frenchmen: Pelloutier, Grifuelhes, and Merrheim.

The great so-called treason cases, the first of which was Almereyda's, served as an excuse for stopping the development of this revolutionary tendency dead in its tracks. This successful outcome allowed the last great defender of the French bourgeoisie, Clemenceau, to play out his part, and in the process to mortgage the country's future.

It was mostly after the "Tiger's" rise to power that the political exploitation of the Almereyda affair reached its pinnacle. The trial of Duval and of those implicated with him was henceforth referred to as "the *Bonnet Rouge* affair," and in the public eye the whole conspiracy centred around Almereyda. Malvy and Caillaux's trials were being prepared in an attempt to link them with "the *Bonnet Rouge* affair" because they had been mainly associated with Almereyda.

Even before Clemenceau took power, in early September, cases which had no connection at all with Almereyda or with his paper—such as the Loustalot or Bolo Pasha affairs—were grouped in *La Victoire* under the general title, *The Mysteries of the Bonnet Rouge*, which became a heading referring to all cases of treason.

In short, thanks to the censors, the nationalists successfully made the public believe in a gigantic conspiracy. ("There is only one treason case," the prosecutor Mornet stated, which Bouchardon had already tried to imply during the investigation preliminary to the Caillaux trial.) That Almereyda had never been directly implicated in "the Bonnet Rouge affair," that his trial was a completely different affair, was completely overlooked. When his case finally went to court the papers hardly mentioned Almereyda. The authorities attached very little importance to the case anyway, and his co-defendants, Captain Mathieu, who had sent Paix-Séailles the documents on the Army of the East, and the latter who had given them to Almereyda, received light sentences, more to satisfy principle than to punish. The first received three months in gaol and the second a year's suspended sentence.

In the sudden spate of invective directed at Almereyda a discordant voice was briefly heard, made all the more touching by the circumstances—Gustave Hervé's. Hervé had reached the heights of chauvinism and an abyss separated him from the pacifism Almereyda had articulated in the first half of 1917. However, when called as a witness in the Malvy trial, he was to react against the ignominy of Perrette and speak in a tone altogether different from the one he had used at the time of Almereyda's death. He paid a last homage to his old friend. "I am perhaps the only one here really to have known him and I can assure you that far from being the total wretch that you perhaps imagine, Almereyda had the finest mind I have ever encountered in any of the more progressive quarters; he was the bravest of all the militants; he was a trustworthy comrade and a polemicist of great influence. It was this Almereyda who exercised an irresistible influence." In Hervé's words a nostalgia for their common past as revolutionaries surfaces for the last time and his testimony sounds like a final goodbye not only to the old Almereyda, but also to the Gustave Hervé of 1910, defender of Liabeuf.

This was but one isolated voice, however, lost in the midst of the public outcry directed against Almereyda-formerly-Vigo: a name rejected in the past by a sensitive and proud child, which had been rediscovered and used for the purposes of hatred, and had returned to strike down the man, better yet, the dead, as an accusation and an insult. As the first biographer of Almereyda wrote, "The name Vigo quite naturally brings into mind a sinister character and a river of gold flowing through the mud of the lower depths."[33]

The old magistrate of Andorra having died long ago, the only bearer of the name in France in 1917 was a twelve-year-old boy.

Jean Vigo

2. Jean Vigo

As soon as the news of Almereyda's death reached Montpellier, Gabriel Aubès wrote to Judge Drioux asking for custody of the child. Emily, who did not have the means to support Jean (did she even want to?), agreed. On the judge's initiative, the possibility of declaring that the child had been abandoned by his mother was considered. Aubès and his niece, however, opposed the measure, not because they had any sympathy for Emily, but because they feared that Jean Vigo might hold it against them at some time in the future.

In October 1917 Jean was still in Paris where the young pacifist writer Jean de Saint-Prix saw him in a café on the rue des Petits-Champs. "Today," he wrote to Mlle. Jane Bagault, "I saw Almereyda's son. The poor child, pale, haggard, and taciturn, is twelve. His poor little soul bears the sorrowful burden of his father's terrible death. . . . They write articles, they speak of 'Jean Vigo' without realizing that he is an unhappy little creature. A lack of feeling."[1]

A few days later the child left for Montpellier accompanied by a friend, probably Fernand Desprès. Gabriel Aubès, being ill, had not been able to come to fetch him.

When the child arrived, he was in a state of physical collapse. The Aubès first thought of hiding him: that proved impossible. At the very least his identity had to be concealed, something much easier to accomplish, for the child's state of health forbade his going out. Jean remained at home, cared for by the Aubès' doctor, a friend, the only person who had been told his real name. After several weeks had passed, Jean's health had improved and his sorrow was less visible. The school year had already begun, but there could be no question of enrolling him in a school in Montpellier; his identity would have been discovered, and not only would the "son of the traitor" have been tormented by other children, but the situation of the Aubès family would also have become untenable. Prudence demanded that Jean Vigo remain as little as possible in Montpellier, and they asked the doctor to look for a school for the child in a nearby city. The administration of the *lycée* at Nîmes refused to accept the Vigo boy, but two ladies, the Ducros, accepted him as their boarder. At the end of 1917 Jean began attending a primary school whose director and his wife were interested in his case. Each Saturday he would go to Montpellier and stay with the Aubès until Monday morning. Jean was sickly and sad; his health was precarious, but he never complained and hid whenever he wanted to cry. The Aubès' doctor and his colleagues called in for consultation were pessimistic.

Nevertheless, at the beginning of 1918 Jean gave the impression of having become used to his new life. During this period he started to write a journal, keeping it at least until August of the following year.[2] It is a strange document. In it we see an observant child who knows how to express himself, and whose precocity is quite evident even though at the beginning his ideas and judgments mostly echo the grown-up world around him: his teachers, the Aubès, and the Ducros sisters. "Today," he wrote on July 4, 1918, "we celebrate American Independence Day in France. The streets, the houses, and the stores are decorated with allied flags floating in the sea breeze. Today we helped the good Americans become Republicans and a free and prosperous nation. Therefore, to express their gratitude, it is the Americans' turn today to come to our aid. Let us fête the Americans and let us show our warm feelings towards them."

These lines are probably mostly an echo of a teacher's speech. His jokes about the incessant jabbering of a lady named Gignoux almost certainly refer to the Ducros ladies. However, after having watched, with Gabriel Aubès, a procession for the pilgrimage to Notre-Dame de Lourdes, Jean wrote: "We were a bit amazed to see that they had the cheek to perform their ritual in the street." One has the impression that he is already expressing a personal feeling here, although one shared by the photographer, an old anticlerical. It is even probable that, on certain particular political issues, the thirteen-year-old boy had more progressive ideas than either Aubès or his teachers. Some of Almereyda's old friends wrote and spoke to him about political problems. On June 4, 1918, after having received a letter from Emile Dulac, Vigo wrote: "Today, the Rappoport trial begins; a turn for the better, acquittal." Two days later: "I have read the Rappoport acquittal (six months of prison with a suspended sentence), he got off rather well." About the condemnation of Malvy and his departure to Spain, Vigo noted: "Poor chap." "Poor man," he wrote on July 19, learning that Duval had been shot, "I feel sorry for his wife and children, I am very upset about it." One day, on the train, Vigo overheard a conversation between two people nearby. One of them "began to tell of his exploits before the war (he was a policeman), he explained the interrogations, the beatings, and other equally cowardly things; I don't know whether it runs in the family, but I felt a profound disgust for this boaster." His feelings about his family origins were very keen. "I," he wrote about a fight, "am not in a habit of letting anyone put anything over on me (I would not have any of the family traits if that were not true) . . . I punched my adversary on the jaw. . . ." Jean speaks directly of Almereyda only once, in reference to the speech made by Gustave Hervé at the Malvy trial: "I read the testimony given by my 'Uncle' Hervé about my poor father, it made me feel good"; and he wrote to thank him. He often wrote to Emily and always speaks tenderly about his "little mother." On July 26 he wrote: "I received a letter from my mother, bad news." And for a month, he ceased using the affectionate adjective "little" beside "mother."

At school Vigo was interested in history; at the Ducros' he read *David Copperfield*. In Montpellier or during vacations the Aubès took him to the movies: on September 22 he saw a Chaplin film. He had made numerous friends: Sabatier, Van Cuneghem, big Lib, little Lib, Roland, etc.

For a part of their vacation in August–September 1918, the Aubès took Jean to the mountains. The climate having done him some good, the doctor strongly advised sending him to continue his studies in a more mountainous region. On their return, the Aubès and Jean stopped at Millau, where it was decided that the child would be placed as a boarder in the local school. M. and Mme. Canac, owners of the Hôtel du Commerce where they stayed, agreed to become his guardians. As at Nîmes, the child was enrolled under the pseudonym Jean Salles, the maiden name of Mme. Aubès, Almereyda's mother, long since dead.

"I am so pleased that I am going to become acquainted with boarding school life," Jean wrote in his journal. He arrived at the Millau school on October 7, 1918, but a week later all the pupils were sent home because of an outbreak of influenza. Those seven days had been filled with little events which Vigo never forgot.

On the first day Jean was a bit uneasy, and wondered how the other pupils would treat him and whether he would be well fed. The teachers, on the whole, made a good impression on him, and he became friendly with Gaston Jougla, from Gabiau. In the evening the parents left, and then their life as boarders really began. "So we said our goodbyes, we wanted to seem cheerful, and we joked, but in reality our little hearts beat rather hard in our chests; being shut away appealed to none of us, but that was the way it had to be, and, in a long line, we slowly climbed the stairs. At the head was M. Lafon, the junior master. This gentleman didn't seem very agreeable. First, we stood at the head of our beds, then at the sound of a handclap, we got into bed. This seemed sad but a few wisecracks made us laugh. The lights were turned off and there we lay in the darkness. Gaston spoke to me, I

'On the first day Jean was a bit uneasy . . .': Tabard in *Zéro de Conduite*

laughed, we both laughed. Finally, the junior master raised his curtain, and told us to keep quiet."

Over the next few days Jean had several tangles with Lafon, the junior master. Wednesday, October 9: "At eight dinner and then bed. I was laughing with Jougla when I heard or rather did not hear the name which had been called out; but I did hear: come to my cubicle. Taking the name to be mine, I got up, and I felt my way over to the junior master's bed. I had stood there barely five minutes when I heard someone cough; I coughed, someone coughed louder, then I started to cough again, when suddenly I felt an arm touch my face; I grabbed it and bit it. The arm was pulled back. I walked around the junior-master's bed. Walking along one of its sides, I sensed the presence of another boarder. I asked his name (which I could not make out). Then we whispered and laughed. Finally the junior master said, 'Labanaire, go back to bed.' I risked a timid 'Me too, Monsieur?' I felt the junior master jump in his bed as he said, 'Who is there?' 'Me, Salles,' I said. 'And what are you doing here?' 'But, Monsieur, you told me to come.' At these words the junior master began to fume and said, 'I did not tell you to come, but since you are here, stay here.' And he laid down again."

Two days later: "It was 8.30, everyone was asleep, when a laugh responded to a sound . . . who laughed? Me. Then the junior master lifted the curtain of his bed and said, 'Whoever was laughing come over here.' Oh! it hurt to have to get out of bed when I felt so warm. But I got up and felt my way over to the junior master's bed. When I got there, he said: 'Are you there, Salles?' 'Yes, Monsieur.' 'Well, you will not leave before 11; see if you feel like laughing about that. . . .'

"Oh! was I feeling sorry for myself. It was 9 o'clock, with two hours to go, and I didn't feel like laughing. I thought it was 11 when 10 o'clock struck, the hour had seemed so long to me. Towards 10.30 I was seized by a strong and violent stomach-ache. I asked: 'Monsieur, can I go to the bathroom?' No answer. 'Monsieur, I have stomach cramps. I want to go, I can't hold it any longer.' Still no answer; he was sleeping. I quickly ran to the toilet, but before I got there I started doing it in my pants. When I returned, 11 o'clock struck; the junior master woke up and said, 'Go back to bed.'"

When Mlle. Aubès saw Jean come back to Montpellier, she at first thought that his identity had been discovered in Millau and that he had been sent home. "I'm so glad," she said when she was told about the flu epidemic. Jean described the scene in his journal, and then continued: "Burials followed one after another, and many people were buried without coffins, in sheets, sad-looking things; to avoid frightening the local residents, two coffins were put in the same hearse.

"In Paris, my little mother got pleurisy and I was frightened, but it is over. My friend Roland died in hospital, poor fellow. He was so nice and sweet. It is sad to die at the age of thirteen! ! !"

Rumours of peace began to circulate. "It is sad for those who have given their lives for their country; no one will be able to tell them, and they themselves will not be able to say: 'It is all over! . . . I can sleep in peace.'"

Jean Vigo was fourteen. He was to remain four years at the Millau lycée. Jean strictly obeyed the order not to reveal his true name to anyone. But he had realized that the head of the school at Nîmes and his wife knew his secret and despite their knowing were still nice to him. Besides, he spent each weekend with the Aubès. At Millau, his isolation became more pronounced. His guardian and the school principal were in all likelihood aware of his identity, but Jean was not aware of that fact. The guardian and his family were quite correct in their relationship with Jean, took him out on Sunday, but that was all. M. Daleinne, the principal, whose history lesson Vigo had liked on the first day, was a fat, unimaginative, pompous man; there were also the headmaster, M. Santt, moustached, with a Vandyke beard, who positively enjoyed slapping students, M. Parrain, saccharine, disagreeable, and ugly, and the junior master, M. Lafon, decidedly not a good fellow.

We might ask if, at the beginning, his situation was any better in relation to the other children. Two of his former classmates[3] describe him as the only Parisian in the school, which already singled him out from the others, all from the south of France. His accent was strange. Besides, Jean was a tragic, delicate, sickly, and nervous boy, and the young southerners willingly made fun of this finicky weakling. "Well, ever since yesterday," he wrote on December 16, 1918, "the pupils do nothing but bother me and I've already had enough! ! There are about fifteen of them, who keep on at me; stop me from having fun, push me around, and in general annoy me." The worst of it all was that his old friend Jougla led the harassment, and Jean had to fight him. From then on, he habitually fought anyone who bothered him, and having fun at his expense soon ended. The beating he administered to Alibert, "a big skinny guy in the first form" who had provoked the fight, even earned him, he excitedly wrote, "the congratulations of the whole playground." His feats earned him the friendship of Bruel and Caussat, who, like him, were in the sixth form, but were already old-timers. Jacques Bruel was the tough guy of the class. He took Jean under his protective wing, and together with Georges Caussat, they became an inseparable trio.

Something that troubled him was that his comrades often spoke of their parents. He himself could not talk of his fallen idol, of his courageous, rich, and handsome father, with whom he had lived in a big and beautiful house such as none of the others had ever even seen. And what could he have said about his mother other than that he loved her and that he lived in fear, thinking how far away she was. At Saint-Cloud, it had been Almereyda to whom he was attached. When his father had gone, Jean became closer to his mother, but she was soon separated from him. The thought that his mother perhaps did not love him upset Jean. So as not to seem to have no parents Vigo told his friends that Gustave Aubès was his grandfather.

His health had clearly improved. He had even become robust, despite the bad food, which consisted chiefly of beans and cauliflower, food which the students never would forget. Jean, Caussat, and Bruel used the best part of their energy resisting adult encroachments by organizing rows, which sometimes created quite a fracas. During the last months of the war, but mostly after it, there was a certain laxity; the junior masters for the most part came from wherever they could be found, and discipline was relaxed. Nevertheless, zeros for conduct had started to pour in, and for long periods it was rare for Vigo and his friends not to be confined to the school on Sunday.

Neither his recovered health nor friendship with Bruel and Caussat induced Vigo to accept the boarding school he so hated. In addition to the rows, he used non-violent methods against his teachers. During his four years at the Millau lycée, he never stopped playing the dunce. Keeping a journal was something a nice boy did and Jean stopped his.

Getting involved in rows or playing the dunce did not allow him to escape entirely the school's dreary monotony. The arrival of a new junior master, a young, sympathetic, and amusing man, was a novelty; but he soon left. The modest feats of a sleepwalking student after a while were no longer astounding, but his death was a real event. The night before he died he had stood at the foot of Jean's bed. "Little sleepwalker," Jean Vigo wrote some fourteen years later, "whose casket was lowered into the playground for the priest's blessing, a priest who sprinkled his holy water on the devil of whom we were all terrified."[4] The little sleepwalker died of Spanish influenza in 1919, and for a long time afterwards the children whispered among themselves that sleepwalking was a warning of imminent death.

That same year it became clear that Jean's state of health, excellent as it appeared, was still not very good; while at school he had an acute attack of rheumatic fever which kept him in bed in the infirmary for quite some time with his feet wrapped up in cotton wool. After his recovery he could run about again, although his bones had become somewhat bent.

For Jean, his vacations with the Aubès were a liberation from constraint. He was reticent about his feelings, but Mlle. Aubès encouraged him to speak out and willingly listened to the rebellious child's complaints and the story of his doings. His relationship with Gabriel Aubès was equally good.

Though Jean continued to be a bad student, he started to take an interest in books, in the arts, and in his grandfather's trade. Jean was a young man now, and he worked for the photographer sometimes in the shop and took some pictures outdoors. As a good craftsman Aubès was struck by the soundness of Jean's eye and by his taste. "Like his father," Aubès must have thought. Aubès, for whom the trade of a photographer in the provinces gave no real satisfaction, did not encourage Jean to follow in his footsteps. Aubès had even less desire to see Jean try his luck in the profession in Paris. That city in his eyes was the cause—together with Emily—of Almereyda's fall. He used to tell Jean that since he was interested in photography he should learn a trade which had more of a future; he should become a movie cameraman. This was also a profession which led to Paris, but Jean still had enough time before him, and if he was to end up in the capital, he would arrive there already mature, better prepared than Almereyda had been for the dangers awaiting him.

Starting in 1919 Jean went to Paris every September to spend two weeks with his mother. One of the attractions of these stays was that they allowed

Jean to see several of Almereyda's old friends again. Now that he was almost sixteen, he felt the need to share the cult of his father with others. At Montpellier he could speak to the Aubès of his father, but the photographer and his family could not be of significant help to Jean in restoring his hazy childhood memories or informing him of his father's personality and life; aside from the fact that the Aubès disapproved of Almereyda's life, from the south of France they had not very successfully followed his Paris career. By contrast, during his stays with his mother, Jean often saw Fernand Desprès and Fanny Clar, both very pleased to see Nono again, and their talks together, in which Almereyda was often mentioned, were pursued in a very friendly atmosphere.

When Emily wrote to the Aubès family in 1922 to express her desire to have her son with her, the idea of seeing his adult friends more often pleased Jean. Gabriel Aubès, in spite of the little sympathy he had for Emily, agreed to send Jean (still at Aubès' expense), to Chartres, near Paris, to continue his secondary education.

The Almereyda affair no longer had the virulent overtones it had had in earlier years, and at Chartres Vigo was able to register as a boarder at the Lycée Marceau under his real name. There he was enrolled in section "First C" (Latin and science), considered the most rigorous programme of study. Lessons at Chartres were altogether more serious than in Millau, and in 1923 Vigo twice flunked his baccalauréat exams, despite a second prize in French composition and an honorable mention in modern history. More than anything else his failure was due to the bad quality of his earlier preparation in Millau, for he had now become a conscientious student. He repeated the year, and won a first prize in French composition and an honorable mention in Latin, and in July 1924 he easily passed the first part of the baccalauréat. When he left the lycée, he was on the honour roll in philosophy and still first in French composition.

We can already see, by this simple enumeration of his scholarly successes, that Vigo had succeeded in fitting better into his surroundings. His antagonism towards the school administration was now no different from that expressed by the other schoolchildren. Whenever the headmaster, a small bearded man, crazy about physical education, boasted about his former feats as a rugby player, Jean made as much fun of him as his schoolmates did, and like them, Jean enjoyed the practical jokes played on the teacher of natural history, a fat, disagreeable man. At the Marceau lycée, in addition to his studies, Vigo found a new outlet for his energies, in sports.

The headmaster had given considerable emphasis to physical education in the school's curriculum. Jean Vigo distinguished himself in sports. We find his name often on the school's list of athletic champions for those years. In the 100-metre dash he particularly distinguished himself. In soccer he was a good goalkeeper and was, with his friend Colin, the principal mainstay of the team.

Among his classmates, Vigo had become friends with Jean Colin, son of two of the boarding school's clerks, who was at the school thanks to a scholarship. Colin and Vigo mostly had a common interest in sports. Vigo's best friend was little Paul Mercier, a student in a lower form. However, the school administration tried very hard to discourage friendships between students in the higher and lower grades, and succeeded to such a degree that Vigo and Mercier could not meet very easily. Sometimes, when Vigo was not at Chartres, he addressed to Colin letters written to Mercier, because of fear of the administration's censorship.

Their vigilance was nevertheless not always so severe. On April 14, 1924, Mercier wrote to Vigo, shut up in the infirmary: "I thought the measles was something serious. When I went to bring you *L'Auto*, the nurse found pocks on my face. She took me to the assistant headmaster; he told me: 'You want to be like your friend Vigo?' The headmaster then came in and said: 'You understand, you're so friendly with Vigo that we're watching you closely.' This year they feel better about you. You are the assistant headmaster's little pet. It's better that way, the two of us don't have to be so careful."[5]

As Colin recalls, Vigo's behaviour, except for his extreme sensitivity, was hardly different from that of his friends. He sometimes had sudden changes in mood, plunging for hours into fits of pensive melancholy.

Vigo spent his vacations, and sometimes his weekends, with his mother in her Paris apartment, 266 rue des Pyrénées.[6] Emily had built a new life for herself with a journalist, M. Dudon, a reporter for *L'Auto* with whom Vigo often talked about sports. Vigo was naturally reserved. In 1917 he had suffered from a sense of abandonment by his mother. The fact that subsequently, from the age of twelve to seventeen, he had seen her only for the token two-week annual visits, had done nothing to heal the old wound. Nevertheless, all this did not prevent the establishment of a cordial relationship between mother and son, at least at first. Vigo must have felt at ease at his mother's, for he often brought his friends Mercier and Colin, and Bruel who was then in Paris, with him; all of them were welcomed by Emily.

Vigo's worship of Miguel Almereyda's memory was what kept mother and son emotionally apart. The adolescent, with the intransigence of his age, must have found it difficult enough seeing his father replaced; so the situation was ripe for a final break between Vigo and Emily, a break which nothing could ever heal.

At Chartres, Vigo spoke about Almereyda no more than he had in Millau. In Paris, in addition to Fernand Desprès and Fanny Clar, whom he saw frequently, Vigo had contacted Eugène Merle, Raphaël Diligent, Gassier, and others. He had decided to work to rehabilitate Miguel Almereyda's memory. He confided his intention to his father's old friends and asked them for help. Vigo must have felt a certain reticence or scepticism on the part of several of them. But he quickly forgot this impression when listening to their accounts of young Almereyda's exploits in his anarchistic period, during his years at *La Guerre Sociale*. It is not inconceivable that, to avoid an embarrassing situation, Almereyda's friends deliberately left out all references to the *Bonnet Rouge* period, the war years, the morphine, and

'Vigo's best friend was little Paul Mercier': Bruel and Tabard in *Zéro de Conduite*

Almereyda's death, emphasizing the heroic period of his life.

These conversations, this preliminary research, had taken place during vacations, and had extended over quite a long period of time. It is not easy to determine chronologically the evolution of Vigo's discoveries or of their emotional impact on him. Certain clues sometimes suggest quite tenable hypotheses, but we have no documents to prove things one way or another. Thus, it is possible that during his years in Chartres, or just afterwards, Vigo wanted to visit Almereyda's tomb; and after an exhaustive search in the Bagneux cemetery, found the grave in a state of total dilapidation. This possibility, although not proved,[7] perhaps contributed to the sudden crystallization of Vigo's resentment towards Emily. We have no need to linger on hypotheses, however, since more precise facts are at our disposal to allow us to clarify partially at least the reasons for the break.

By reading Albert Monniot's book[8] Vigo angrily discovered the details of his father's murder, and the part he had inadvertently played in it by buying the shoelaces which were used a few days later to strangle Almereyda.[9] In this angry state of mind Vigo learned about the legal brief, abundantly quoted by Monniot, which had accompanied the murder complaint presented by Maître Morel, the lawyer on whom Emily had relied in 1917 to defend the interests of the child Jean Vigo. Vigo indignantly discovered that, to support the thesis that Almereyda had been murdered, the lawyer had agreed with almost all the arguments presented by *L'Action Française*; and by his insinuations, Morel presented his father almost as if he were a criminal executed by his highly placed accomplices so that he would not reveal any compromising secrets. Almereyda's rehabilitation had become Jean Vigo's principal preoccupation, and he never forgave his mother for having let the lawyer use the political situation of 1917–18 to ensure the successful outcome of their suit.

Vigo never doubted his father was innocent. Even more, in his eyes Almereyda was a hero. Something which at first was only an emotional conviction became after his first inquiries a rational schema, although a confused one which he was attempting to fill out and support with definite proof. During his vacation in 1924–5, he put together his first file which aimed to prove that Almereyda had not been a traitor during those last years of his life, and, in addition, that he had never ceased being a revolutionary. He perhaps unconsciously was more interested in Almereyda's youth than in any other period of his life. He met with people who had been with Almereyda during the *Bonnet Rouge* days, but he never addressed himself to the friends Almereyda had made after 1911. We can easily imagine the painful, confused feelings his attempt to shed light on the events which had occurred between the establishment of *Le Bonnet Rouge* and the declaration of war up to the final drama at Fresnes, must have caused him.

Once back at Chartres after the vacation, Vigo turned back into the schoolboy everyone knew, more interested in sports than in anything else, and manifesting a certain originality in his French compositions. His classmates, however, were surprised by the sudden and uncompromising antimilitarist statements he sometimes made. Aside from that, he never lost an opportunity to berate in a friendly way those of his friends who were sympathetic to the Camelots du Roi, the Bonapartists, and other "patriotic youth groups."

The cordiality with which Almereyda's old friends had received him had given Vigo a new assurance. Eugène Merle, who had become "the most Balzacian [journalist] in Paris,"[10] wrote to him in October 1924: "You can absolutely count on me, in life as in death." Jean Vigo adopted this motto of friendship, made popular by Ghione's film *Topi Grigi*, for the rest of his life.

Jean Vigo finally left Chartres in June 1925 after having spent three years at the Lycée Marceau which, added to those in Millau, constituted a good seven years in boarding school. At twenty he had had enough deprivation of liberty, and the influence of the antimilitarist ideology which had animated Almereyda's life, together with the political line adhered to at that time by the French Communists (among whom was Fernand Desprès), could only increase his aversion to the possibility of spending time in a military barracks. Vigo told Colin that he was prepared to do anything to get out of doing military service. It is possible that he did something foolish then so that he would not be in good health when summoned for his physical examination. If

Jean Vigo and Paul Mercier

true, the consequences of his action were soon to extend dangerously beyond what he had foreseen.

Vigo was to have taken his physical in December 1924, but he succeeded in getting it postponed for a year. In the meantime, he hoped to enrol in a university, which would allow him to get additional deferments. Only, when the time came at the end of June 1925, in Paris, for the second part of the baccalauréat, he missed the philosophy examination. A letter to Mercier after the October examination period shows that nothing had yet been settled. However, when classes started in 1925 Vigo attended courses taught by Brunschwig, Bouglé, and Delacroix at the Sorbonne. According to a letter to Mercier dated December 30, Vigo was thinking of passing the examinations for a certificate in ethics and sociology in March and in psychology in June. Vigo may have sent these details to his friend just to satisfy the curiosity of his immediate entourage. In fact, Mercier had written to Vigo on December 10: "You tell me not to tell anyone what you are going to do. That's hard, not at school, but at home. Every time I go home they ask me what you are going to do. What can I answer? It's embarrassing." It is likely that Vigo had told Mercier about his decision to make a career for himself in cinema.

At the Sorbonne Vigo had not made any friends and he continued to associate mostly with Fernand Desprès. A few days before Christmas at

Desprès' home, he met the brother of Jean de Saint-Prix, Pierre. The young pacifist and revolutionary writer had died a short time after the Armistice. Pierre de Saint-Prix was struck by Vigo and identified him with his dead brother. In a letter in which he told his mother of his feelings upon meeting "Almereyda's son," he wrote: "How everything is renewed in different individuals!"[11]

The most pressing problem for Vigo at the beginning of 1926 was his approaching army physical. On February 11, Mercier wrote to him: "You must have taken your physical on Wednesday, how did it turn out: well or badly? Are you so upset that you have forgotten to write to me?"

Vigo had fallen ill. His relationship with his mother grew more strained each day, and his nostalgia for those with whom he had a real home increased. The letters received by the Aubès were full of sadness and discouragement. They responded by inviting him to come to stay with them, and once again Jean arrived in a poor state of health. They took care of him for months, first in Montpellier where he was treated with ultraviolet rays, then in Palavas where the doctors sent him to take sunbaths. Vigo did not believe that he was seriously ill and tried to find out about the possibilities of obtaining some small job on Abel Gance's production, *Napoléon*. It was then discovered that Vigo's lungs were affected, and Gabriel Aubès sent him to Font-Romeu, near the Spanish border, very close to Andorra where his forefathers had come from, for a cure.

At first Vigo stayed at a hotel while waiting for a room, which he got on August 2, 1926, in Doctor Capelle's sanatorium, Espérance. He did not reveal his state of health to his friends from Chartres. "What are you doing in a sanatorium?" Mercier asked him. "Heliotherapy; that word scares me; what is going on? Are you worse? Are you hiding something? I don't understand. Whenever someone asks me what you are doing I say nothing or I say that you are at your photographer-uncle's in Montpellier. Everyone asks me whether you have passed your philosophy oral; I avoid answering. Try to help me out of the bad position you've put me in."[12]

Vigo's condition did not appear serious. "Jean is very happy," Fernand Desprès wrote to Pierre de Saint-Prix.[13] Desprès, however, feared the effect this extra burden might have and tried to help Vigo bear it. It was at his request that Pierre de Saint-Prix, who was then in Perpignan, went to Font-Romeu to visit the convalescing Vigo, and that Mme. de Saint-Prix wrote letters of introduction to some important local people to try to interest them in Jean Vigo. At the same time, Mme. de Saint-Prix sent an affectionate letter to Vigo in which she made him promise to come and see her as soon as he returned to Paris "which must be very soon." Vigo was very touched by the attention paid him by someone who was chiefly for him the mother of "Jean de Saint-Prix whom, some nine years ago, I saw in a café on the rue des Petits-Champs for the first and . . . the last time. He said little—and I can't remember what he did say—but I do remember his silence. He was dressed in black, and because of that his body seemed even more frail and his face even more pallid. I was sad. He looked at me . . . with sadness too.

He was probably thinking about how the death of a man involved in politics reveals the screaming jackals among his former associates. And he thought that there I was . . . a spectator, suffering from a double loss: loss of a loved one and loss of his memory which was being sullied. A few days later he wrote of the 'lack of feeling' of those people who revealed to me in my youth the filthiest dimensions of life."[14]

Fernand Desprès arrived at Font-Romeu in the second week of September to spend part of his vacation near Vigo. Neither he nor the Aubès, any more than Emily, could afford to pay the medical bill, but Eugène Merle for the time being solved the problem. Everything seemed to be working out, and in November 1926 it seemed that Vigo was almost cured. His brief stay near Andorra had given Vigo a vital sense of his Catalonian roots, and he enthusiastically took part in research to help Pierre de Saint-Prix, who, with Desprès' encouragement, was preparing a novel centred around the Catalonian conspiracy[15] which had recently been discovered and crushed. Before returning to Paris at the end of November 1926, Vigo went to Perpignan to obtain some Catalonian literature, and his enthusiasm was so great that he had the misfortune of being taken for a police spy.[16]

Vigo hoped finally to be able to begin his cinematic apprenticeship in Paris. He had recently been in contact with Francis Jourdain, whom he had not seen since 1914. Very much a part of Parisian artistic circles, Jourdain offered to introduce Jean to a "few cinematic bigwigs."

The following three months spent in Paris were unhappy ones for him. Mercier wrote to him on January 14, 1927: "You seem very busy these days, you say you spend your days doing things. What's happening?" It is likely that Vigo was feverishly pursuing his research on Almereyda and desperately trying to find a job which would allow him to leave his mother's house. Then he again became ill. "Why have you returned to Font-Romeu?" Mercier asked him at the beginning of March. And at the end of the same letter: "By the way, you do not write anything about your parents; how is your mother: well, I hope."[17] His relapse and his bad relationship with his mother took Vigo back to Font-Romeu in a pitiable state. A rise in the price of transportation and hotels kept Fernand Desprès from coming to his friend's side, and Vigo had to bear this new trial alone. Most of the letters Vigo wrote from Font-Romeu, notably those addressed to Desprès, Mercier, and the Aubès, are missing. However, we can retrace his mental state through his correspondence with the Saint-Prixes, which continued throughout his stay.

His friendship with Jean de Saint-Prix's mother and brother had an enormous importance for Vigo. He could write or speak to them of his father as if they were friends sharing his sorrow. He associated his memory of Almereyda with his image of Jean de Saint-Prix. On May 19, 1927 Jean Vigo wrote to Mme. de Saint-Prix, who had just sent him her son's philosophical work, *La Conscience comme Principe spirituel*: "I would have indeed liked to have Jean de Saint-Prix as a friend—no—he is my friend (understand me: my father *is* my best friend)." Through the young writer's work, Vigo realized that pessimism does not preclude energy and enthusiasm, and that an intense spirituality can be a source of revolutionary strength.

Vigo revealed his fears, his uneasiness, and his timidity to his new friends. "So much kindness towards me makes me a little hard to deal with. I shrink awkwardly into myself as soon as anyone pays too much attention to me, for I don't believe I shall ever understand how anyone can pay any attention to me. And still more kindness! Even if it delights me it still dismays me a great deal. A feeling of humility is far from what I feel even if there is nothing in the concept of humility to displease me. What I feel stems from the fear of not being deserving now and of causing deception later on. It is so terrible when one has to withdraw emotional or spiritual feelings, or has them withdrawn from one. That is why my friends give me the greatest joy and the deepest sadness—and why for me they are the best possible stimulus."[18]

However, in moments of depression, familiar figures in his life (Almereyda and Jean de Saint-Prix) took on a morbid turn. Almereyda no longer was someone whom Vigo in a burst of energy wanted to defend and rehabilitate, nor was Jean de Saint-Prix someone who, by his writings, his energy in the struggle, and the lucidity of his pessimism, helped Vigo endure his misery. Both became for Vigo brothers in misfortune whom he would have to, whom he already wished to, join in an early death.

Matters for concern came to him from Paris as well. Emily was in a great fit of moral despondency; she and Dudon had separated and she was looking for work. Vigo could do nothing for his mother. If he had had the means, he would have helped her with money (as he would do later). However, he could no longer love her and this caused them both suffering for which there was no possible solution.

But it was not long before a new element was added to Vigo's life. In August 1928 Mme. de Saint-Prix was worried about not having heard from Vigo for a long time. Després reassured her: "He has something on his mind. That is the only possible explanation for his silence."[19]

Fernand Després had hit the nail on the head. Vigo had, by then, known Lydou for several months.

Elisabeth Lozinska was the daughter of a manufacturer in Lodz. She was nineteen in 1926 and was completing her studies in Switzerland. At the end of the year Lydou had gone to Font-Romeu for treatment. Her condition was serious. Completely discouraged, she had to stay in bed for most of her first year in the sanatorium.

Both Vigo and Lydou had lived very isolated lives and the awakening of their curiosity in the other patients in the clinic was one of the symptoms indicating that their spirits had improved. After a survey of their surroundings they decided that the only interesting resident was Claude Aveline, who had arrived from Switzerland in the autumn of 1926 accompanying his very sick wife. He was the author of several literary pamphlets, but at the time was chiefly known as an editor. Aveline was soon nicknamed "the great man," partly out of mockery and partly out of real interest, for Vigo wanted very much to meet him but was too timid to take the initiative. However, Aveline was an intimate friend of Pierre de Saint-Prix; and one day, when Aveline introduced himself after referring to their mutual acquaintance, Vigo was extremely happy and confused.

"The great man" turned out to be a young man barely four years older than Vigo. Besides, though his success as an editor had given him a certain confidence, Aveline still thought of himself as a beginner in what really interested him: creative writing. Thanks to that fact, Vigo was able to overcome his reserve. A short time after their first meeting, during the long walks he took in the woods with his new friend, Vigo told Aveline about his problems and his plans. He spoke to him of Almereyda and of the documents he had already collected for his father's rehabilitation. He dedicated all his willpower to his own and to Lydou's cure in order to be able to plunge back into the fray—to work, to create, and even to get involved in politics.

In the meantime, Vigo's monetary situation had become desperate. Merle's business affairs had become very troubled and he no longer sent money. Fernand Desprès' salary at *L'Humanité*—at that time the salary of a skilled workman—did not even allow him to take his annual trips to visit Vigo. When Desprès was able to give Vigo some money, he usually used outside funds which he probably obtained from the Saint-Prixes. Francis Jourdain for his part tried to allay Vigo's scruples and to contact some old acquaintances. "Your father left some good and true friends whose faithfulness is beyond dispute. . . . Why then should they be forgetful bastards?"

Vigo's problem was therefore to find remunerative work for the rest of the time he had to spend in Font-Romeu. Claude Aveline was still an editor and he decided to share the correction of proofs with Vigo. However, this collaboration between the two friends went even further, and Vigo became a sort of secretary to Aveline. Among Aveline's papers there is, assiduously copied out by Vigo, the first act of an opera based on Voltaire's *Zadig* (a project subsequently abandoned), and numerous excerpts from Anatole France's works (in which Aveline had already become a specialist).

Vigo was subsequently able to reduce the cost of his treatments. An improvement in their health allowed Lydou and Vigo to leave the sanatorium for a nearby chalet for the last months of their stay there.

Vigo read a good part of his time in Font-Romeu and even wrote a little. He had never had a literary career in mind, having definitely decided to work in cinema ever since he had left Paris in 1926. But he had no idea of how to set about entering that profession. Vigo's hopes rested on Francis Jourdain and his contacts. For the moment he read books on film and thought about certain statements, such as the following by Jean Epstein. "This form of photography in depth sees the angel in man, as one might see the butterfly in a cocoon." Vigo quoted and commented on this idea in an October 1928 letter to Mme. de Saint-Prix.

In the same letter Vigo announced that both he and his fiancée were cured, and that they had decided to settle on the Côte d'Azur after a brief stay in Paris. They arrived in Paris in November 1928 and on the thirtieth Fernand Desprès sent his impressions to Pierre de Saint-Prix. "I saw Jean and his

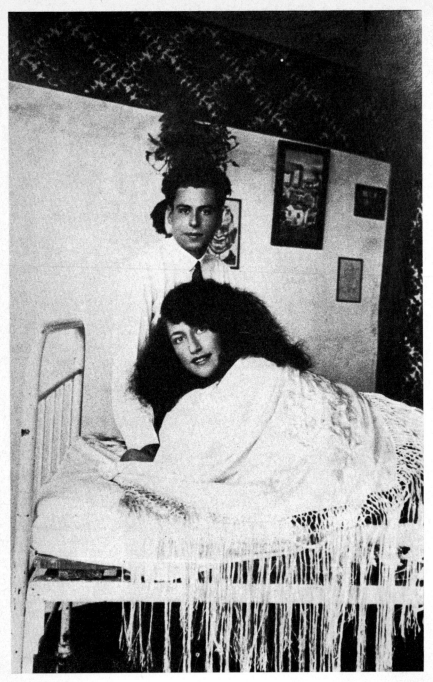

Jean and Lydou

lady. She looks pale and emaciated, and he was in the grip of his cramps. Paris does neither of them any good. Their situation is more desperate than ours. Jean, burdened with the responsibility of a wife, is leaving for the south *without a job*, with a useless letter of recommendation in his pocket. Were I in his shoes, I'd feel desperate. He has never worked and perhaps he is physically incapable of working."

In Paris, however, the few timid overtures Vigo had made were apparently bringing results. Thanks to another newcomer in the field, Claude Autant-Lara, to whom Francis Jourdain had introduced him, Vigo had succeeded in joining Franco-Film which was branching out into Nice. Introduced by Mme. de Saint-Prix, Vigo had also gone to see Germaine Dulac, who had received him very cordially and had promised to help him at Franco-Film, where she knew everyone. Company crews were continually being constituted and dissolved and Germaine Dulac's intervention could, according to Vigo, be decisive should an opportunity present itself. In the meantime, Germaine Dulac asked him to clarify in writing what his background was and what he wanted to do. The answer to either question was not a simple matter.

Vigo and Lydou left for Nice in the first week of December 1928. They stayed at 19^A Boulevard de l'Impératrice de Russie with Janine Champol, Almereyda's old friend and little Nono's nurse. Age had not impaired Janine Champol's vivacity and intelligence and she continued to express forcefully her sympathies with what the Paris Commune had represented.

She was happy at having her "little Nono" with her, and once again assumed her former nursely function by watching over the couple's health. Georges Caussat, his old friend from Millau who had just finished his medical studies in Montpellier, was an intern in Nice. He was constantly with them and, to save money, he finally moved in for a while with Vigo. In the Franco-Film studio a job as an assistant cameraman awaited Vigo. He still had about ten days of freedom which he used to explore the city with Lydou, to find an apartment, and to assemble the papers for their marriage. Lydou's papers were not in order; once again Mme. de Saint-Prix had to be asked for help, and she solved the problem by contacting the Ministry of the Interior.

By the end of January Vigo and Lydou were married and had settled near the studio in a villa, Les Deux Frères, on the Avenue Paderi, in the Bas-Fabron district. Francis Jourdain had designed their furniture and Eugène Dieudonné, the old anarchist ex-convict, had made it for them. "I feel," Vigo wrote to Mme. de Saint-Prix, "that our life will be a very happy one. That means that others will be as pleased to see us as we will be to see them."[20]

At the Franco-Film studio Vigo was to assist the cameraman, Burel, in the production of a film called *Vénus*. His responsibilities were ill-defined and not very interesting, and the pay was quite meagre. But he was in the studio, near the cameras, and for the moment this initiation into the world of cinema was enough to satisfy him.

A month later there was no work for Vigo, and without the help of Lydou's father the couple would have been penniless. When the couple left Font-

Vigo's villa in Nice, 'Les Deux Frères'

Romeu, Hertch Lozinski, the Lodz manufacturer, had gone to France to meet Vigo and to see their situation first-hand.

He was satisfied, was present at the wedding on January 24, and helped them settle into the villa in Bas-Fabron. He continued to send Lydou an allowance. The manufacturer also announced that as soon as his business permitted, he would give them a small amount of capital to give Vigo greater freedom of action as he began his chosen profession.

Vigo continued to stay around the studio, but, his curiosity satisfied by watching the shooting process from close up, he soon became quite bored with the whole thing. The possibility of trying his hand at a film of his own did not seem feasible even in the distant future; then, in the middle of 1929 his father-in-law sent the promised gift—a sum of 100,000 francs—which allowed Vigo to spend some time in Paris and to buy a second-hand Debrie.

They tried the camera everywhere they could. Vigo had decided to film the animals in the zoo and he carefully noted the time when the light was best to photograph each of the animals: the elephants at 3.00 p.m., the monkeys at 3.15, the boar at 3.45, etc. He ended by botching all his shots except for those of the crocodiles and the ostriches.

Vigo could now think of doing something of his own. He had a camera, a sum of money, and the free time. Not even envisaging any project which might involve expensive studio shooting, he could only consider a documentary film on Nice. He had no preconceptions about the subject he had chosen, only a certain hostility. First, because he would have to stay in Nice, and he was convinced he could succeed only in Paris; and then his attitude towards the city itself had become ambivalent. Although he loved the setting in which he and Lydou had been happy, he hated its being a meeting place for the rich. Once he had settled on his subject, his first unconscious step was therefore to withdraw from it.

Vigo started by seriously researching his subject. The thirty-odd works he read or consulted gave him a good knowledge of the history and archaeology of Nice and of the surrounding countryside. In his notebooks he set down Nice's loyalty to Rome against Hannibal and Carthage, the construction of a monument in memory of the victory of Augustus, whose reign was so destructive to the city, and the construction of the road between Arles and Rome. He did not overlook Saint Barnabas preaching the gospel during Claudius' reign or the names of the first martyrs of Nice, Celsus, Nazaire, and above all, Saint Dolores, killed during Nero's reign. Nevertheless, he was somewhat perplexed by all of these notes about facts which were so much dust.

Although there were the ruins of Roman arenas at Cimiez, Vigo's only response to them was one single cinematic idea. He thought that after an establishing shot, the camera should move through what was formerly the lions' entrance and discover a fat milk cow peacefully nibbling the grass. He searched fruitlessly around the city and its environs for traces of the temple of Apollo, which, it was said, had been turned into living quarters for merchants.

As he got further into the city's history, Vigo discovered an increasing number of ancient monuments; with Brun's *Promenades d'un Curieux dans Nice* as a guide, he visited them assiduously. He was keenly interested by rooms dating from the fourteenth century, particularly the nuptial alcove with Ionic pillars which had been used by Maurice de Savoie and Marie-Louise Christine and now sheltered the most destitute beggars. He had already realized that he could do nothing with history itself, but certain monuments, like the church of Saint Augustine, seemed to him to contain elements which could serve as a starting point. The image of Saint Nicholas of Tolentino, the city's lawyer before Our Lord, was in the church. Luther had officiated at religious services there, and Garibaldi had been baptized there. Yes, those could become important themes; but the visual possibilities were quite insignificant. A pietà by Louis Bréa, also in the church, was of no great help. Near it, a *graffito* from the sixteenth century, a naked man and woman arguing, surrounded by flowers and leaves—Adam and Eve in their earthly paradise—was much more amusing.

Vigo visited the Catholic, Protestant, and Jewish cemeteries, and he was struck by the vulgarity of the Prat cemetery. Of all the dead things he had seen, the bad taste of some of the graves there offered the most promising visual possibilities.

Jean Vigo

After weeks of work, Vigo concluded that ancient monuments could be of no conceivable help to him. He decided to annul history, to approach it as if it were a parenthesis between two extremes: the state of nature without man, and life in a modern city. He planned to shoot two thousand feet of film for the first part, about half of it to be selected later for use. In his notebook Vigo wrote: "It is important that the presence of man or of any of his works be nowhere evident. The marvellous countryside should be there alone, just as nature has made it. The countryside placed under the tutelage of the sky and the influence of the sea."[21] The sky and the sea would become the first two of the three themes constituting the opening. The film, Vigo thought, should begin with the sky. First the sky would be clear and then full of heavy, turbulent clouds. The sky would be seen at sunset with dark clouds, followed by clouds moving at different speeds. Then the sky would again become turbulent and filled with soaring gulls. The seagulls would descend towards the horizon. In that way, the transition to the second theme, the sea, could easily be made. The sea was to appear only briefly. First, a variety of waves of different sizes, then a wave of medium size would be followed from the moment it gathered to the moment it exhausted itself on the beach. The third theme, the land, would then be introduced: the land of the soft rolling hills of Saint-Raphaël, with sand and trees, and the landscape of Monte Carlo, abrupt and sprinkled with pebbles. Then, the plains and small dry mountains, next, the canyons, giving way to triumphant mountains covered in green, and then snow, and finally ice.

This was not much for one thousand feet of film, and once there, how could he motivate a transition to the city, to man? While mapping out his itinerary, he had almost achieved the desired transition, but only by ignoring his academic division into themes and his decision not to show the works of man. According to some of his notes, we see, in fact, that there was another version; after the sea, Vigo moved on to rivers, one flooded, the other bone dry, and ended by showing sewers. Sewers, a work of man: man had made his appearance. Vigo probably then retraced his steps, and in his search for a better transition, ended up with ice—and a dead end.

Vigo was quite attached to his symbolic waves, and in his new outline, he retained all of the opening; then, after the wave had exhausted itself on the beach, he intended to insert a shot of the plain and the valley, followed by the ebb of the sea, then a bigger wave which would be seen only as it gathered. The camera was to have filmed the wave from a slight angle. This was to be followed by a shot of a mountain slope, the ebb of the sea, and once again the big wave which, rather than expiring on the beach, would crash triumphantly over some rocks.

The film was then to have passed to the land, a rocky crag surrounded by mountains. These shots of mountainous terrain were to progress into a panoramic view seen from a bend in a hill road. The supposed victory of the big wave would then be revealed as a defeat, for it too would be shown ebbing, followed by other big waves hurling themselves against the rocks and ebbing back in a demonstration of futility. This was to be followed by a landscape of snow, the snow starting to melt, and then a snowman. A work of man, the snowman was to announce man's presence.

Man's appearance was to have led to a change in visual style (the images would be out of focus), and gradually a landscape of houses, hotels, and harbour would emerge from the images as they came into sharper and sharper focus. We would then see a long shot of the sea: solitude disturbed only by a lone ship. The sea, now calm, would, Vigo stressed, appear as "if it were standing at attention." Mastered. A shot of some ebbing foam would dissolve into a tree in bloom. The sea, still calm. We would still see the same tree, only this time we would see fruit being picked from it and then a single cypress tree followed by a telegraph pole with wire climbing up into the sky, extending to infinity. An aerial view: Nice. The heart of the city would rise up into view.

At this point Vigo had to interrupt his work. His and Lydou's health had again worsened, and in the autumn of 1929 they went to Paris to consult specialists.

Vigo took advantage of his stay to become acquainted with young Parisian film-makers, Mitry and Lodz; he also met Boris Kaufman, a cameraman of Russian origin.

Boris Kaufman is often confused with Mikhaïl Kaufman,[22] Dziga Vertov's brother, and cameraman on the most important of the Kino-Pravda films. Boris is perhaps the third Kaufman brother, the youngest, but it is also possible that Vigo and Kaufman deliberately created a myth. In any event, it seems that Boris Kaufman had indeed learned what he knew about film in the Soviet Union, and through an association with the Kino-Pravda group.[23]

Kaufman showed Vigo two of his films and Vigo immediately asked him to help with the documentary on Nice. Vigo's villa had a guest-room, and Vigo persuaded Kaufman, who had never been to Nice, to move in as soon as he could.

Vigo probably started to direct Kaufman's camerawork according to the outline for the opening as it existed before his departure to Paris. They started by taking shots of some of Vigo's beloved waves, but the problems of distinguishing one size of wave from another soon became apparent. The "medium size" and the "bigger" waves looked alike on the screen. The shots of the mountains looked like postcard views. Did Vigo finally realize that from the very outset he had been evading his subject? At the end of 1929 he changed direction and only concerned himself with the modern aspects of the city. Vigo still had no overall outline and, with Kaufman's help, started working on a shooting script. His hostilities to the city remained the principal source of his inspiration, and he started to put everything in order in a first outline which was both simple and direct.

A. Nice is a city which thrives on gambling.
B. Everything in Nice is aimed at foreigners.
    1. The big hotels, etc., etc.;
    2. the foreigners arrive;

> *3. roulette;*
> *4. those who make their living at it.*
> C. *The natives are basically no more interesting than the foreigners.*
> D. *Besides, everything in Nice is dedicated to death.*[24]

Death! It was now possible to do something with those horrible cemeteries he had visited with the *Guide Brun*. He immediately jotted down, "graves, graves, a few examples of the grotesque," and as soon as he could he rushed off with Kaufman to film them. A nude statue with a nest and some dirty water between its legs overjoyed them. They tried animating a marble dove by having the Debrie dolly backwards. By rotating the camera they tried to suggest the fall of an angel leaning on a broken cross. However, in most of the shots they did not disturb the immobility of these funeral monuments.

Vigo wanted a shot of a woman in mourning, weeping at the end of a row of gravestones, to follow the funniest of the monuments. The camera was to move slowly towards her. Just as it was about to pass her, a hat held in someone's hand would appear in the foreground, raised up and down. In front, row after row of graves. The camera would turn back to the widow, but she would no longer be there. There would only be a simple grave with no name on it. Then, brief glimpses of the tombs of great men, Herzen, Gambetta, etc. The camera would make a movement as if saluting four cypress trees. After a series of quick shots of increasingly dilapidated graves, the camera would linger on a tombstone almost buried in the earth, with the city lighting up in the distance behind it.

To conclude this cemetery sequence Vigo had considered a nightmarish variation. After the tombstone half-buried in the ground would come a statue of a child under a huge bell, followed by a death's head, some pyramids, a photograph of a marble book, and the inscription, "Entrance to the Tomb." At that point, the camera was to have fled through the cemetery to the exit, quickly crossed an arbour, knocked at the closed shutters of a convent, then entered, and in a shot taken from the centre of the courtyard, panned right round the cloisters. One door would be open. The camera would rush towards it. The door turns out to be shut. The sky. The sea.

Vigo's intention seems quite clear. The original reason for the shots of the cemetery was to dedicate Nice, a city of gamblers, to death; and in fact that is their function in the finished film. However, when faced with the theme of death, Vigo was once again seized by his obsessions. That grave, beside which Vigo hoped to see a widow mourning, but which, unmarked, untended, was destined like the corpse it sheltered to disappear into the earth—surely this grave, for Vigo, represented the tomb of Almereyda? To avenge himself on society, Vigo wanted to mock the graves of great men, to make fun of Gambetta's bust.

In the rest of the nightmare, reference to Vigo's personal feelings is made in a more veiled way, but there is no mistaking the significance of the child, the death's head, and the flight towards a door believed open. However, both of these sequences expressed pain, and he promptly eliminated them, keeping only the mockery.

The cypress trees interested Vigo. He still wanted to link them to the telegraph poles. But no longer in order to follow the wire to infinity as if it were a road leading to heaven. Rather the reverse; he wanted to close the circle. The sequence was to start by tilting up the cypress's trunk until the top had been reached. The camera would then come down again. Then, the same upward movement would be repeated, but before reaching the top, the audience would realize that it was now a telegraph pole. Once the camera had the telegraph wires in frame it would follow them to the next pole. The descent, from further away this time, would be along the trunk of the original cypress tree. Once again Vigo was straying from his subject, evading it by going off on tangents of personal feelings or clever effects.

He quickly put himself back on the track. To introduce the city he decided to use the last part of his first outline: a panoramic view, with the heart of the city rising up to meet the camera. Then the whole city of Nice would start spinning and that would be followed by a roulette wheel.

The ball skips around. A hand throws in a chip. The ball slows down. A hand slides a chip along the table. The ball slows down. The croupier makes a sign with his finger. The rake pushes the chip back. A hand plays with some chips. The ball slowly skips around. Close-up of the ball. Distorted view of the gamblers' faces. Impassive faces of the croupiers. A stack of chips seen in close-up. The rake. The stack of chips seen from a distance. The ball is spun again. The numbers on the green cloth. Travellers leaving the station. Travellers sitting on their suitcases. Commissionaires. Hotel employees. Taxis. Cars. The interpreter. A hotel door opening. Bellboys. A porter hurrying along. A terrace being swept. A restaurant. A headwaiter adjusts his tie. The hotels seen upside-down right themselves. A waiter checking the parting in his hair. A gnarled tree becomes a palm tree. A palm frond. A street cleaner's broom. A wave depositing garbage on the beach. The street cleaner sweeping. The casino on the promenade. A small pile of garbage near the street cleaner. The sea. The broom. The street cleaner leaves, pushing his cart. A view of the promenade desolate and treeless. The beach chairs being set up. The sea. The gulls. The lines of trees. The clear sky.[25]

Vigo felt that he had got to the heart of his subject. With Kaufman he shot the street cleaner and his broom, and waiters preparing a café terrace for customers. They shot the palm trees just when they were stripped of their old fronds. They filmed the Négresco Hotel, the Rhul, the Palais de la Méditerranée, first upside-down and then right side up. The scenes in the Casino, with the nervous gamblers and impassive croupiers, were more difficult, and were left until later. To film the Promenade des Anglais, empty but already swept and with its chairs ready for the tourists, they had only to arrive early, and that was quickly done.

The Promenade des Anglais, the very centre of Nice's tourist trade and a favourite subject for postcards, had, up until then, hardly inspired Vigo. He realized he had been wrong, and decided to get as much as he could out of the location. To catch strollers unaware, Vigo and Kaufman built a cardboard box to conceal the camera, and frequently went hunting. Their trophies were splendid: lots of ladies with parasols; bearded old men, bald men, one with a monocle reading a paper; a number of women, one of whom was superb, "super-beastly," as Vigo described her in his notes; another seated with her legs crossed; a gypsy, a woman scratching her leg; a paralytic in his wheel-chair being pushed by a servant, some close-ups of a roll of fat on the back of a man's neck, another's prominent ears; a woman showing her thighs as she sat, a beggar, a pedlar, "an old dynamo on two feet," Vigo noted, delighted; a parakeet vendor, more street cleaners, a legless cripple who stops, looks, pushes off again; a close-up of earrings and necklaces, another mass of parasols of different shapes and sizes; a woman selling dogs, and so on. The quality of the photography, however, varied considerably.

After the Promenade des Anglais, Vigo moved on to the beaches. For a time he was preoccupied by the theme of children hurt by adults. He imagined a child at play, carefully constructing sandcastles; huge feet appear and crush them. Vigo then dissolved to: *The sea. Follow a wave. It expires on the beach. Appearance of the castle cemetery.* He also wanted to film a happy, handsome, naked child on the beach, and take "a lot of close-ups" of a woman in a bathing-suit with a lovely figure in a number of poses. Vigo loved bodies. He would have liked to show them at play in beach games. Suddenly, however, the arms of young people throwing a ball back and forth became associated in his mind with the muffled arms of a paralytic pushing at the levers of his wheelchair. *The paralytic's motionless legs, the legs of the attendant pushing the chair. The ball lands on the head of one of the players, who sinks to his knees. The ball bounces away and rolls towards a legless cripple, who looks at it, hesitates, and then continues on his way.*[26] Vigo also wanted to draw a parallel between people tanning themselves in the sun, and men delivering coal, and Negroes.

Actually, there wasn't much on the beach that lent itself to this kind of filming. Here a man with his trousers rolled up to sun his legs; there a fat, bored woman; elsewhere some very ordinary-looking swimmers: that was about all they found.

Using what they had already shot and the ideas they had jotted down, Vigo and Kaufman decided to get the beginning of the film, the lead-in to the subject, down on paper.[27]

1. Overall view of Nice. 2. The heart of Nice rises up towards the camera. 3. All of Nice is sucked up towards the camera. 4. Which finally absorbs it. 5. [Illegible] 6. In the sea. 7. The sea. 8. Ebb and flow. 9. Seagulls flying. 10. Seagulls landing on the waves. 11. Seagulls flying. 12. The woman with the parakeet. 13. The parakeet vendor. 14. The sea throwing garbage up on the shore. 15. The street cleaner's curved broom. 16. The street cleaner. 17. He sweeps up some garbage. 18. The hotel on the promenade. 19. The cleaner looking at the hotel. 20. He makes a gesture of helplessness. 21. He pushes his cart. 22. A paralytic's wheelchair pushed by a servant. 23. The

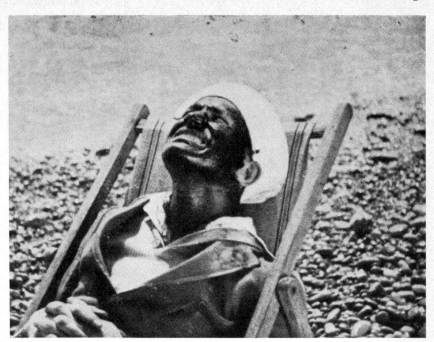

A Propos de Nice

arms of youngsters playing with a medicine ball. 24. They kick a football around. 25. The ball rolls to . . . 26. A legless cripple. 27. He wonders whether to return it, and then goes off leaving the ball there. 28. The ball rolls along on its own and bounces. 29. The ball's trajectory. 30. End of the trajectory of a bowling ball. 31. A game of "boules." 32. The ball rolls. 32a. The bowlers crouched in strange positions as they wait. 33. The roulette ball rolls. 33a. A roulette wheel. 34. Contorted faces of gamblers. 35. Expressionless, ordinary-looking faces of croupiers. 36. [Illegible] 37. A stack of chips in close-up. 38. The croupier's rake. . .

Vigo still thought that the crux of the film should be gambling. However, he had already given a good deal of emphasis to the Promenade des Anglais, and after filming the game of "boules" had become interested in various aspects of Nice's local colour: the *ciapa-cans* (Nice's dog-catchers with their donkey-drawn wagons), children carrying huge pies, or *socca*, Nice's pizza-like dish, the public washing-places at La Vierge du Malonat or on the rue du Pertus. So Vigo finally arrived in the old city, the slums. He saw an old woman washing her laundry in the gutter, mounds of garbage, cats, a dog urinating, children scavenging for rotten bananas, young men playing *morra*, the mutilated fingers of a young boy. He also filmed the sky in the old

A Propos de Nice

quarter, a sky hemmed in by cracked walls and dilapidated roofs. Vigo passed on to the fish market, the beggars asleep on benches, the fish vendors, some huge fish, the prostitutes in the Place Masséna, and the shoeshine man with a wooden leg at the Place Garibaldi.

If Vigo had abandoned all the reading and research he had done about Nice, he had not forgotten the words of Alphonse Karr in a letter to a friend which he had found quoted in a tourist publicity brochure. "Leave Paris," Karr wrote, "where the sun shines for only half an hour; come here, plant your cane in my garden. The next day when you awake you will see that roses have bloomed on it." Vigo may perhaps have wanted to realize Karr's joke on film in the sequence devoted to the theme of flowers, a theme he wanted to elaborate on. Kaufman had taken advantage of a short stay in Grasse to film the flower harvest, and Vigo wanted to film the rows of baskets at the flower market in Nice and the flower-vendor on the Quai Saint-Sébastien. He wanted to return to the cemetery when the graves were covered with flowers; and to conclude the sequence all he would need to do was wait for the battle of flowers.

It was now the beginning of 1930 and carnival was approaching. Having decided to concentrate henceforth on Nice's tourist attractions, leaving open the possibility of reversing that decision at the editing stage, Vigo obtained

A Propos de Nice

permission from the Comité des Fêtes to film the construction of the parade floats. During the parade and the flower battles, he and Kaufman set themselves up on the stand reserved for photographers and cameramen. They soon realized they had made a mistake; but when they tried to film more freely by moving closer to the floats or mingling with the crowds, they constantly had problems with the police. Even so they succeeded in getting a good many shots; but on average the quality was poor. They had been delighted to find "super-beastly," their old friend from the promenade, battling away on one of the floats. But the only really exceptional shot consisted of a group of women dancing on a high platform, filmed from several low angles and at different speeds.

During the entire period of preparation and actual filming, not only had a general plan not been established, but Vigo was not even sure what style the film should have. As we have seen, at various points he seemed to be after a sort of symbolism. Then he had become attracted to harsh realism in the Von Stroheim manner, notably in the sequences where he planned to use the paralytic, the legless cripple and certain particularly grotesque figures from the Promenade. But he was also interested in the possibilities offered by expressionism. Since the carnival was to be featured in the film, he thought of staging a scene: customers seated at restaurant tables, the waiters arrive, and the waiters' faces are effaced while the customers put on their masks.

To these general indications of intention, we might add Vigo's interest in formal experiment. This interest was already evident in the sequence with the cypress trees and telegraph poles; henceforth it turns up in a less schematic way. Like most admirers of *Entr'acte*, Vigo had not passed up the opportunity of filming a real funeral in speeded-up motion. Now he had a scene from the carnival—the women dancing on the platform—in slow motion. Like everyone else, he had been struck by the grotesque effect created by speeded-up motion and the natural solemnity of slow motion. So by linking these two shots, he wanted to inject some of the carnival grotesquery into the funeral and some of the funeral solemnity into the carnival. A quite fortuitous element—the eroticism of the images of the dancing women—prevented him from doing so. But although the eroticism upset his plan, it gave him other ideas. The vulgarity of this eroticism was an invitation to satire; and eroticism and satire were calls, beyond all theories on style and expression, to which Vigo was ready to respond.

Eroticism and satire enabled him to break the bonds of a straightforward documentary on Nice, which already seemed too narrow. Now he could not only incorporate the speeded-up shots of the funeral, but even some of the shots he had taken himself when he was trying out the Debrie: the crocodile and the ostrich, a shot of a priest taken from a window, a soldier on horseback encountered while wandering about the city. These few shots now seemed insufficient. Vigo decided to reinforce the antimilitarist and anticlerical potential of the film. So he and Kaufman proceeded to film warships and troops. They tried to make a church totter by shaking the camera as they filmed it.

By the middle of March 1930, Vigo and Kaufman had shot thirteen thousand feet of film. The time had come to stop shooting and to begin putting the film together.

Several of Vigo's original ideas had proved impossible. All the staged scenes had been abandoned, not only because of the practical difficulties they presented, but also so as not to clash with the spontaneity of the actuality material on which Vigo wanted to rely. He had restricted himself to asking a few acquaintances for a pose, an expression, a gesture.

The gambling sequences had created some serious problems. They had been given reluctant permission to film the roulette wheel, chips and rake while the casinos were closed; but there was no question of filming the croupier's head and hands, and even less of being allowed to prowl with a concealed camera while the casino was packed with gamblers. Nevertheless, they tried, but each time their suspicious movements gave them away, and once they had been spotted they had to give up all hope of doing any filming in the gaming rooms. On the other hand, they were allowed all the freedom they wanted in the ballroom.

The gambling motif, however, couldn't be omitted from the film. They got around the difficulty by using dolls, and this also allowed them to eliminate all the shots of tourists arriving at the station, which were of pitifully bad quality. Using a toy train and cheap dolls, they shot, frame by frame, the arrival of the tourists, who were promptly raked in by the croupier. So gambling became a minor motif in the opening sequence.

Once they had decided to stop shooting, Vigo and Kaufman had at their disposal a mass of fragments and half-sentences which would be difficult to mould into a rational and coherent argument. But then, that had never been the intention.

Vigo, an admirer of the Russian films made under the NEP period of Soviet film-making, had always thought of using "montage-attraction" and the Kino-Eye techniques in some sequences. The extensive use ultimately made of these techniques was due to the unexpected disparity of the usable material. Vigo and Kaufman were therefore obliged to link the fragments together so that they would enrich each other by creating a series of associations. Kaufman's presence could not help but encourage Vigo to adopt this solution.

Their work was finished by the beginning of May. Since the film aimed beyond the city of Nice in its intentions, Vigo christened it *A Propos de Nice*, and he added a subtitle: *Point de vue documenté*.

Now that the time has come to analyse the completed film, one is faced by a problem posed by so many films, and by all of Vigo's work: the film as we now know it is not the film shown in 1930. As the censor's certificate (no. 39751) indicates, *A Propos de Nice* was eight hundred metres long (about twenty-six hundred feet). The prints which now exist and the original negative are mutilated and invariably shorter. This mutilation is particularly damaging in the case of *A Propos de Nice*, because the unity of the film resides in the precise relationship between shots, and which the slightest cut can destroy.

How can we best summarize the film? Among Vigo's papers is the following attempt in the form of a press release. "Jean Vigo and Boris Kaufman have just finished their film, *A Propos de Nice*. Blue sky, white houses, dazzling sea, sun, multi-coloured flowers, a joyful heart: such, at first glance, is the ambience of Nice. But this is only the appearance, ephemeral, fleeting and haunted by death, of a city of pleasure. Beyond this earthly aspect, the young film-makers of *A Propos de Nice* have tried to show the *evolution* of a city."[28] This press release reveals little of Vigo's intentions. Later, when he tended rather to saddle the film with a little too much ideological ambition, he would indicate its meaning more accurately.

The carnival had become the film's central motif. An all-pervasive carnival which turned everything into a carnival: the architecture of the hotels, the people on the Promenade, the army, the navy, the clergy, the cemetery, love, and death. A carnival which sometimes makes one laugh, but more often creates a sense of unease. On two occasions, however, the carnival is forgotten: towards the middle of the film, with the squalor of the old city, and at the end.

Now let us try to describe the film, from notes taken during screenings at the Cinémathèque Française and in film clubs in Paris in 1950.

A Propos de Nice opens with fireworks, followed by four superimposed

A Propos de Nice

aerial shots of the city,[29] dissolving to a roulette wheel. The toy train arrives and the doll-tourists are raked in by the croupier. More aerial shots, enclosed in time by waves which are still framed by a palm tree seen in a gyratory movement from bottom to top, and by a street cleaner. His appearance announces the preparations for the carnival. These preparations continue with six shots showing the making of huge puppets and masks, alternating with three shots of waiters setting up tables on a terrace. After a shot showing a mouth being painted on an enormous puppet, we see a palm tree being spruced up. After being juxtaposed for a moment with a little potted palm, the tree is shown again, spreading its fronds nicely out towards the top of the frame. The Hotel Rhul, the Palais de la Méditerranée and the Hotel Négresco, which were upside-down, are righted. The statue is added, then a tracking shot along railings seen in shadow on the sidewalk, and everything is ready.

Now for the promenade. There is nothing very extraordinary about the Promenade des Anglais, actually: ladies, gentlemen, a newspaper vendor, armchairs and beach chairs, a beggar, a photographer, a dog, a gypsy, a street cleaner with his cart. The time has come to leave the Promenade, looking at it from above, from higher and higher up until it is replaced by a very prosaic seaplane slowly landing on the sea. So slowly, in fact, that its flight is interrupted by another shot of the Promenade. But when the plane finally

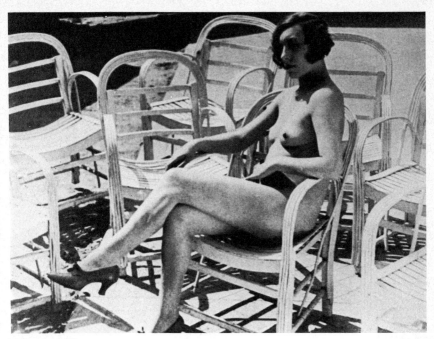

A Propos de Nice

stops, the Promenade is left behind. The seaplane is followed by sailboats, soon mingled with tennis players who dominate for a while, and then give way to a game of "boules." The start of an automobile race occasions a brief return to aquatic sports, but then the Monte Carlo Rally returns. It is a limousine driven by a wealthy woman, however, that stops in front of a palatial hotel with a carpet on the sidewalk. A man eating. Another even more expensive car arrives with a chauffeur and lackey. Fortunately an old greybeard takes us back to the Promenade.

But the Promenade des Anglais is oddly different. The women, all middle-aged or old, are hideously ugly. One, who might be the most elegant of them all, is followed by a shot of an ostrich, and then "super-beastly" reading a newspaper. The joys of ugliness announce the carnival. The peaceful musicians, the pedlars, and the seagulls can no longer change the course of events.

Yet there are still young legs, young thighs, a watchful old man. A young woman seated on the terrace changes costume five times, after which she is clothed only in her shoes. The outline of white sculptures suggests that people go to the beach, and the sailor sunning himself turns black. And since, in addition to the ostrich, Vigo had a crocodile, he brings it in here, only for it to give way to the Palais de la Méditerranée. The absurdity of the hotel's façade and arcades is finally interrupted by the narrow strip of sky in the old city banked by ruined walls and roofs. Yet, everything up there is more beautiful than the street intersection below. Not so much because of the washerwomen in the public laundry, or the children carrying their huge pies, or the games of *morra*. Rather, because of a child whose fingers have been eaten away by fire or leprosy. And sewers, garbage, a cat.

Luckily there is a paradise for rich old ladies, tuxedos with gigolos inside them. But for the shot of that rich old woman's face, what a dead end! FOR THE CARNIVAL HAS COME! The giant dolls live, they walk, and some of them are so lifelike that they have human faces in their bellies. "Super-beastly" is part of the revels, as are the ribbons and the horse they festoon. But on the ground, those same flowers harvested by the hands of the women of Grasse are trampled underfoot. And the only hands they touch before they are crushed are those of "super-beastly" or a policeman. That is why the little dog and the dolls with guitars seem so melancholy. The melancholy is broken by the women dancing on the platform. And although the penguin and the black effigy are made of pasteboard, the general and his horse really are flesh and bone. The other effigies are neither flesh nor pasteboard; they are marble and they are in the cemetery. No matter, for it is carnival time! The military parade, the fleet in the Bay of Villefranche, and the women dancing, dancing, dancing, are proof of that. The priest looks first at the posters, then pauses on the edge of the sidewalk. He does not cross the street in front of the dancers' swaying thighs, and the funeral is rushed through in a second so that the women, the paralytic and "super-beastly" can go on. Not only shoes are shined now, but naked feet as well. Next a beard, a donkey, decorations; a shot from under a sewer grating presents the legs of people stepping over the empty space. We then realize that a cemetery exists because of death. The women continue dancing, but slowly. The bust of Gambetta on his tomb is shown not only from the front but from the back. The other statues are more or less stationary (for, ultimately, only the angel knows how to, can, and wants to fly). But this no longer matters, for although the women continue dancing, they do so more and more slowly. However, that makes them no less vulgar, and only the intrusion of the waves and the palm trees allows peaceful contemplation of the grieving mother, of the woman who veils her face, and of the sky. Everything would be fine, except for a sudden obsessive search for seated women's sexual organs. Even when the women are carved in stone, all we see is a moist nest! Why bother changing the subject by introducing new waves or cypress trees when they are no longer able to redress things? The older woman with her sexual organ plastered across her face, she understands. She and her friend smile on the dancers who again seem to be going into a frenzy. Confronted with a factory chimney, the older woman nods her head with more than approval: her desire turns into utter ravishment as the chimney gets bigger and bigger. But then hasn't this huge chimney become a cannon? The proof is the decapitated head of a giant carnival effigy. Of course there is smoke and the blackened faces of workmen cracking jokes. But the chimneys can return, for their function is indeed the expulsion of smoke so

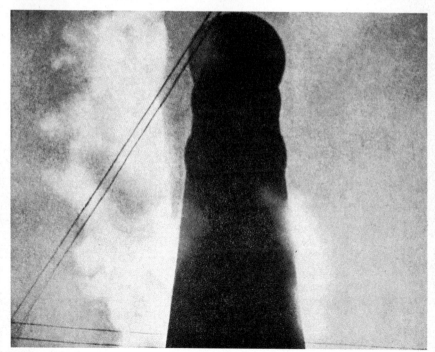

A Propos de Nice

that it will not asphyxiate people. The cemetery has not been able to kill the carnival. It would be over by now, even if this was not really the end.

A Propos de Nice was not merely an opportunity for Vigo to prove that he could conceive, shoot, and edit a film. Speaking in Paris before the Groupement des Spectateurs d'Avant-Garde, he was to extract a theory from his experience and present an outline of what, in his view, social documentary—cinema with "a documented point of view"—should be. At the end of his talk Vigo made a profession of revolutionary faith. "In this film, by showing certain basic aspects of a city, a way of life is put on trial. In fact, as soon as the atmosphere of Nice and the kind of life lived there—and not only there, unfortunately—has been suggested, the film develops into a generalized view of the vulgar pleasures that come under the sign of the grotesque, of the flesh, and of death. These pleasures are the last gasps of a society so lost in its escapism that it sickens you and makes you sympathetic to a revolutionary solution."

Vigo's comments, in fact, were apropos of *A Propos de Nice*. Rather than just creating a film with several points of view, he had succeeded in introducing subversive feelings into the film. It was the film itself—after he had finished it—that helped him to organize his feelings and channel them into a revolutionary ideology.

At first glance, the film's aggressiveness may seem impersonal. The tendency to ridicule the military and the clergy was quite widespread at the time, and although doing so may have given Vigo the pleasure of drawing closer to Almereyda, the way he did it remained rather generalized. When he attacks middle-aged women, on the other hand, his anger seems to have deeper roots. In a sequence which has disappeared, "a shot of an old woman, apparently decomposing although still alive" is followed by, as a critic complained, "an allusion in bad taste: a hole dug in a cemetery."[30] Did Vigo back down and cut the sequence out himself? Anyway, Vigo had only to express his hatred for something to be delivered completely from it. We will see this later in *Zéro de Conduite*, where Vigo openly uses the personal and confessional.

Beyond its feelings and ideologies, Vigo's first film has a style. Finding an artistic tradition in which to insert *A Propos de Nice* is a difficult task. We have indicated that Vigo, haunted by memories of *Foolish Wives*, admired Von Stroheim—a name brought up by several critics. We have also pointed out that for one shot he found inspiration in René Clair. But mostly we have followed him in his search for an approach, guided in that search by his admiration—an admiration shared by his collaborator—for Soviet filmmaking. The German avant-garde is another possible influence—Vigo could have seen one or two films at least (by Ruttmann and Richter)—as are certain French experiments prior to *Entr'acte*. But by 1929–30 Vigo had not had a chance to see very many films. His opportunities in Nice were limited, and his stays in Paris were rare.

Like most members of the avant-garde, Vigo felt attracted to formal experimentation. We have seen how he was tempted by a circular construction in the sequence with the cypress trees and the telegraph poles. But he had resisted.

He had also been attracted by changes in camera speed; and this time he did succumb. However, in his case one senses a sort of joyous personal rediscovery of the cinema's means, rather than any influence from his predecessors. Moreover, he uses speeded-up and slow motion with specific ends in mind, and this too distinguishes him from other avant-garde film-makers with their often gratuitous effects.

Among the young, the term *avant-garde* enjoyed great prestige in 1929–30, and Vigo was happy to see himself classified under that heading. All the more so because at the time the expression could imply artistic as much as social audacity. Even today his work is presented under the same label, which, despite its fall from grace, is vague enough to be convenient. However, from our present perspective, it is unfair to put *A Propos de Nice* in the same category as that jaded avant-garde with its slick audacities. Facility, as a matter of fact, is totally absent from *A Propos de Nice*. When Vigo tries to use facile techniques to make a stone angel fly or to associate the waiters sweeping a café terrace with workers building the carnival floats, he fails. When the beauty or ugliness of a palm tree or of a woman dazzles us, it springs from the discovery-creation of Vigo's eye (later to become almost infallible). Even if the lack of facility gets in the way, it never lessens the sudden shock created by the beauty of a palm tree or the ugliness of a woman. This absence of slick effect means that whenever he does strive for effect the result is always naïve. Yet the roughness and naïveté in no way prejudice artistic expression: Vigo in *A Propos de Nice* is a primitive.

In that spring of 1930 Vigo's problems lay elsewhere: he had to elucidate the revolutionary message of *A Propos de Nice*, and to present the film in Paris in the hope, if possible, of finding a commercial distributor. A good part of the hundred thousand francs had been swallowed up, and the little money the film might earn would be very welcome. In the meantime, the remnants of the gift from Lydou's father allowed them to set off happily in May 1930 for Paris, where they stayed at the Hotel Corneille on the rue Corneille.

The obvious place in Paris—ideal in Vigo's opinion—for the première was the Vieux-Colombier, home of the avant-garde film for some years now under the management of Jean Tedesco. Invitations, bearing a still of Vigo, Kaufman and their camera, were mailed, and a press release was sent to the papers. *Le Soir*, the paper for which Fanny Clar wrote, published it:

". . . One should not look for the more conventional aspects of the Riviera in this film. Although the atmosphere of Nice is part of it, the film-makers were after something else.

"They have tried to capture, in the elements of a particularly representative city, a certain way of life and its destiny.

"*A Propos de Nice* will be shown at the Vieux-Colombier on Wednesday, May 28."[31]

The evening before the screening, Fanny Clar reminded *Le Soir*'s readers of the impending event, specifying the time (3.00 p.m.) to avoid any possible confusion with the normal daily programmes at the Vieux-Colombier, which was currently showing *Menschen am Sonntag*, a film not much to the taste of admirers of the avant-garde.

We know very little about this first public screening. Fanny Clar was there, of course, and two days later she published an article in which her only reservation concerned the repetition of shots.[32]

Vigo knew the article was to appear, and expected as much from the kindness of his old friend. More significant, because more spontaneous, was an article which appeared on the same day, much to the astonishment of Fernand Desprès, in "the reactionary *L'Echo de Paris*."[33] *L'Echo de Paris* was a morning paper, so its review of *A Propos de Nice*, signed Luc Anri, is very likely the first review of a Vigo film ever to appear.[34]

This review reveals the same failure as Fanny Clar's to understand the repetition of themes, but it was laudatory; and Vigo needed encouragement, for he was having doubts about his film. "He is persuaded now that he has not made a complete flop, but he still has a good many doubts about the excellence of the film," Fernand Desprès wrote to Pierre de Saint-Prix,[35] asking the latter to send Vigo a letter complimenting him on his film. Both friends were at the screening, and so were Caussat and Bruel. The film critic from *L'Humanité*, Léon Moussinac, had also been present, and he was planning to write about the film. Moussinac's opinion carried a good deal of weight with Vigo, for he was both the Communist Party's spokesman and one of the most distinguished film critics of the day. Fernand Desprès must have "worked" on his comrade and colleague at *L'Humanité*. In any case, he felt he could tell Pierre de Saint-Prix, and very probably Vigo as well, that the article by "Moussinac in next Sunday's *L'Humanité* will be even better" than those previously published in *Le Soir* and *L'Echo de Paris*.[36] However, after the first showing at the Vieux-Colombier, aside from the two articles already referred to, nothing much appeared in the papers. Apparently, not enough critics had gone to the screening. They had to be rounded up at the first opportunity, and that opportunity presented itself very soon.

The first screening had been attended by the organizers of the Groupement des Spectateurs d'Avant-Garde, which was made up of young people avid for everything which was or appeared to be new in cinema. They immediately invited Vigo to bring his film to their June screening, which was to be devoted, like the one in May, to young French film-makers. The May screening had been quite a success.[37] The Paris correspondent for *Close Up* spoke of it as the "first really significant cinematic event in Paris in a month," and the season was far from an uninteresting one.[38]

Vigo could not let such an opportunity slip by and decided to prolong his stay in Paris, for he had been asked to say a few words to introduce his film. He had never addressed an audience before and thought it wise to prepare a text beforehand.

Once again the screening took place at the Vieux-Colombier, on Saturday, June 14, at 3.30. "Jean Mitry spoke first in a somewhat confusing although penetrating manner about certain young film-makers whose principal defect, he said, was their tendency towards abstraction."[39] Mitry's film *Un Coup de Dés* followed, and Vigo then spoke. "He acquitted himself beautifully," Desprès wrote to Saint-Prix. "That surprised me, coming from such a shy young man. But he has sincerity."[40] ". . . He spoke shyly and with sincerity," wrote one journalist, "then, seeing that the audience was with him and liked him, he grew more confident, more positive, more sure of himself and his subject."[41]

Vigo had entitled his talk: "Towards a Social Cinema." It was not only the first time that he had spoken in public, but also the first time that he had ever put his thoughts about the cinema down on paper.

In his short speech, Vigo made a profession of revolutionary faith. Before that, however, he stated that he had no intention of "making revelations about social cinema" or of "strangling it with a formula." For him, the quest for a truly social cinema began with getting away from technique for technique's sake and from over-subtlety. "In the cinema," he said, with youthful delight in amusing comparisons, "we treat our minds to the sort of refinement usually reserved by the Chinese for their feet." He immediately added the corrective that it was just as dangerous to be condescending as it was to be over-subtle. "On the pretext that film is an art born yesterday, we baby-talk just as daddy babbles to his darling so that baby can understand." Vigo then protested that: "The camera, after all, is not an air-pump for creating vacuums."

The battle over the sound film was still raging in 1930, and Vigo touched on the question by affirming that a step towards social cinema would be taken "when people stop trying to decide whether a film should *a priori* be silent, or as sonorous with sound effects as an empty jug, or as 100 per cent talkie as our war veterans, or in three dimensions, in colour, in smells, or in what-have-you." Vigo's catalogue clearly reveals his preference for the silent cinema. He did not want to get involved in an aesthetic dispute which he considered pointless, but the metaphor with which he brushed the dispute aside was, to say the least, unexpected. "For," he continued, "to take another field, isn't it the same as asking a writer to tell us whether he wrote his latest novel with a quill or a fountain pen?" After being led to commit this blunder by his penchant for funny comparisons, Vigo, lost in unfamiliar terrain, cut his argument short by stating that in any case these disputes "belong in fairs," and that the film industry was governed by "the laws of the fairground." Here he was being only mildly malicious. He was harder on film audiences when he said, still speaking about social cinema, that one had to "awaken other echoes than those created by the belches of ladies and gentlemen who come to see a film to help their digestion."

Vigo proposed *Un Chien Andalou* as an example of a proper approach. "A crucial work in every way: the assurance of its direction, ingenuity of its lighting, perfection of visual and conceptual associations, good dream logic, admirable confrontation between the subconscious and the conscious. . . . From a social point of view an accurate and courageous film." The most polemical passages of the Buñuel and Dali film are referred to, the prologue in particular. "Our apathy, which makes us capable of accepting all the monstrous acts men have perpetrated, is severely challenged when we are unable to bear the sight of a woman's eye cut in two by a razor on the screen." His conclusion: "*Cave Canem*. . . . Beware of the dog, he bites. . . . Any step towards social cinema confronts the cinema as a whole with a provocative subject, a subject which bites into flesh."

So far, Vigo had only spoken in general terms about social cinema. He wanted to talk to his audience about something more specific—*the documented point of view*—a precise approach to the making of social documentary. "The camera should be directed at something which must be recognized as a document, and which during the actual editing must be approached as such.

"Obviously, conscious posing or acting cannot be tolerated. Unless the character is taken unawares by the camera, the *documentary* value of this kind of cinema is impossible to attain.

"Anyone involved in making social documentaries must be thin enough to slip through the keyhole of a Roumanian lock and capable of catching Prince Carol jumping out of bed in his shirt tails: assuming, that is, one thinks such a spectacle worthy of interest. He must be small enough to fit under the chair of a croupier—that great god of the Monte Carlo casino—and believe me, it isn't easy."

And so the *point de vue documenté* is revealed as a resurrection of Kino-Eye: an impossible resurrection, as Vigo himself unconsciously demonstrates. In joking about "Prince Carol in his shirt tails" or alluding to his problems while trying to film in the casino, Vigo was describing the very reasons why the Russians had failed. As Georges Sadoul says: "The development of a real 'cinema-eye' is dependent on the invention of a camera as light, mobile, and sensitive as the human eye itself."[42]

But Vigo was no theoretician, and any attempt to place him within a particular school or tradition is only of relative importance in a study of his work. The interesting thing is that in his contradictions while considering the problem, Vigo shows himself torn between what he feels to be his duty as a man and his nature as a creative artist. He distinguishes between the two, making it clear that the first is more important. "This kind of social documentary demands that one take a position, because it dots the 'i's. If a social documentary does not commit us as artists, it does commit us as men. And that's worth at least as much." Vigo seems almost to regret that this is so. Trying to list examples of how the objectives of the *point de vue documenté* could be properly implemented, he begins by expressing a desire "to reveal the hidden reasons behind a gesture, to extract from the most mundane person caught off guard a hidden beauty or a caricature." Here, Vigo is already treading on ground where taking a social position is no longer crucial. He corrects himself immediately. He wanted to feel committed as a man, and still referring to *A Propos de Nice*, he concludes by stating that he was "accessory to a revolutionary solution."

The audience enjoyed Vigo's caustic verve, and some of his amusing turns of phrase were greeted by great bursts of approving laughter. A receptive atmosphere was thus created for the screening of *A Propos de Nice*, and the film was greeted by applause, at times both enthusiastic and unanimous. Everything had turned out very well, and all that remained now was to wait for the reviews. Fanny Clar and Fernand Desprès faithfully stood watch.

Le Soir was a radical paper inclining to the left. Fanny Clar had explained to the somewhat puzzled desk editor that a film by the son of Almereyda, a victim of the reactionaries, was going to be screened, and that a reporter must be sent both to review the film and to interview Vigo. A young man was chosen for the task: Charles Goldblatt, who was trying to make a living as a journalist after spending several years with Copeau's theatre and doing his military service. It was the first time he had ever interviewed anyone or met a film director, and Goldblatt was rather awed.

He noticed a young woman who seemed to be very much at her ease, as though she belonged, so he told her he was a newspaperman and asked to see M. Jean Vigo. Lydou ran off to look for Jean, who was equally excited at the idea of making a statement to a newspaperman. They were soon chatting easily together, however, and Vigo gave Goldblatt a copy of his talk. Fernand Desprès, for his part, got a copy to Léon Moussinac, whose article they were still awaiting. The next day, *L'Humanité* covered the screening, using a photograph with a caption, and a short note.[43] The photograph showed a woman in white with a hat, and the caption read: "This remarkable specimen of the bourgeoisie—winner of the battle of the flowers in Nice—is shown running wild in *A Propos de Nice*, an excellent film by Jean Vigo and Boris Kaufman which was shown yesterday. . . ." The note, entitled "Towards a Social Cinema," was scarcely any longer, but it ended by announcing that a longer article would appear shortly.

The articles by Goldblatt and Moussinac appeared the following week. Goldblatt thought that the June 14 screening "would find a place in the history of French cinema." His article was long—it summarized Vigo's talk—and very favourable. His only reproach: "At times the film's rhythm becomes tiring, sometimes because it is too frenetic, sometimes because it is too slow." He concluded: "Here we have some young people on whom we can count; they know where they are headed."

Only the last part of Moussinac's long-awaited article, "Documentaire," was devoted to Vigo's film. "Special praise to the film *A Propos de Nice*. A documentary, yes; but one which, as its authors obviously intend, goes beyond the restrictions of the average documentary, and aims for social commitment." From that point on, Moussinac simply quoted from Vigo's talk, as Goldblatt had; he quotes about a hundred words before concluding: "That is why *A Propos de Nice* is not only an attempt at real cinema, but also an attempt to pillory a certain world. Bravo, young men! It is a fine though rocky road you have chosen."

It seems that this second screening of *A Propos de Nice* evoked no other comments.[44]

The results of these two screenings were discouraging: four articles, of which at least two, and probably a third, were gestures made by friends. Nothing appeared in the *Revue du Cinéma*, the forum for the younger critics. Charles Stenhouse, who kept a close eye on Paris film activities for *Close Up*, and who had expressed such interest in the first programme of young cinema presented by the Groupement des Spectateurs d'Avant-Garde, said nothing about the second. He mentioned only one film by a young director shown in Paris during the month of June: *J'avais un fidèle Amant*, by Francis Winter and Robert de Ribon. It is true that the same issue of *Close Up* carried an article in French on Vigo's film, but once again the author was a friend, Maurice M. Bessy, and his benevolent attitude was clear from the article: "An interesting piece . . . an odd film. Jean Vigo confessed to me that he was greatly impressed by *Un Chien Andalou.* . . . Although conceived on the basis of a carefully worked out script, the film seems at times to lack coherence. . . . Nevertheless, it is a film which deserves attention, and there are several gems of invention and some amusing gags in it."[45]

The results were meagre, adding up to an insignificant succès d'estime. The commercial side was hardly better. The possibilities for distribution did not seem encouraging, and the outright sale of the film—the solution preferred by Vigo because he was counting on the money to produce his next film, another documentary, this time on Lourdes, for which he had already done the research and started the treatment—seemed even less of a possibility. He planned to learn his craft by making another two or three short films before attempting more ambitious works. The little interest expressed by the distributors stopped Vigo's plans cold.

His stay in Paris was dragging on, no prospects for work seemed imminent, and he had to start thinking about the immediate future. Vigo did not want to abandon the cinema, so he decided to start a project he had often thought about: setting up an organization to show films in Nice. The idea interested him, and he hoped to reap some profit from it. There was no question of starting something like the Ursulines or even the Vieux-Colombier: the milieu was hardly suitable, and anyway Vigo probably no longer felt quite the same enthusiasm for enterprises like that. He envisaged the creation of a film club which would function according to the possibilities for programming and depending on the degree of interest created by its existence. His model was to be associations of a popular nature like Les Amis du Cinéma.[46]

His club, which he called Amis du Cinéma after its predecessor, would present—for members only—films which had been banned or cut by the censors, just as the Amis de Spartacus had done earlier for Soviet films in Paris.

Vigo used the end of his stay in Paris to find out about programming possibilities, and as soon as he returned to Nice he started to work on the project. The principal obstacle to its realization was his lack of contacts in Nice. He mentioned his idea to a group of interns at Saint-Roch Hospital. He had been introduced to them by Caussat, and he often passed his evenings in the duty room with the interns who would kill time by playing cards, reading, or chatting. Caussat, already won over to the idea, supported Vigo as well as he could, explaining to his friends what this new phenomenon, a film club, was. They convinced only one of the young interns, Maurice Nicolas. Nicolas, however, proved a notable recruit, for once he had agreed, he would not balk at any task. Lydou completed the staff, and the four of them were ready to get things going. However, the stay in Paris had affected the Vigos', especially Jean's, health. Everything had to be postponed; and they left for Peira Cava, where they stayed almost two months.

Vigo must sometimes have been terribly depressed by this perpetual threat of a relapse. In Paris, after one of the showings of *A Propos de Nice*, Mme. de Saint-Prix had told him (referring to her dead son): "Jean would have been happy." At Peira Cava that phrase troubled Vigo, and he wrote to her. "I am happy to be close to the friend of my longest and most fruitful silences, who achieved what I would have liked to do."[47] His search for this kind of approval was not a good sign. He had again fallen into a state of depression. Even when news from Paris announced that the possibilities for commercial distribution of *A Propos de Nice* had become very good, he did not dare believe it entirely, and being both timid and proud, he started constructing defences against the possibility of another defeat. "I have real hopes for *A Propos de Nice*," he wrote to Saint-Prix, "but until the final papers are signed, I will keep my doubts, for I refuse to exercise my back by kowtowing before anyone, and that isn't likely to endear me to anyone, is it?"[48]

Fernand Desprès sensed that Vigo was once again in a bad way, and as usual, he hastened to Vigo's side. By the beginning of September things had taken a turn for the better. Desprès wrote to Pierre de Saint-Prix and described Lydou and Jean's happy life together, dancing and having fun like two children. But the old family friend was still worried. "She looks good, seems strong. He is still frail. One of them will win out. Isn't that what always happens between sick people? I hope I'm wrong. After all, death is the supreme defeat."[49]

The physical and spiritual crisis Vigo went through at Peira Cava was not as serious as the one he experienced at Font-Romeu. He soon realized that he did not have to fear a real relapse, and he no longer thought of himself as a nobody, he no longer felt isolated. First of all, he had Lydou, and then there were the friends he had made through Fernand Desprès. He could even be of service to his friends by pulling strings, as he did for Caussat. Caussat was having problems with his military service, and Vigo asked Mme. de Saint-Prix to intervene. During the very height of his depression, in August 1930, the feeling of having a certain power, even of the most tenuous sort, must certainly have helped Vigo overcome any feeling he might have that he was the most unfortunate of mortals.

During his last weeks at Peira Cava, Vigo's taste for work returned, and he spent a good deal of time on his film club. Sometimes he even travelled to Nice, or sent Lydou there. Things went so well that, when they finished their rest cure on September 15, they were able to schedule the opening programme of the Amis du Cinéma for the nineteenth. At the beginning, only Vigo knew where and how to obtain films. Lydou took care of the financial side. She was not only treasurer, but ran the box-office on the days of the screenings. Caussat's function—he had the title of secretary—consisted of picking up the films on his motor-cycle. Often the films did not arrive in time; in which case Caussat and his motor-cycle became even more useful, since someone had to go all over Nice, and if necessary to nearby towns, looking for substitutes for the missing films. Nicolas was named vice-president of the Amis du Cinéma, but in fact he was stuck with being the group's speech maker, and he had to introduce and comment on the films before they were shown. At the beginning this was not without its problems: Nicolas knew nothing about the cinema. Most of the time he had not seen the films being shown, and the prints always arrived too late to preview them before the screening. He got some information on the films from *L'Art Cinématographique*, and from magazines given to him by Vigo. Vigo was able to give him some ideas, but even he was not very well informed. The fact that Nicolas was able to get by was mostly due to his training at medical school in the art of bluff.

Vigo had managed to get Germaine Dulac to come and inaugurate his group. The first showing took place on the evening of September 19, 1930, in a lecture hall on the Boulevard Victor-Hugo, in an old disused chapel which has since been torn down. At the last minute everything seemed in danger of collapse: the fire inspector, after examining the projection box, made entirely of wood and without any fireproofing, announced that he would not allow the event to take place. Caussat left on his motor-cycle in quest of a patron influential enough to have this ruling reversed. Vigo and Nicolas plotted and planned. The audience was already in the hall. Although it was rather sparse, the organizers were pleased. They had not expected so many people. Finally the screening was allowed to start. Maurice Nicolas (from whom I received most of this information) was struck by Vigo's determination and by his hostile disdain towards anything which represented authority or the established social order. This surprised Nicolas, coming as it did from a young man he had always thought of as quiet and reserved.

Later screenings took place in various suburban cinemas on the nights they were normally closed to the public. The winter promised to be a particularly harsh one. Inside the box-office, despite the fur coat she wore, Lydou shivered while Vigo argued with the projectionist, surrounded by reels of film from Marseilles or Paris which Caussat, as usual, had collected from the station at the last minute. Nicolas, meanwhile, sized up the audience and rehearsed his speech with an eye on his notes. Bit by bit they succeeded in collecting a faithful and sympathetic audience. The first solid core consisted of friends who subsequently recruited acquaintances from different sectors of Nice's middle class—doctors, architects, painters, a few civil servants, some high-school pupils, a very few university students. (The university at Nice was not nearly so big then as it is today.) When they started showing Soviet films, a more popular element, comprising Communists or Communist sympathizers, started coming. Among his friends, Vigo made no secret of his sympathy for this segment of the audience, but Nicolas noted that "he was not at all the comradely sort you can pat on the back; he kept his distance with a friendly but somewhat haughty smile which kept everyone in his place."[50]

During the first months, when they came to count the receipts after a screening, there was often not enough to pay for the hire of the auditorium and the modest salaries offered to the projectionist and the usherettes. Vigo and his friends would discuss the situation over a drink at the nearest bar, and agree that they should have faith in the future. They would then bid Nicolas goodnight. Caussat would straddle his motor-cycle, Lydou and Vigo would balance themselves on it, and the three of them would vanish into the night heading towards La Dominante, the name they had given their new villa perched on the top of the Tenon hill.

During the film club's first two weeks, Vigo received two bits of good news. Pathé-Nathan had agreed to programme *A Propos de Nice* at the Ursulines some time early in October; and, in November, Vigo was invited to present his film at a congress of film-makers and critics which was soon to meet in Brussels.

From the first days of October Vigo bombarded Desprès with questions about the audience's reaction to *A Propos de Nice* at the Ursulines. "If you should go," Desprès wrote to Saint-Prix, "would you please observe the audience's reactions? Being so far away makes Jean very apprehensive; he wants to know which sequences the audience reacts to, with smiles, mutters or applause. He asked me to tell him. But I cannot get off early enough in the evenings to go to the Ursulines."[51]

Vigo could not resist satisfying his desire to see things at first hand, and a week later he was in Paris. He also did not want to miss out on any chances for work which might perhaps present themselves while the film was being shown. Desprès thought Vigo wanted "to become assistant to a known director: René Clair, Tourneur, or Abel Gance."[52]

A few weeks before his departure, Vigo had written to Georges Charensol asking him about the possibilities of getting a job as a second assistant to René Clair.[53] At the same time, Francis Jourdain approached Maurice Tourneur, a friend from his youth. Although these expectations proved abortive, the screenings of *A Propos de Nice* at the Ursulines gave the film an incomparably larger audience than had the two showings at the Vieux-Colombier, and, by making Vigo's name known, they allowed him—for he was present at most of the film's showings—to enlarge his circle of contacts in the artistic world. He met several people there who were to play an important part in his career, for example, the actor René Lefèvre, who, after having been present at a showing, expressed a desire to meet the film-maker. Lefèvre was to return, bringing with him a friend whom he introduced to Vigo. Albert Riéra was his name, and Vigo happily discovered that their families were closely related. For someone who had suffered since

'La Dominante' in Nice

childhood from a sense of having no family, this discovery made the occasion quite a sentimental one; Vigo immediately became friends with the young painter.

Beginning to become known had some more concrete and immediate results as well. The contacts on which Vigo depended had already become stronger. To Germaine Dulac, Vigo was no longer merely Madame de Saint-Prix's protégé, and to Moussinac, he was no longer only Fernand Desprès' friend; he was someone whose work they both now knew. They joined efforts in an attempt to get Vigo a contract for a short film from Gaumont-Franco-Film-Aubert.

Vigo was to start work on it in December 1930 or January 1931. He therefore had plenty of time to go to Brussels to participate in the "Deuxième Congrès du Cinéma Indépendant."

The Congress had been organized through a decision made a year earlier by a group of film-makers and critics, including, among others, Eisenstein, Moussinac, Cavalcanti, and Robert Aron, gathered together at a château in Sarraz, Switzerland, through the efforts of Mme. de Mandrot, who was herself interested in the future of the cinema. Afterwards, the meeting had been christened the "Premier Congrès du Cinéma Indépendant." It was therefore the second which took place in Brussels from November 27 to December 1, 1930. It was attended by most of those who had been present at the château, and by Germaine Dulac, Richter, and a whole group of young film-makers and critics: Ivens, Vigo, Lodz, Auriol, and Bourgeois. The working sessions were dedicated to a search for methods for fighting censorship, and the rest of the time to film showings.

The young film-makers were pleased to have their films shown to members of the Congress and the public on the same bill with films like *Earth, Hallelujah, Melodie der Welt, Man With a Movie Camera, Drifters*, etc.

The neophytes, besides Vigo, included Henri Storck. The year 1930 had been his first as a film-maker. He had already experimented with abstract images and had made an animated film by painting directly on celluloid. But his first film to be shown to an audience was *Images d'Ostende*, one of the films shown at the Congress. Storck earned his living by making newsreels in Ostend, and his first film consisted of a selection of shots he had taken in the course of his daily work. The selection had been determined by memories of his childhood walks through the city. He confided that he had wanted to "show the friendliness and life that exist in inanimate objects: the wind carrying away a chair, the sea moulding the sand," and he nervously asked the English critic, Oswell Blakeston, "Do you think that will be realized by the cinéastes at the Congress?"[54]

His doubts were well founded. In *Images d'Ostende* there are endless shots of the sea, and towards the middle of the film Vigo created a disturbance by crying out, "Water. Nothing but water," a cry which was immediately taken up by a chorus of young voices. After the screening, Storck suppressed his nervousness and sought out the person who had started the row so that he could politely explain the film to him. It was now Vigo's turn to be embarrassed, and as a result of the long conversation the pair got to know each other quite well.

We do not know how the majority of critics present at the Congress reacted to the younger generation's films. They did not, however, please the critic from *Close Up* very much. Speaking about a documentary by Kaufman and Lodz, but probably referring to a whole group of films, Oswell Blakeston wrote: "These people do not MAKE pictures. They shoot hundreds of feet and SELECT. It is too easy. One must MAKE."[55] As for *A Propos de Nice*, Blakeston simply refers to the article by Maurice Bessy already published in *Close Up*.

The Congress decided to create the Association du Cinéma Indépendant, which Vigo and his Amis du Cinéma joined. Like many other similar ventures, both prior and subsequent, the Association led nowhere. Aside from the customary manifesto, the only trace which remains of the meetings in Switzerland and Brussels is a 16 mm. burlesque filmed by Eisenstein at the château in Sarraz with members of the Congress as the cast. But are there any prints still in existence?[56]

For Vigo the Congress had a certain importance. *A Propos de Nice* had been shown to an international audience, and possibilities for distribution had emerged in Holland and Sweden. He had also been able to see some films and, by extending his contacts, to ensure a wider selection of films for his club.

Vigo returned to Paris immediately to start work on the film he had been commissioned to do by G. F. F. A. (Gaumont), thanks to the support of Germaine Dulac and Léon Moussinac. G. F. F. A. wanted to start a new series of short subjects under the general heading, *Journal Vivant* (*Living Newspaper*). The person in charge, M. Morskoï, decided to start with documentaries about sports, centring them around well-known athletes. Vigo was allowed to select an assistant, and he chose Ary Sadoul, whom he had met through Francis Jourdain. Ary was the son of Jacques Sadoul, the revolutionary.

The film he had been selected to direct was a short about swimming with Jean Taris, the swimming champion. After several sessions with the star— during which Taris had to explain the sport to Vigo, who knew nothing about swimming—Vigo had prepared an outline, just before leaving Brussels, which covered the different styles of swimming and also incorporated details of the champion's career and exploits. The producers were now in a great rush, and Vigo had to construct a shooting script out of the three short typed pages on which he had jotted down his ideas in some sort of order.

After another session with Taris, this time at a swimming pool so that he could see him in action, Vigo took two days to prepare a shooting script which consisted of fifty-six shots. Most of the actual shooting was done at the swimming pool at the Automobile Club de France; through its glass portholes underwater shots could be taken. The two studio shots presented no problems, and they were able to proceed quickly to the editing and to the addition of a soundtrack.

The result was not just run of the mill. Vigo's attempt to make something not quite conventional was evident. Both the interest and the limits of this short film lie therein. Vigo did not have much to say about swimming or about Taris. The champion's bodily proportions and the perfect ease with which he moved his body through water interested Vigo more. He followed Taris' movements while he dried himself, the camera doing a wandering study of the champion's entire body, ending up at his feet. When the camera once again moved upwards, Taris was in his bathrobe. As we see, Vigo had not lost his taste for certain formal effects, in this case perfectly motivated and done without calling attention to themselves.

Vigo did not like the film very much. When he had occasion to see it again a few months later in Nice, he thought it quite frankly bad, with the exception of a few underwater shots. The strange image formed by a man's head under water had struck him, and he foresaw its dramatic possibilities. He was not to forget when he came to make *L'Atalante.*

The film centred around a "didactic [demonstration] of the crawl," with a commentary spoken by Taris. Vigo allowed himself a little fantasy at the beginning and end of the film. Over the titles there was a soundtrack backing[57] consisting of a chorus of little girls asking, *Mother, do little boats floating on water have legs?* After the credits and the mother's answer, a crowd roars its approval, then the voice of an announcer briefly enumerates the champion's feats. At the same time the camera tracks forward towards a megaphone until it fills the entire screen. Then silence—and the screen fades into black; a voice shouts, *On your mark!* The film then begins.

After a dozen shots of Taris swimming, the interview begins. While he dries himself, Taris gives some brief biographical information, followed by four general observations.

1. *Every man floats?* We see a huge fat man in the water.
2. *Water is as much man's domain as it is a fish's.* We see underwater acrobatics (somersaults, distorted bodies, etc.).
3. *Undoubtedly there are a few movements one should know, but all one really has to do is to get into the water.* We see different people playing in the water.
4. *You do not learn how to swim in a room.* We see a thin woman with frazzled hair, flat on her stomach on a stool, doing arm exercises. In the background, a lifesaver on proud display.

Then Taris gives a lesson on the Australian crawl, both swimming and talking to us. One must admit that the lesson demonstrates that one cannot learn how to swim from a film either. At the end, some underwater shots in slow motion. For the last shots, Vigo wanted to "create something avant-garde" by using trick effects. A feet-first dive is run backwards, and Taris suddenly seems to fly out of the water. Immediately after, we see him dressed in a suit, an overcoat, and a hat. He jumps and lands by the side of the pool. He waves at the camera, and, in a superimposition, he leaves, walking on the water accompanied by a little tune on a saxophone.

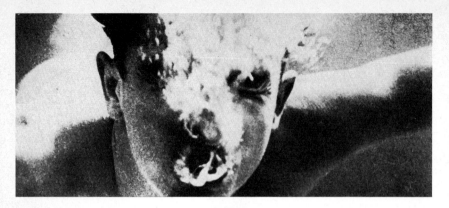

Taris

A few months sufficed for Vigo's work to become influenced by the avant-garde. From this time on, he was aware of the fact that the only audacity which counts is one involving a new and happy blend between an ornamental form and a realistic content.

However, at the beginning of 1931 the chances of making good use of his recently acquired knowledge in new projects seemed remote. Financial problems were accumulating dangerously. The few hundred francs he had received for *Taris* were of little help, and *A Propos de Nice* had not brought in very much. As for the film club, it was just about breaking even. This was an improvement, but it was clearly out of the question to expect a profit, even a modest one, in the coming months.

At G. F. F. A. Vigo had been promised other films in the *Journal Vivant* series, but he would have to wait. In the meantime, he went frequently to the studio in Nice hoping to find work. He was willing to accept anything, even a very humble position on a production. Germaine Dulac had contacted Jean Grémillon about his production of *Daïnah la Métisse* in Nice. Vigo had to try very hard to get a position on the production crew. He probably had promises made him, but they were never fulfilled. Henri Storck, on the other hand, did succeed in getting hired as script boy on the same production. This was the first time that the job of keeping track of continuity was ever incorporated into a French production. Even before the shooting started there was a disagreement between Storck and Grémillon. Immediately afterwards, Vigo arrived and loudly accused Storck of having taken his job. Storck quit the production, but Vigo was not hired in his place. After the Brussels row and this argument in Nice, the two young film-makers became close friends. Storck soon moved into Vigo's home, where he amused Lydou, three months pregnant and exhausted, with his Flemish stories.

The disagreement with Grémillon was quickly forgotten, and he invited the two young men to share an excellent lobster dinner with him. They remembered the dinner for a long time, because their poverty did not allow them to eat at elegant restaurants. Still, they both remained without work, and Storck left to try his luck in Paris or Brussels.

Vigo now decided to do something which he had formerly refused to consider: to sell the Debrie. Towards the end of April Storck found him a buyer willing to pay 20,000 francs. That was not much, but Vigo no longer had any alternative. He was in debt, and the month of May promised to be a critical one. The only thing he insisted on was that he be paid 10,000 francs down in cash. A few days later the prospective buyer proposed a sum of only 19,000 francs, and Storck, disgusted, no longer wanted to serve as a go-between. But Vigo wrote to him in May: "Storck, you are a bastard if you even dare think, 'I want nothing to do with this deal,' and if you want no further part in it for fear of 'seeming like a horrible Jew.' You must continue to help me. If I don't sell the Debrie, I've had it." By the end of the month he was asking a minimum of 15,000 francs from a buyer who offered him 12,000. Then, towards the middle of June, he got some money. He was offered a loan of 8,000 francs, the lender taking an option to buy the camera for 14,000 francs; Vigo received 5,000 in cash as soon as the camera had been shipped. With those 5,000 francs he paid his most pressing debts and anxiously awaited the remaining 3,000 francs to cover approaching maternity expenses. When the child, a girl, Luce, was born on June 30, Vigo had not yet received the money. By the end of the year he had still received no further payment, nor any news of Pelster, the buyer. Pelster was a Dutchman involved in avant-garde film-making, "and who eats it," as Vigo wrote with only one thought in his mind, to beat the Dutchman's head in at the first opportunity.

All these problems did not prevent Vigo from getting extremely excited when he heard that Charles Chaplin had arrived in Nice. Vigo succeeded in getting an appointment with him, but the conversation faltered for lack of a common language. Chaplin made the gesture of offering him a photograph, but Vigo, in his confusion, refused it, and left the meeting with the feeling that his life was becoming one failure after another.

During these preceding months Vigo had been in desperate straits. Lydou's pregnancy was an extremely difficult one. Each day she became weaker, victim of all sorts of painful afflictions. Some nights she had shivers which made her teeth chatter, and Vigo's efforts to help her were of no avail. Then, in the middle of the night she would suddenly become feverishly hot, with a temperature of over 102 degrees. Opportunities for work came up, such as a short documentary for G. F. F. A. in Paris, or as assistant to a director, Champreux, who was to film the Tour de France from June 15 to August 15. Vigo could not accept any of the offers because he could not leave Lydou alone, "in this city of Nice which is a desert for us," as he complained to Storck.[58] A few days afterwards he confessed to his friend that the next morning he would be forced "to wander around Nice and try to beg the small sum necessary for the noon and evening meals from charitable souls."

To pay for the hospital in advance, he again had to borrow, and it was only after the child was born that he and Lydou received some money from Poland. They used it in an attempt to restore Lydou's health by sending her again to Peira Cava. Their spirits had been affected. "Sudden fits of depression set their behinds down in our chairs, spit into our dishes at mealtimes, hide themselves in our sheets, leave their fingerprints on the margins of the pages of our best books, and nip at our heels if we risk taking a walk."[59] Vigo tried to do a little work, but he complained of a lethargy which ruined every effort and left his script wasting away in its cover.

When he returned to Nice he was offered a job on one of those productions in two versions which were very common at the time: a film based on Verneuil's "very Parisian" play, *Pile ou Face* (*Heads or Tails*). The shooting script had already been turned out by the co-producers, G. F. F. A.—U. F. A.; everything else had been decided upon and provided for, and Vigo's role was to consist simply of supervising the filming of the actors in the French version. After a great deal of hesitation, Vigo was prepared to accept the offer so that "he could eat for a few days," and get to Paris at the beginning of November with the hope "of doing a little better there."[60] Things were held up, and Vigo was finally dropped from the French version. He bitterly mocked the vain scruples he had had, judging his attitude as a "terribly amusing dilettantism."[61]

However, Vigo did manage to go to Paris and got a contract from G. F. F. A. for a second documentary on sports, on tennis this time, with the tennis champion, Cochet.

He asked Goldblatt to collaborate with him, and together they went to see Cochet seven times to acquire some basic notions about tennis, to learn about his career, and to have him explain the finer points of his art. Some of these meetings took place on a tennis court, and by the end both were speaking about tennis with a glibness infuriating to their friends familiar with the sport. After this preliminary research, G. F. F. A. gave Vigo the usual twenty-four hours to prepare a shooting script for final approval. Vigo was staying at the Muse Hotel, which was quiet only when the whores were not at work; but his writing had to be done that night, and the conversations Vigo could overhear in neighbouring rooms aroused his curiosity and caused his mind to wander. So he and Goldblatt moved into one of Riéra's rooms on the rue du Four for a night of work. It was very cold, and the only heat in the room was provided by an alcohol heater; the only light was from a kerosene lamp. As the hours went by the two friends started to feel afflicted by a strange sickness. However, they had work to do; they continued, and only much later did they suddenly realize that they were being poisoned by vapour from the kerosene lamp. Goldblatt struggled to his feet, and found enough strength to open the window before he passed out on a couch. Vigo could not get up. On the script he managed to scrawl, already half-unconscious, "This is our testament," and then passed out. Since the window was open, the air cleared, and a few hours later they woke up, feeling intolerably sick. Goldblatt led Vigo, who was worse off than he, to the nearest drugstore, where the appearance of these two ashen-faced, bizarre-looking young men was greeted with suspicion. The owner's distrustful attitude brought them completely back to their senses, and they were able to finish their work in the prescribed time.

This film was entirely different in conception from the film on swimming. It was structured around poetic variations on tennis, as played by children, with a few technical notes on Cochet's style of playing. The end satirized, without malice, the idolatry of the champion sportsman.

The title and credits were to be accompanied by a drum roll, and the film was to open with tennis balls hitting a drum. The balls were thrown by a child who, after each throw, would clap his hands behind his back, making a sound exactly like the sound of the ball. More balls, against a wall, and children playing with them. Still more balls, at the back of the court and against the sky, others always returning to their point of departure. A child bouncing a ball on the ground ended this introductory sequence.

This was to be followed by a racket hitting the bouncing ball. The camera would back away and discover Cochet getting rid of the ball with an abrupt movement of his racket, sending it over his shoulder without even bothering to watch where it went. Over this a voice asking, *Tell us, M. Cochet, why do you play tennis?* As the ball lands on a jet of water, bouncing up and down like an egg, Cochet answers, *I always wanted to. That's all.* And while the camera moves up along the stream of water, continues on its way into the sky, and descends to a baby who is learning to walk, and in the process falls over on his behind, Cochet speaks about the inevitability of the sport. When he begins praising the animal joy of children, light, air, movement, freedom, the camera has already started tracking among a great number of naked children enjoying themselves at a tennis court. The games they play are all different and improvised, but all involve a tennis ball, a racket, or a net. They play tennis, one with his bare hand, another with a piece of wood, a third with a racket, while Cochet's voice encourages them, *Hit the ball, wherever you can, however you can, whenever you can.* At this point the first technical explanation of the sport was to be introduced. Cochet explains that a child holds the racket under his arm, supporting its weight with his whole body, that when older he learns to support the racket's weight with his entire arm, and that finally, by trying to extend his reach, he learns to hold the racket with the tips of his fingers. Before going deeper into the subject, Cochet would add that a child should be allowed to play and discover the sport which suits him, which pleases him best. We would see a small child hitting a punching-ball consisting of a tennis ball hanging from the branch of an apple tree which is being shaken by other children.

The variations became even freer. A ball would bounce into a baby carriage with a sleeping baby in it who awakens and sucks the ball. This is followed by a shot of a baby being breast-fed. This sequence is not very clear in the manuscript available for study; the last variation, however, consisted of a ball being eaten by a grown-up performing conjuring tricks.

During Cochet's demonstration the camera would not leave the children for a second, and their actions are very closely related to the champion's feats, and to his explanations of the style which, he says, one cannot acquire, one can only improve on, and of how he personally had to work on his backhand.

Towards the end, the film was to take on satirical overtones. After being in considerable difficulties, Cochet would save the situation with two great plays. The voice-over commentary has already stated that a tennis player proves his worth by playing and not by sitting over a cup of coffee. A shadow passes over the children, and a solemn group of men in high hats and black gloves enters the court: the selection committee. In a circle they argue around a bust of Cochet. Gathered together, the children crouch down, the camera lifts, and discovers a mob, a veritable herd of children. Cochet's voice concludes, *Be ambitious and tenacious, fair enough. But great champions, or those who strike us as great, are more than just examples; they are accessible gods.* Accompanied by a Chopin lullaby and by a heavenly choir, Cochet appears in the sky on a big white cloud, with two rackets as wings.

If this project seems to be more authentic in its inspiration than Vigo's previous documentary, it is not because tennis interested Vigo more than swimming, or Cochet more than Taris. It is because the subject had become no more than a pretext, a point of departure, and Vigo had focused on a theme which was very close to his heart: respect for children and for their freedom. All discipline imposed from the outside was suspect to him. He liked sports and had been a football player with great team spirit, but all group exercises struck him as military training. To him, sports involved the harmonious development of a child's love of play, and must be chosen by the child in complete freedom. Vigo refers to children, but to him these children are symbolic of mankind, and especially the weak and the wretched. He would later explain himself better in *Zéro de Conduite*. But already, in this script for a short film about sport, his ideology shines through; and it contains a phrase which might almost be his motto: *Hit the ball, wherever you can, however you can, whenever you can.*

The script was approved by G. F. F. A., and the project was turned into a more ambitious one. Three versions of the film were to be made, French, German, and English, to be co-produced with U. F. A. The length, at first to have been the same as *Taris*, was expanded to about thirty-three hundred feet. Vigo thus had a chance to elaborate his script. A production crew was selected. Vigo took Goldblatt as his assistant, and since Kaufman had previous commitments, Michel Kelber was chosen as director of photography, with Walter Wottitz as his assistant. The shooting was scheduled to start at the beginning of February in Monte Carlo. Problems developed, but in late February Vigo still believed that he had the job. He then learned that, upon reconsideration, his script had been rejected; and a few days later the company abandoned the project. "I haven't had much luck with film-making," he wrote to Storck, "but, to be frank, that's the least of my worries; I have two hands and will surely succeed in holding on to something or someone. When you know what you want you are patient and tenacious."[62]

Vigo had known for a long time what he wanted, and he had never stopped being tenacious. As for being patient, he could afford that luxury now because his film club was doing well, and because Hertch Lozinski's imminent arrival temporarily solved his financial worries.

The Amis du Cinéma had progressed. Local people of some influence— Mme. Greta Prozor, M. Muratore, and various newspapermen, particularly André Négis—were supporting the efforts of Vigo and his friends. From suburban cinemas they had moved to the centre of town, first to what is now the Studio 34, and then to what is now the Cinéac on the Avenue de la Victoire. Henceforth they could count on attendances more than large enough to pay their expenses. The local snobs had become interested in these "different" films being shown on Sundays. Curiosity seekers from the cosmopolitan world of the big hotels started attending, and soon their audience contained its regular share of sophisticates.

The film-club movement in France was again becoming an important phenomenon. A federation had been created, and at its second congress in 1931, Vigo was elected to the executive committee. The possibilities for programming had increased, and during the two years of its existence, the Amis

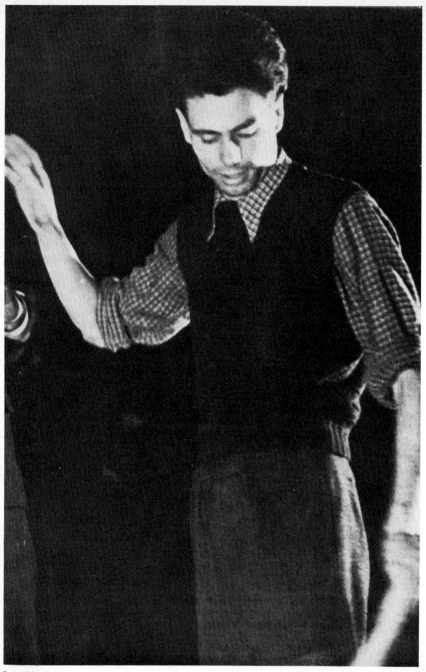

Jean Vigo

du Cinéma showed a distinguished selection of works by Dovzhenko, Turin, Preobrajenskaya, Eisenstein, Fischinger, Richter, etc. Most of the time Nicolas continued to introduce the films, although Vigo occasionally did so for films he particularly admired, such as Carl Junghans' *So ist das Leben* (*Such is Life*). Whenever possible, Vigo asked the director of a film for a statement which could be read at the screening. Sometimes the club arranged programmes illustrating a theme. For instance, for the first session in April 1931, they chose Anatole France as their theme. They showed Feyder's *Crainquebille*, Berthomieu's *Sylvestre Bonnard*, and a documentary lent by the Anatole France specialist, Jacques Lion. Then Claude Aveline gave a talk in which he recalled an interview with Anatole France about the cinema.[63] Even that did not end the programme. Anatole France was abandoned, and two documentaries were shown, as well as Lupu Pick's *Sylvester* (*New Year's Eve*).

Directors came to introduce their films. Germaine Dulac came with *La Souriante Mme. Beudet* and *Thème et Variations*. Vigo wanted to show works by the younger generation, and Storck, as yet pretty much of an unknown, presented his *Train de Plaisir* and *Idylle à la Plage*. Jean Painlevé came twice, the first time on November 11, 1931. Vigo and Painlevé had never met. They were to meet at the station and hurry straight to the cinema where the screening was to begin a half-hour later. Jean Painlevé often told the story in film clubs of his meeting with Vigo. "I got off the train and looked for Jean Vigo. He had written to me that he would be at the station, and that I would easily recognize him: tall, blond, the Legion of Honour on his lapel. That struck me as somewhat peculiar. So, since he had a photograph of me, I let my beard grow for two weeks before my departure, and put my films in a suitcase after telling him that I always carried them in a knapsack. I approached people who fitted the description he gave me, but got nowhere. At the exit I felt a hand on my shoulder, and a small dark-haired man said, 'You are Jean Painlevé, aren't you?' I replied, 'Yes.' 'Despite your disguising yourself as a hairy stranger, I recognized you.' 'I must admit that I wasn't as lucky with you, for I approached several people in vain.'

" ' Secret for secret,' he replied, 'you are not the first person I tapped on the shoulder; one of them even dropped the package I have here and fled.' "

Painlevé had to shave before the screening, and they arrived late. There was a crowd at the entrance to the cinema. Painlevé was quite pleased. But in reality, he said, "they were a bunch of loafers attracted by the shouts of some madman asking for the person in charge. From close up the man seemed to be a gentleman, quite well dressed, and rather upset. 'What do you want?' Vigo asked. 'Oh, so you are in charge. I must congratulate you, I've been here an hour and . . .' 'But excuse me, who are you?' 'Who am I? That's a good one! I'm Jean Painlevé, and I've come to give my lecture, that's who! . . .' Vigo paled under his tan. I saw he could do with some help, so I addressed myself to the imposter: 'What do you mean, you're Jean Painlevé? I'm Painlevé!' 'Well, that's a bit much!' And he appealed to the crowd, unfolding a local newspaper: 'Please take me to the projection booth, it is time to start,' he said, pointing to a photograph illustrating the article announcing my arrival. It was without a shadow of a doubt a photograph of our madman in a white smock in front of a microscope. I realized then that he was quite serious, quite respectable-looking—in short, that he made a better impression than I did. Vigo's conviction faltered. I made another effort—at the time identity cards did not exist—and said, 'All right, you give my lecture.' 'Certainly I'll give *my* lecture,' he answered. Vigo was livid. 'Say something,' he begged me. But what? I couldn't convince him of the truth just like that. Then I remembered the films. 'And do you have films?' I asked sarcastically. 'As many as you,' he answered. I looked around for my suitcase which I had left at the edge of the crowd—gone! That was the last straw. This was Nice, but even so! The suitcase could not have gone very far since the scene had lasted only a moment. I looked around and noticed a 'helpful porter' at the corner of the street nonchalantly making off with it. I rushed out and grabbed him, and he meekly returned the case. I hurried back into the cinema, ready for a riot if my rival insisted. But I saw Vigo doubled up with laughter, in violent reaction. The gentleman was a practical joker, former director of the Pasteur Institute and a local celebrity. Since a block already existed of a photograph of him, it had been used with the article about me to save money—one laboratory smock being as good as another. The result: free seats for him and his wife."

That evening there were two showings and Painlevé had to repeat his lecture. Even so they had to turn people away. Vigo took Painlevé to his home to sleep, and the practical jokes continued. They were to continue for several years. "Jean Painlevé is quite a guy," Vigo wrote to Storck.

Through Painlevé, Vigo met Maurice Jaubert, who was also a friend of Storck. His friendship with Jaubert constituted a new experience for Vigo: it was the first time he had been on close terms with a religious believer. Jaubert's ideas, which were to direct Vigo's attention to the problems of film music, must have interested him very much.

At the beginning of 1932 Vigo was convinced that staying in Nice would make any career in films impossible. Even when the studios on the coast were flourishing, he had been unable to find any substantial work, and now that they were failing his chances were even slimmer. The principal reason which until now had kept him from thinking seriously about moving to Paris was strong opposition from their doctors, who firmly urged the unsuitability of the Paris climate for both Vigo and Lydou. But they had both become sceptical about the supposed benefits of the coast. Only rarely were they both in good health, although this at least had the advantage that one could nurse the other. They did not believe that their health would be any more menaced in Paris than it was in Nice. They had to leave the city from time to time anyway to rest in the mountains, and that they could do as easily from one city as another. In Paris, at least, there was some hope of finding work, and almost all of their friends were there: Aveline, Riéra, Storck, Kaufman, Goldblatt, Painlevé, Lodz, Altmann, Aron, and all of Almereyda's old friends who had become theirs, Fanny Clar, Raphaël

Diligent, Fernand Desprès, Eugène Merle, and Francis Jourdain.

However, at the start of summer Vigo was still in Nice. His father-in-law had come to see Luce and had again helped them out, but Vigo only succeeded in paying off his most urgent debts. They needed to save for the cost of removals and an apartment in Paris. They also needed to store up energy, which they did by going to the mountains at Pelasque, near Nice. "We are enjoying a period of outward tranquillity," Vigo wrote to Storck on June 9, "and our worries are less frantic.

"When you eat well, go to sleep at eight, spend the day relaxing on easy chairs, do little walking, and even less talking, the results are astounding. First, you freeze all your problems, all your debts; they can even increase. And if your kidneys hurt like hell, well, you just go on. The future gets no brighter, and our so-called material, moral and artistic situation remains as brilliant as it would be after a thousand overtures made to proper and improper persons. But at least love does not suffer. A look is as sustained as it should be, and a caress too. A shoulder is always ready for your tired head, and the hand is never withdrawn. In much the same way, a business appointment seems like something out of an avant-garde film. A telephone call comes from friends who are much too sad. You answer and you wait for their visit. You can do a lot, so long as you don't forget to lose your watch."

Ten days later Vigo was in Paris looking for work and for an apartment. Luce was in Nice with Janine Champol, and Lydou stayed in the mountains to rest.

After a month Vigo still had not found any real possibilities of work. He spent his time on little projects which never led anywhere, for minor producers like Daniloff or Trivas. Lydou's health continued to worry him. After she joined him in Paris, it was necessary to send her back a few days later, this time to Leysin, in Switzerland, where the climate reputedly cured lung diseases. All of Vigo's ideas, one after another, remained inoperative for lack of opportunity to implement them into a film. He had not even written a short article Storck had requested for the Belgian magazine *Kamera*. When Storck saw him in Paris on July 23, he found him very demoralized.

At this point, Vigo met Nounez.

Jacques-Louis Nounez was a businessman with connections in industry. The son of a big Camargue breeder, Nounez had a taste for horses. He was fifty-four years old, and until now had shown no interest in the film industry. But he loved films, was an enthusiastic admirer of Charlie Chaplin, and also liked Renoir and René Clair. His attitude towards social problems was an understanding one, and he was a friend of Léon Blum. Of distant Jewish ancestry, he was very sensitive to human suffering.

Nounez had learned that the European film market lacked one category of film—those of medium length, somewhere between short subjects and features. He investigated the situation and proposed to produce six films a year, each about four thousand feet in length, in what were then felt to be the two genres most appropriate to films of that length: comedy and fictionalized documentary. To keep the films from being too expensive, no stars or known directors were to be used. This involved finding intelligent scripts, and young directors anxious to be given a chance.

Nounez had met René Lefèvre, the actor, in horse-racing circles. Nounez spoke to him of his projects, and Lefèvre suggested Jean Vigo, whom he had met after a showing of *A Propos de Nice*.

On July 23, 1932, when Vigo left, accompanied by Storck, for the Place du Palais-Bourbon where he had an appointment with Nounez in his office, he was somewhat sceptical. He knew very little about Nounez, or about the exact reasons why he had been summoned, but he had already lost his illusions about French film producers. The last one he had seen, to whom he had proposed an adaptation of Aristophanes' *The Birds*, had turned him down in no uncertain terms: "Above all, no documentaries."

Nounez knew all about Jean's childhood and remembered the *Bonnet Rouge* affair and Almereyda's tragic end. He was immediately attracted to the nostalgic and sorrowful side he thought he detected in Vigo, rounded out by a lofty spirituality which retained no grudges or hatred.[64] He treated Vigo paternally and with great tact. Vigo was surprised, and quite delighted at finding someone who was "very nice,"[65] who loved good films, and above all, who was willing to give him a chance to work. Vigo told him about some ideas he had been nursing for some time: a film about boys at school based on his own experiences, and another about prison life based on the experiences of the former anarchist, Eugène Dieudonné. Nounez, on his part, spoke to him of adapting some of Georges de la Fouchardière's works into films, of a film about the Camargue and its horses, and of a personal idea which could be turned into a film on middle-class hypocrisy. No decision was made, and nothing was signed on that day, but, in principle, the film on the Camargue and the film about schoolboys were retained as possibilities. The interview had lasted more than an hour. Vigo left full of enthusiasm. He went to find Storck, who had been waiting for him in a café, and they immediately began work. Together they went to the Phototone Studios in Neuilly, and to the Taponier Studio on the rue de la Paix, to inquire about rentals and about the quality of the equipment.

Despite the slow progress of Nounez's plans, the horizon looked bright. During August Vigo did research on the Camargue, and early in September he left for Leysin to draft a script and rejoin Lydou, whose health was much better. He himself felt full of life. In a few hours he wrote the article he had promised Storck, "Sensitivity of Film Stock." He also continued to work on a script about the Camargue. He had started on this project first, not only because Nounez seemed to prefer it to the other, but also because it was something new to him, and he did not want to risk being caught unprepared. As for the film about boys at school, it had long been thought out in his head, although he had no ideas as yet about how it should be filmed.

Before the end of September Vigo returned to Paris with the Camargue script, which he immediately gave to Nounez. Things moved along slowly, but for the time being Vigo's good spirits were unshakeable. For Lydou's return on October 1, he gathered his friends, Goldblatt, Painlevé, and Riéra, who went to the station to wait for her, disguised as important officials in magnificent top hats rented from a costumier on the rue de Seine.

Nounez's projects really began to take shape towards the middle of October with the decision, for a start, to make the film on the Camargue. According to the production plans, it was to be a fictionalized documentary four thousand feet long without professional actors. It would of course be shot on location. One reason it had been chosen as the initial project was the difficulty of finding free studio space over the coming weeks. Although nothing had been signed by the end of October, Vigo was preparing for a first visit to the Camargue at the beginning of November. Then he was to have returned to Paris to put the finishing touches to the script; and finally go to the Camargue again with Kaufman and Riéra for the actual shooting, which was to have lasted six weeks, from the middle of December until the end of January. While waiting, Vigo went riding each morning at Maisons-Lafitte to familiarize himself with the subject. "Oh! You should see me break in a thoroughbred," he wrote to Storck.

Vigo was forced to do some things which were not half as much fun. Nounez, who was just starting out in the film business, still did not understand very much about it. Being very busy with his other affairs, he left Vigo to cope with the work a producer normally does, drawing up the budget, fixing salaries, and so on. Vigo, already installed with Lydou in the apartment they had found at 23 rue Gazan, facing the Parc Montsouris, was playing the businessman—and very badly, at that. He was both clumsy and naïve. Out of a total budget of 172,000 francs, he set aside 40,000 as his salary and a total of only 85,000 francs for the rest of the crew. This proportion perhaps corresponded to the amount of work he would do compared to the others, but they nevertheless found it quite preposterous. Moreover, he drew up the budget like a rank beginner, listing each item separately. Storck also reproached him for leaving the budget with Nounez, and not going back to see him or asking for it for a whole week. Storck found Vigo "too much the gentleman, too eighteenth century in business matters, riddled with absurd scruples."[66]

It is not altogether impossible that the reluctant way in which Vigo handled the business end of the proposed film—and the scepticism with which he prepared for his first trip to the Camargue—was his way of expressing hostility towards the subject. A study of the proposed script and its accompanying notes, if they still exist, might help to explain whether Vigo helped torpedo the project so that it could be replaced with something more to his liking. Nounez had probably been warned against documentaries, whether fictionalized or not. At any rate, early in November Nounez finally abandoned the idea of making a film on the Camargue. He now wanted to commission three comedies, each four thousand feet in length, to be immediately followed by a feature. Possibilities were thus opened for the realization of some of Vigo's projects, such as the film on children and the film on prison life. It was known that Nounez had come to an understanding with the Gaumont company for using their studios, and everyone was optimistic. Vigo immediately started writing a scenario, incorporating a partial breakdown into scenes, for the film about children which he had provisionally titled *Les Cancres* (*The Dunces*).

On November 4, Lydou's birthday, Vigo invited a few friends—including Lydou's sister Genya, the Kaufmans, the Goldblatts and Storck—to a party where, over caviar canapés, smoked mackerel and a good supply of wine, they celebrated the prospects of better luck with speeches, dances, sermons, songs and, the next day, a general hangover.

Vigo finished writing *Les Cancres* in a week, but by the beginning of December he had still had no opportunity of submitting it to Nounez, and the worries began. He became short and sharp with his friends, which was a bad sign and also offended the more susceptible among them. The personnel —including several friends—who were to work on the production and who had already been more or less hired, started to complain, for they were waiting for work and a salary which now seemed problematic. They were left hanging in mid-air. Lydou, always aggressive and even unjust when it came to defending what she considered Vigo's interests, got involved, and bitter arguments broke out. They could still laugh and drink at Riéra's, but for Vigo and his poorer friends the next days promised to be anxious ones. Finally, on December 12, 1932, Vigo, summoned by Nounez, left with *Les Cancres* under his arm to have dinner with the producer. After listening to Vigo stammer through the script, Nounez, who had already made his decision, agreed and gave him full freedom within the limitations set by a modest budget of about 200,000 francs. At the same time Nounez informed Vigo that the Gaumont Studios would be at his disposal for about a week during the holidays, starting December 24.

3. Zéro de Conduite

Vigo filming *Zéro de Conduite*

Jean Vigo's attitude towards his subject—childhood inhibited by adults—
was governed by two experiences: his own childhood years spent in Millau
and Chartres (above all, the four years in the first city), and his father's in
the children's prison at La Petite Roquette. His father's stories had made him
very familiar with the prison; and later he was shocked into a deeper understanding when he came across Almereyda's description of the routine imposed on the children in an old issue of *L'Assiette au Beurre*.[1] Although
Vigo's setting is a school rather than a prison, and although there are no
obvious traces in his script of the brutality with which children were treated
in La Petite Roquette, certain details were directly inspired by his father's
prison life. However, the most important influence on Vigo's sensibility was
the association of his father's troubled childhood with the suffering he had
endured personally after his father's death: he had come to identify one
childhood completely with the other. This resulted in Vigo's extreme sensitivity to anything concerning a child's vulnerability in the adult world. Even
as an adult, his memories still caused him suffering, and for a long time he
had wanted to free himself through a film. Towards the end of the shooting
of *Zéro de Conduite*, from the roof of a house in Saint-Cloud, Vigo told a
journalist friend: "This film is so much my own life as a kid that I'm anxious
to go on to something else."[2]

Vigo, however, wanted to broaden the base of his initial inspiration with school reminiscences recounted to him at his request by his friends and collaborators; but in the end he made little use of these accounts. In the first versions of his script, at least one obvious literary influence could still be detected: *Le Grand Meaulnes*. At that stage, the school attic played an important part in the action, and the children wanted to make it their "retreat." In the first outline for the projected film, the children emphatically declare: *If we must be prisoners, at least let us choose our prison, let's be happy and have fun there, so that we will want to stay there for the rest of our lives.* Later, referring to his film, Vigo said: "How did I, a grown man, alone, without schoolmates or playmates, dare venture down the paths of *Le Grand Meaulnes*?"[3] But, in fact, in the final script this "Grand Meaulnes" side was very much toned down, while in the film its traces can be discerned only with difficulty.

On the other hand, when Mlle. Antoinette Aubès saw the film, in many instances she recognized the stories Vigo had told her during his childhood vacations.[4] In the film, the four principal child-characters, in fact, are Caussat, Bruel, Colin, and Tabard. We are already well acquainted with the first three: Caussat and Bruel come from Millau, Colin from Chartres. Tabard is a new name, that of the boy who, at the beginning of the story is as frail as a girl, and whose friendship with the older Bruel provokes the school administration's evil suspicions. Vigo later said that the administration tormented and spied on Tabard, "whereas what he really needed was a big brother, since his mother did not love him."[5] In the same text, Vigo speaks of "kids on their way back to school, abandoned on an October evening in a schoolyard, somewhere in the provinces, far away from home, yearning for a mother's affection, a father's camaraderie, if the father is not already dead." We need go no further to recognize in Tabard the Jean Vigo of Millau. But Tabard is also little Mercier from Chartres, and Vigo then becomes the older, protective friend, the film's Bruel. Having played both parts in the tender friendships of schoolboys, Jean Vigo is present in both characters, but since *Zéro de Conduite* above all refers to Millau, it is Tabard in particular who represents Vigo. However, it is also true that there is something of the young Vigo in Caussat. In the film, Caussat is trying to play the hardboiled, knowing tough. After spending a Sunday afternoon with his guardian's daughter, playing innocent games involving a goldfish bowl, he boasts to his friends of his daring feats. In the same text introducing *Zéro de Conduite*, Vigo addresses himself directly to his childhood girl-friend, reminding her of the scene in the film: "Do you remember how I loved to watch you climb up on the piano and hang the goldfish bowl from a wire which we had strung up, the two of us, our hands touching? You used to cover my eyes with your handkerchief, smelling so nicely of your mother's lavender, because I looked at your plump, babyish thighs. And then gently, as one does with the sick, you would remove the festive bandage, and in silence we would both watch the goldfish bowl."

Everything in the fictional Caussat and Bruel not attributable to the young

Zéro de Conduite: 'Innocent games involving a goldfish bowl' (*above*) and Gas-Snout at the window

99

Vigo—nearly everything, that is—is drawn directly from the surly Caussat and the husky Bruel Vigo had known in Millau. Even though the Colin of the film has become the cook's son, he is the Colin Vigo knew at Chartres. Among the children who play minor roles in *Zéro de Conduite* we can recognize echoes of Millau—Durand, who could mimic animal cries, the sleepwalker who died of Spanish influenza, and the acrobat.

Just as he had done with the children, Vigo started from reality to create his adult characters, but reality as seen through the eyes of a rebellious, hurt child who, now an adult, could revenge himself through satire. His characters are so far from their models, and their personalities have been so mixed together, that any attempt to determine their origins is doomed to failure. All we know is that the nicknames Gas-Snout and Dry-Fart come from Millau, and that the principal at Chartres—a good-natured man, for all his attempts to discourage the friendship between Vigo and Mercier—was a small, bearded man.

One striking thing is Vigo's hatred for Gas-Snout, the head supervisor, who becomes the one really odious character in *Zéro de Conduite*. This is because Vigo, in defining the character, used mannerisms borrowed from the guards at La Petite Roquette in Almereyda's day; for instance, pretending to leave, then suddenly returning to catch a prisoner (or schoolboy) doing wrong.

As for that magical character, Huguet, the junior master, he probably derives from the impression left by the only congenial supervisor at Millau, the one who remained at the boarding school for only two or three weeks.

Let us return to Vigo, preparing himself, script in hand, to make his film in those last days of 1932. When Vigo had submitted the script to Nounez, it still was entitled *Les Cancres*. Vigo did not like the title and considered it a temporary one. Once he was sure the film would be made, the final title spontaneously suggested itself to him: *Zéro de Conduite*, that awesome zero for conduct which, at Millau, had often kept Vigo and his friends from going out on Sundays.

As soon as he had shown Nounez the script, Vigo busied himself making the first massive cuts which had become necessary. The script had been planned for a film about sixty-five hundred feet long, and he was now limited to about thirty-nine hundred feet. He started by cutting out a montage which summarized school life and which tried to show, to the rhythm of clapping hands, drum-rolls and the words *Kept in on Sunday*, the constantly repressed spontaneity of children. The sequence was to have been very fast, amusingly done, and to have broken up the chronological sequence of events.[6] In this section, Vigo was still making concessions to his love of trick effects.

These exercises, however, never became gratuitous, but were always conditioned by an exacting search for concise expression or for poetic effect. For instance, the children rush out into the schoolyard. Suddenly there is a handclap, and the image freezes on the screen like a still photograph, held there for a few seconds. The children who had been playing and running, their flight arrested, remain in uneasy balance, in a pose both painful and comic. At another moment the children walk towards the camera. They reach it singing. Suddenly, with the children's mouths held open on a high note, for a few seconds both the image and the song freeze. The scene in which they approach the camera singing is run backwards: a stern voice, *Kept in on Sunday!* The children are dragged violently backwards: a door shuts on them. A brief trill on a flute provides the final comment.

Vigo took advantage of being forced to make revisions in the script by also reworking it for emotional reasons. To a tenderness stripped of all sentimentality he added a healthy feeling of respect for children. In his first drafts he had strongly emphasized the malice with which the teachers interpreted the children's behaviour, especially the friendship between Tabard and Bruel. In the final version of the script—in so far as there ever was one—or at least in the film itself, he retained the niggling, equivocal spirit of the staff. As for the children, he decided not to shoot, or to cut out after shooting, any sequence which might give rise to the slightest scabrous idea in the viewer's mind: scenes such as the one in which two children amusing themselves in the dormitory bring their mouths together to chew the same piece of gum, and are caught by the supervisor. Vigo in fact went too far; for example, he cut out a scene in which the boarders are washing themselves at the sink in the morning. They are all in shirt-sleeves; one of them, the better to wash himself, is bare-chested. The head supervisor appears, rushes to the bare-chested boy with a blanket, and screams, *Aren't you ashamed, you miserable wretch!* The scene was a good one, and all the odium fell on the teacher. However, Vigo eliminated it because the child did not react to the adult's insolence, as another child does when he swears at a teacher in a sequence which remains one of the film's key scenes.

Vigo's vigilance was not limited to matters of morality. Just as young Almereyda, at the time of *La Guerre Sociale*, had arrested, judged and punished a stool-pigeon, the child-conspirators one evening punish a sneak in the dormitory. But Vigo did not want to taint a child, so he cut the sequence. Two adults speaking of children call them *dirty brats*. First, the railway employee as he shuts the carriage doors; the shot stayed in the final version, but the insulting remark was suppressed. In another sequence, one which Vigo did not retain, an antique dealer being courted by the young teacher, Huguet, speaks to him about his *dirty brats*. Huguet simply turns his back on her.

The production crew for *Zéro de Conduite* was more or less the same as the one planned for *La Camargue*: Boris Kaufman, assisted by Louis Berger, on camera, and Albert Riéra as Vigo's assistant. Vigo asked Henri Storck to join the crew as production manager, and Maurice Jaubert to provide the music. Goldblatt, a dabbler in poetry, was to write the lyrics for the song the children sing. Pierre Merle, son of Almereyda's friend, rounded out the group.

Casting the actors and extras did not create any great problems. The extras, notably including about twenty children, played a relatively important part in the film. One of young Merle's functions as assistant was to round up boys from schools, and a teacher friend from a boys' school in the 19th arrondissement helped out by entrusting Vigo with some of his pupils. For one of the principal parts, Vigo had already chosen a boy who lived near him at 34 rue de l'Amiral-Mouchez, and whom he had met in the Parc Montsouris. Louis Lefèvre, the film's Georges Caussat, was the terror of the neighbourhood, delightful, bizarre, and crude. He had a gift for telling fantastic stories which took place at the bottom of the sea or on the moon. Very sensitive, under his brutelike mask, he wanted to be left alone. Without leaving the building in which he lived, Vigo discovered two more actors: the superintendent, M. Blanchar[7], to portray the head supervisor, M. Santt, known as Gas-Snout, and Michèle Fayard to play the little girl.

Bédarieux, a poet, brought along his son Gérard, a pale lad with fine features and long hair, to play the part of Tabard. Bruel was played by Constantin Goldstein-Kehler, Coco Goldstein to his friends and on the credits, from the Boulevard de la Chapelle. Colin was played by Gilbert Pruchon, a lad from Pré-Saint-Gervais. Almost all of the child extras were from the 19th arrondissement, the most typical of all the working-class neighbourhoods in Paris. Those not from that neighbourhood came from the rue Letort or the rue Lepic, and the social unity of the children's world was not disturbed. Where could one find better nurseries for poor, lively, and rebellious children?

For the firemen he needed, Vigo invited painters who, despite the humiliating comparison suggested by the role, accepted. First, Raphaël Diligent, who used to draw for *La Guerre Sociale* and *Le Bonnet Rouge*, and was one of the signatories to the group letter protesting Almereyda's arrest. Then there was Félix Labisse, brought along by Storck, for whose first film he had written the scenario. He in turn brought a friend to play the elegant young lady Huguet encounters during the school walk. The other two firemen were played by Georges Patin and Georges Vakalo.

Vigo needed a man of distinguished presence as the Prefect. For some time he had been friendly with the poet Louis de Gonzague-Frick, the closest friend and testamentary executor of Laurent Tailhade, who in 1901 had defended young Almereyda. Frick agreed to don a full-dress Prefect's uniform, since it was to be subjected to the insults of rebellious children.

For certain parts, professional actors had been engaged. But even Jean Dasté, trained in Copeau's theatrical school and playing his first film role, participated in the venture as a friend. He had met Vigo a few months earlier through Goldblatt and Riéra, and had become one of his constant companions. Strictly speaking, therefore, there were only three professionals: Robert le Flon as the supervisor Parrain, known as Dry-Fart; Larive as the fat and repellent teacher; and the dwarf Delphin as the school principal. Le Flon and Larive were veterans on the cast lists of French films. Delphin had a long artistic career behind him, dating back to before 1914 when he had been a singer with Xavier Privas. There were still a few small parts to be filled. Georges Berger became the guardian, and Storck, the priest.

Nounez had given his final consent on December 12, 1932, and had informed Vigo that the studio shooting was to start on the twenty-fourth. During the few days remaining before shooting was to begin, the production crew was feverishly busy. Vigo sketched out a plan for the dormitory, the film's most important set, and Storck designed the principal's office. On the evening of the thirteenth, Vigo, Storck, and Kaufman stayed at La Coupole until four in the morning, discussing the sets. Working all day on the fifteenth, Vigo and Storck prepared a budget, a shooting schedule, and a list of sets and props, while Riéra put the actors on call and took care of practical matters at the studio.

At Gaumont, two studios, F and G, were given over to the crew. The dormitory was to be installed in F. Careful attention had to be given to the props, since the principal's office installed in Studio G was to be successively and above all rapidly transformed, by shifting flats around and the addition of props, into the guardian's dining-room, the attic, the chemistry classroom, the school study hall, and the refectory.

The entire crew spent the evening before the big day at Gaumont, preparing the sets and the lighting, and the next morning at nine shooting began. The Gaumont employees ironically watched the modest preparations of the young crew, whose oldest member was not yet thirty. Nounez, full of goodwill, watched the proceedings, and was very surprised to see the dwarf Delphin appear dressed all in black as the principal, swathed in a huge beard of the same colour, with a magnificent, shiny new bowler hat, and clutching a prayer-book in his tiny hands.

They started with number 72 in the shooting script, a scene which a few days earlier had existed only as the following simple description: *In his office, the school principal tells the head supervisor: 'You know, the school Commemoration Day is near. Perhaps we could cancel the punishments.'* Vigo had prepared some notes. He had the principal and the head supervisor enter the room with their backs towards the camera. The head supervisor remained in the foreground, near the camera, with his back to it. The principal, looking very dignified, continued on his way to the mantelpiece, on which, with some difficulty because it was too high for him, he carefully placed his hat under a glass cover. After glancing at the supervisor, the principal turned his head towards the mantelpiece, and adjusted his tie, hair, and beard as though he could see himself in the mirror, where only the reflection of the supervisor was visible. He moved towards the desk, his arm out, put his feet into a foot-comforter perched on a footstool, and motioned to the supervisor to sit down. When he sat, the principal's very short legs remained dangling in the air. There was a moment of very solemn silence. The principal was about to speak.

For the first time, Vigo found himself in a studio as director in charge. Gradually, he took control. It was also his first attempt at dialogue. In *Taris*, there had only been a commentary, and anyway it was only a small film. The principal was about to speak; but not the sentence from the script. Vigo had soon realized that the dialogue he had written for the script could only

Zéro de Conduite: Delphin as the Principal

serve as a guide, and he started to rewrite lines as the shooting went on. Every morning when he went to the studio, he took a train which went by a roundabout route so that he could rewrite the dialogue during the journey. We will return to the dialogue later. Meanwhile, the principal was starting to speak:

> *Our Commemoration Day, Monsieur*
> *Santt, is approaching . . .*
> *Isn't that so?*
> *Our little*
> *merry-making . . .*
> *Isn't that so?*
> *Above all, above all,*
> *above all no trouble,*
> *no escapades!*

The crew felt that Delphin's acting was bad. Besides, he was very touchy, and when the exhausted Vigo exploded towards the end of the day, he declared that he wasn't coming back. More than once subsequently Vigo had to send Storck as an ambassador to negotiate with Delphin in his strange attic room at 70 Boulevard de Clichy, furnished to his size, where several years later he gassed himself to death while out of work.

According to schedule, all the scenes in the principal's office and in the guardian's dining-room were to be shot on the first day. Despite frantic efforts which continued late into the evening, they had not finished shooting the office scenes when the exhausted crew was finally dismissed, and Vigo was worried.

On Sunday he went for a drive in Saint-Cloud with Storck in search of exterior locations. On Monday the studio personnel were on holiday, and the crew took advantage of the fact to rehearse with the children, actors, and extras.

On Tuesday the twenty-seventh, they were able to finish the office scenes, and to shoot the scene in the guardian's dining-room between Caussat and the girl, but Storck was sick and had to stay in bed the next day, looked after by Lydou.

The pace had to be speeded up, the crew was already small, and Storck's absence, even if only for a day, threatened to upset their schedule. The crew ate their meals on the run in a small bistro near the studio. On the first day during lunch Vigo completed his casting by hiring the proprietor, Mme. Emile, to play the part of "Mother Beans" the school cook. He had already found a technician among the studio personnel who, clad in dark glasses, would make a suitable nightwatchman for some of the dormitory scenes.

On Wednesday, they managed to shoot the scenes in the kitchen and the school refectory. In order to save time, they dispensed with a set for the latter scene. The necessary props were simply placed in the already constructed dormitory set, and the scene was shot from a high angle.

The next day they went on to the dormitory where the most complicated sequences, those that demanded the most care, were to take place. There they were to spend a little less than four days, working at a constantly increasing pace.

Relations between the crew, who never lost their sense of humour despite their fatigue, and the managing director of Gaumont, M. Thau (considered unbearable), had become acrimonious. Delphin still complained about Vigo, whom he found a hard taskmaster. The children, who were enjoying themselves immensely, fighting with huge pillows spilling out feathers and dragging chamberpots about, were becoming intolerable. Vigo became ill, but insisted on carrying on, and by the evening of the thirty-first, had a fever of 104 degrees. André Négis, sent by *Ciné-Monde*, watched the shooting that day. "No small task, I assure you, to guide, to discipline, to draw something out of twenty kids recruited from all over the place, uprooted from behind shop-counters, from schools, from garrets, from sidewalks. Vigo has carefully hand-picked them out of Paris. He even followed them in the street on occasion, at the risk of being taken for a person of dubious morals. But whenever this little man wants something, he really wants it.

"And so, at this moment, with his sunken eyes, his hollow cheeks, his feverish cough and his temperature of 102 degrees, he should be in bed. But shooting continues, expenses pile up, and there he is, hoarse, on edge, railing, swearing. Since he has no voice left, Riéra has lent him his: a magnificent instrument, a real loudspeaker of a voice. Vigo whispers in Riéra's ear and

Riéra bawls: 'In your beds, boys, goddammit! In bed with your eyes shut! Everyone got that? Then we'll run through it once more.' Lights. Camera. It seems to be all right, but it isn't. The scene must be done again, to give firm shape to this barely malleable, dough-like mass: kids who have never acted before and are having a whale of a time.

"The wind machine is brought forward. A small pile of feathers is put on the edge of a bed, the propeller turns, hurling a whirlwind of down into the head supervisor's face as he enters the dormitory. This, retaken three times, uses up three packages of feathers. The air is snow-white with them, we are covered with them, we breathe them, we eat them. 'Here, Jean, drink this.' A charming young lady with magnificently wild hair steps forward, a steaming cup in her hand. She is Mme. Jean Vigo. When Vigo asks, 'What is it?' she explains, 'It's an infusion of mallow, mountain cat's-foot, colt's-foot, and red poppy.'

"And Vigo docilely drinks it down, as much to soothe his cough as to wash the feathers down."[8]

Vigo had gone to the limit of his endurance, counting on Sunday and Monday for rest. But he had gone too far. His fever did not subside; on Monday he was terribly exhausted, and precautions had to be taken against pneumonia. Everyone had to be told not to come. Riéra and Storck had the task of coming to an agreement with M. Thau at Gaumont about the practical problems caused by the postponement. M. Thau reacted badly, and the discussion was not calm. The possibility of continuing to shoot without Vigo was even considered; finally, the studio administration agreed to a three-day interruption, and arrangements were made to start work again on Friday the sixth.

The news, however, had been relayed to the Vigos in such a manner that for a moment the couple thought that Riéra and Storck were secretly trying to continue shooting. Vigo's reaction, and especially Lydou's, was extremely violent. "Lydou, furious, acted like a stupid cow," Storck wrote in his diary, outraged by the injustice. "After the infinite care Riéra and I took not to offend Jean's vanity, I am disgusted by Vigo's attitude, and most of all by Lydou's."[9]

Vigo's situation was tragic. After so many years of waiting, his bad health threatened to destroy his great chance. Vigo and Lydou felt hounded by bad luck, expected some catastrophe, and even betrayal by their friends. However, a little reflection on the situation was enough to calm everyone down.

On Friday Vigo was at the studio to finish the dormitory scenes. Even though there was no question of more than one take of any scene, he was there until the end of the day. He had only one day of studio time left and still had a lot of work ahead of him. In the evening, before leaving, Vigo finished off the scene in the attic in a half-hour.

The next day, Saturday, January 7, Vigo shot the classroom and study hall scenes, still doing each take once, and sacrificing several shots from the script. Whatever the situation, the crew had to leave the studio by midnight at the latest. At ten to twelve the managers of the Gaumont studio were pacing the sound stage, looking at their watches. After midnight the stage technicians and electricians had the right to a whole night's salary, at an overtime rate twice their normal wage. And one scene still had to be shot!

In this scene Blanchar, playing the part of the head supervisor, was to indulge his two vices, curiosity and lasciviousness. Since eight that morning, Blanchar, respectable superintendent of a building, had awaited his moment. Finally at ten minutes to midnight his hour had come. He hurried towards the desks, smeared his hands with glue, flashed through stacks of religious cards hoping to find those somewhat less sacred images that certain wicked schoolboys secretly procure for themselves. Vigo, mastering himself despite his fatigue, his eyes bright with fever and his voice hoarse, guided him through it: "The cards, Monsieur Du Verron, there, the cards. . . . Oh! Oh! What is it? Oh! Oh! That's right. . . . Ugh! Religious cards! That's it, throw them away. Now, hurry, the glue, for God's sake, the glue! Smear it all over your hands, no, more glue than that! Shit! Shit! Not so slow! Now the tangerines! Into your pocket! Faster, for God's sake! Monsieur Du Verron, the chalk! That's it; and now, right in your face, the door, Monsieur Du Verron, the door, there. . . ." And finally, his voice broken, "Cut!"

Vigo with an anxious look turned towards Storck who answered, "Twelve seconds." Vigo then put on his hat, and planting himself in front of the studio's representative announced to him, "It is seven seconds before midnight, Monsieur. I have finished. Good night."

Work in the studio had lasted eight days.

After the pandemonium of the last day, Vigo and his friends needed some sort of relaxation. A bistro in Montmartre provided the opportunity with a memorable battle of hard-boiled eggs. That was the beginning of a tradition for Vigo and his friends. The sport, however, was to be perfected; later on the projectiles would become fresh eggs.

On the Monday, Vigo and Riéra returned to Saint-Cloud to finish scouting the exteriors where they were to start shooting the next day. Saint-Cloud, with its village atmosphere, provided Vigo with just the setting he desired. Besides, he was very attached sentimentally to this area where his father had lived during the last part of his life.

On Tuesday, January 10, the shooting of exteriors began. The whole day was spent on the pupils' excursion led by the absent-minded junior master, Huguet. That same evening in the station at Belleville-Villette, working until five-thirty in the morning, they shot the first two scenes in the film, the schoolboys returning from vacation.

The next day Vigo needed firemen, not those who appeared in the film, but real firemen who could provide him with an artificial and controllable rainstorm. They good-humouredly appeared after having run down to the city hall in search of their uniforms. They then unscrewed a fire hydrant and connected up a fire hose, quite happy to be at work without having some holocaust to worry about. But just as things were to start, rain clouds burst in the sky, and with a certain melancholy they had to roll up their fire hoses. The rain proved capricious, and the work difficult. It took the whole day, but by eight that evening the shots of the return from the excursion were in the can. The weather got no better on the following three days. Except for the scenes with the priest, very little was shot. Vigo was in a hurry to get to the scenes in the schoolyard, some of which were crucial.

After repeated requests, the inspector of the Versailles school district had authorized shooting in the yard of the Saint-Cloud school for boys. At first it had been a matter of half a day's work, perhaps during the Thursday afternoon holiday so as not to distract the students from their studies. The crew did, in fact, arrive on a Thursday, but after having piled a huge stack of lights and supplies under a roofed-over part of the schoolyard, they took the yard over for more than a week. The school principal was extremely interested in the filming, but he was immediately appalled by the boys, and feared they would set a bad example for his pupils. "Those are real little hoodlums you have there," he told Vigo. And in fact, after three weeks of film-making, the boys were running wild. The script had something to do with it. They had been asked to say "shit" to a teacher, to rebel, to sing in their dormitory while demolishing everything, to bombard the local authorities during a school ceremony, to gallop down streets *en masse*, and to express the feelings of a rioting mob.

Vigo was in a hurry because Kaufman had to leave on Sunday evening, January 15, for Switzerland, and it seemed desirable that, even if he could not shoot all the schoolyard scenes, he personally should shoot the most important one. Vigo had had an authentic Aunt Sally stall from a carnival installed in the courtyard—*Noce à Nini patte en l'air*—to serve as the platform for the officials invited to the school's annual commemoration day celebrations. They worked on these scenes all the morning and afternoon of the day on which Kaufman was to leave.

The only scenes still to be done were the other schoolyard scenes and the sequence on the roof. But the rain and snow which had first slowed the work down now stopped it altogether. Arguments had started between Nounez and Bedoin from Gaumont about fees and the overextended budget. Once again, scenes had to be shortened or amputated, and each take done hastily and only once. Vigo had to sacrifice a scene, the rhythm of which he liked, which was to have served as a transition between the recreation period in the schoolyard and the scene in the study hall supervised by the amiable junior master. It is worth recalling because it provides an excellent example of what a "gag" was to Vigo. Thanks to Huguet's complicity, Caussat, his map in his pocket, succeeds in escaping the head supervisor's suspicions. To cover himself, the boy kicks a ball rolling in the middle of the courtyard. A windowpane is broken, and the head supervisor immediately appears. Caussat is punished —kept in on Sunday—and comes back into the courtyard just in time for the ball to hit him on the head, and then go straight up into the air, breaking another windowpane higher up in the building. A gesture of helplessness on Caussat's part, for he is now confined for two Sundays! Caussat prepares to return to the courtyard, cautiously this time. The head supervisor disappears through the doorway to his office. The ball returns. Caussat, to avoid it, throws himself to the ground, and the ball continues on its way towards the supervisor's office. The supervisor hastens to shut the door, on the window of which one can read "Head supervisor." The window is broken. Out comes the head supervisor again, and Caussat, speechless with rage, is about to be punished again. Furious, he swoops on the ball and tries to break all the windows he can, but each time he misses. He then decides to aim at the head supervisor, who is now coming out of the door. Just at that moment, Huguet, the junior master, is making his way towards the classroom. In the process, without losing his distracted look, he forces the head supervisor slightly off his course. So the ball goes past the supervisor, who stops, waiting for another broken window. The ball, in fact, having missed the supervisor, does seem headed for another window. Huguet takes off his hat to salute the supervisor, and in doing so catches the ball in his hat. He puts the hat and ball back on, making it seem as if he had a huge head on his shoulders, and followed by the delighted boys, he goes into the classroom.

Vigo had already filmed some shots for this sequence, but it had to be abandoned; it demanded a precision impossible to obtain while he was restricted to one take for each shot. Despite all his sacrifices and thanks to the bad weather, the exterior shooting was completed only on Sunday, January 22, after nine and a half effective days at work.

Vigo took sole charge of the first rough-cut. Friends who saw him during his work-breaks found him very discouraged, doubting the value of his film. He had realized that, despite the preliminary cuts, and despite all the items sacrificed from the script during shooting, he had still exceeded the required length. He still had to cut another thousand feet. This time it involved the amputation of already living material. He had a painful choice ahead of him. He would have to decide whether to concentrate on the clarity of the whole, and choose those scenes and shots which, irrespective of their inherent quality, could help one to understand the action better, or whether to choose the most authentic and appropriate sequences without worrying too much about overall rhythm and so forth. In short, given the practical impossibility in which he found himself of attaining an ideal unity, he had to choose between unity of action or unity of style. He opted for the second solution, prepared to add a few explanatory subtitles if they proved necessary.

Having finished a first-cut, still without sound, Vigo had to take a brief rest before undertaking the final cut. He returned to Paris in the beginning of March, in good health, but he immediately had to care for Lydou, who had been stricken with diphtheria. On March 4, Vigo screened the edited version for his crew.

The result was disappointing. It was felt that the film lacked clarity and action. The crew felt that until the middle it was a documentary with too many confusing jumps, that the rhythm faltered, that the lack of a carefully worked-out script was very obvious, that the acting was bad, that everything except intention was unclear; in short, that the film was amateurish.

Maurice Jaubert was working on his score. Two years earlier, Jaubert had written a film score for the first time, for one of Storck's documentaries,

Ostende, Reine des Plages, sonorized by Painlevé. By the beginning of 1933 he had composed his first symphonic work, *Le Jour* (Paris 1931), and he was working on his *Suite Française.* He was already reacting against the musical heritage of the 1920s, that glorious and varied era of Schönberg, Hindemith, and Stravinsky, and of the sensualism of the young French school, a heritage he found disappointing. In music, he was no longer looking for introspective and detached perception. Haunted as he was by social preoccupations linked to aesthetic ones, the sound film seemed to him to be an ideal field for action.

In 1950 Joseph Kosma recalled the disdain with which composers had greeted the first sound film scores: these scores were only the careful and rather more effective heirs to the role of accompaniment fulfilled by music in the time of the silent film. Jaubert reacted against this state of affairs. "Out," he said, "with those ascending scales when a character goes upstairs, and the descending scales when he comes down."[10] And he embarked on a search for a new relationship between the images a director offered him and the music those images evoked in him.

Jaubert asked to see the edited version several times. He had liked the subject of *Zéro de Conduite.* This religious believer shared the same views, the same nobility, the same youthfulness, as Vigo the atheist. But he also liked the way the subject had been treated, and in his score Jaubert matched Vigo throughout with an ease which gives an impression of simultaneous creation, from the pranks at the beginning (in the train) right through to the children's final revolt and their departure over the rooftops. He never abandons Vigo—quite the contrary—even when Vigo plunges headlong into the extraordinary slow-motion world of the torchlight procession. The score for *Zéro de Conduite* was an unqualified success, and from then on Jaubert was clearly the foremost composer of film music in France.

By the end of March the soundtrack was finished, and the film was ready for distribution.

Zéro de Conduite had departed quite considerably from the original scenario—from the literary conception of the first version, and even the working script Vigo was preparing as the shooting went on. The film opens in a third-class compartment in a train. Hunched up in a corner, a man sleeps, his hat pulled over his eyes. Seated in the middle of the bench is Caussat, returning to school after the holidays. During a stop, he is joined by his friend Bruel, and for the rest of their journey they show each other the tricks they have learned during the vacation.

The first shots of Caussat alone are flawed. Vigo wanted to give the impression of a child outside a child's environment. The first moments, when Caussat is quiet, daydreaming, a bit anxious, sad maybe, are good; but as soon as he moves, his movements are too brusque. When Bruel appears the scene develops beautifully. Jaubert's music conveys both the rhythm of the train and of the boys' game, which consists of an exchange of vacation discoveries, done in a spirit of emulation with each attempting to outdo the other. One rubber balloon is nothing. But two will make a girl's breasts which can be caressed. Bruel takes out a flute and plays it: Caussat finds that amazing

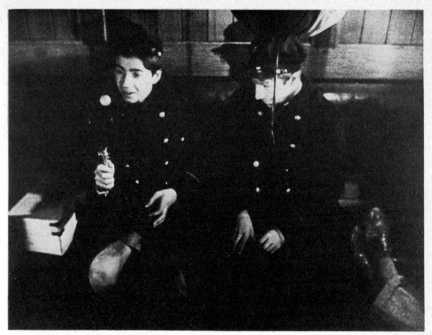

Zéro de Conduite: Bruel and Caussat in the train

enough, but Bruel goes even further—he can play it with one nostril. Caussat has some feathers, he sticks them everywhere, even on his behind, turning himself into a rooster or some such bird. A pause. Each of them prepares a new marvel which will crush the other's. With the same movement they both draw enormous and identical cigars from their pockets. The train is moving at full speed. As the boys, sitting back comfortably, draw on their cigars, the smoke inside the compartment is echoed by the locomotive's smoke appearing outside the window. The compartment becomes hazy and dreamlike: a halo surrounds the lamp and the balloon floating in the smoke. But the boys end up feeling queasy. In his corner, the body of the sleeping man is shaken by the movement of the train. They are just arriving at their destination, and Caussat points to the man, saying, *He's dead. Let's get out of here.* The train arrives at the station, and they both rush for their luggage.

If one had to select a single sequence from Vigo's work representative of his style for an anthology, one ought to choose this opening of *Zéro de Conduite*. Three key elements of his method can be seen in it. First, everyday reality full of carefully selected details (a third-class compartment, schoolboys with skinny legs in frayed uniforms); then it moves through the bizarre (the children's objects and toys), to develop into fantasy (the hazy atmosphere of the compartment).

The arrival at the dimly lit platform of a small provincial station has nothing

111

remarkable about it. We meet Dry-Fart (*We won't have any fun again this year*, remarks Bruel) and the "dead man" from the train: Huguet, the new teacher, well-mannered, eccentric and dusty, with his luggage under his arms and his coat dragging on the ground. We see Colin (*Old Colin, the cook's son, "Kid Beans"*), the new boy Tabard, the silhouette of the latter's mother, and of course the other children. Dry-Fart coldly welcomes young, smiling Huguet, and in a disagreeable voice orders the students on their way in double file and in silence.

It is the first evening in the dormitory. The children are already in bed. The taciturn head supervisor, M. Santt, nicknamed Gas-Snout, makes his appearance, and supervisor Parrain (Dry-Fart) informs him that the pupil Tabard will spend one more night with his mother at a hotel. Gas-Snout is supposed to say not a word during the entire film, and yet from the beginning we feel that he actually does talk. However, no matter. With his velvet-padded walk he crosses the dormitory, and the best part of the film begins.

In the middle of the dormitory, isolated in his cubicle, Dry-Fart gets into bed, and the lights are turned off. At once the noise starts: the boys amuse themselves by imitating animal cries, accompanied by whispers and stifled laughter. An explosion, and the laughter gets louder. The supervisor calls out from his cubicle, *Durand! To the foot of my bed!* The pupil named makes a move to get up, but he is forestalled by Caussat, Bruel and Colin. They haven't been summoned, but they didn't really hear who exactly had been summoned by the supervisor, and they are so used to it. . . . There they are, on their feet, filmed from a high angle, one on each side of the supervisor's cubicle. Sensing another presence, they each cough, then cough again. Bruel extends his arm and in the darkness feels along the other side of the cubicle. Caussat either bites his finger or pinches his arm, and Bruel cries out. Dry-Fart sits up, alarmed.

DRY-FART: *Who's there?*
CAUSSAT: *Caussat, Monsieur.*
BRUEL: *Bruel, Monsieur.*
COLIN: *Colin, Monsieur.*
DRY-FART: *I didn't summon anyone . . . any of you three. You're there, so stay there until eleven o'clock!*

He lies down and goes to sleep. The clock strikes nine. A long pause.

The children were now to have longer speeches. Vigo knew that the sound system at his disposal was bad, and that in addition, the diction of several of his actors and in particular of the children left much to be desired. To obviate these problems he often had his actors repeat the same words or phrases in their lines.

For some time, the children have stood there without moving or speaking. Suddenly Colin doubles over and lets out a cry.

COLIN: *Monsieur, I've got a stomach-ache. . . .*
BRUEL: *Monsieur, can he go?*

COLIN: *Oh! I've got a stomach-ache. . . .*
BRUEL: *Monsieur, he has a stomach-ache!*
COLIN: *Oh! I've got a stomach-ache. . . .*
CAUSSAT: *Well, can he go? He has a stomach-ache!*
COLIN: *Ooh!*
CAUSSAT: *Go ahead! Don't worry about that idiot!*

Colin disappears from view. A pause.

DRY-FART: *Caussat, Bruel, Colin, are you there?*
CAUSSAT AND BRUEL: *Yes, Monsieur.*
DRY-FART: *Go to bed!*
CAUSSAT AND BRUEL: *Thank you, Monsieur.*

The camera pans to the right to follow one of the children to his bed, then moves forward to pick up the other, then pans to the left towards Colin's empty bed and waits for him there, just as Colin comes running in.

If I had to pick out the most beautiful single line in this poem that is *Zéro de Conduite*, I would choose Colin's rapid return to his bed where the camera, like an accomplice, waits for him.

After they have regained their beds, a sleepwalker rises and walks around the dormitory. The nightwatchman makes his rounds.

These scenes in the dormitory show Vigo in a moment of complete control over the cinema, which bends obediently to his desire to re-create the sense of delicious intimacy he had dredged out of his childhood memories. Here, the editing, the camera movements, the composition and inner rhythm of the images, the dialogue, the lighting, all is fused into a harmonious whole which was probably one of Vigo's most ambitious dreams.

The next morning the children are slow in waking up and getting out of bed. When the head supervisor passes through the dormitory, they jump up as though on springs, only to get back into bed as soon as Gas-Snout has shut the door. He suddenly reopens it to surprise the shirkers. Dry-Fart has only to select the usual scapegoats: Colin, Caussat, and Bruel, kept in on Sunday.

The relation between image and sound in this scene again creates confusion, for we are never sure who is speaking, Dry-Fart or Gas-Snout. Another scene in the same sequence brings to mind a film Vigo admired, *Maedchen in Uniform*: the scene in which, as the head supervisor makes his way through the dormitory, the children jump up as if coming to attention. Leontine Sagan's film was made in 1931, and Vigo had seen it in France in the summer of 1932.

In the schoolyard during recess. . . . Some of the children play with a ball. Others smoke cigarettes in the latrines. Still others amuse themselves by tormenting the one child who is in a latrine for a proper reason. Caussat, Bruel, and Colin, as usual, are plotting. They even have a map spread out in front of them. Tabard is alone. He is attracted by the trio, but feels rejected. One of the supervisors is approaching, but Huguet, without seeming to, covers the conspirators' retreat, and they take refuge in the study hall.

Zéro de Conduite: 'the children jump up as if coming to attention'

The recess sequences are rich in atmosphere, but they hardly help us understand the action. We see the three conspirators, intent on their map, with Tabard kept at a distance and Huguet protecting them, but it is not easy to understand what they are saying, and difficult even to know what it is all about. On the other hand, the whole atmosphere of a boarding school is created when we see the youngsters smoking in the toilets or watch a door being jerked open to reveal a kid with his trousers down indignantly yelling: *Swine!*

As soon as they have entered the study hall, the trio have to exit through the window, for the head supervisor is coming. Gas-Snout takes advantage of the recess period to search through the desks. Perhaps he hopes to find something forbidden. Disappointed, he steals the children's candy. Huguet is bored. He would like to join in playing ball, but he too feels he is being watched by Dry-Fart and Gas-Snout. To amuse himself, he ambles through the courtyard mimicking Chaplin's walk, delighting the children hidden behind a wall. A group of pupils alternately appears and vanishes behind the wall of the latrine, depending on whether Huguet has his back turned or is facing them. Soon, Huguet's Chaplin imitation and the children's game of hide-and-seek turn the whole courtyard into a "respectful parody" (the words used by Vigo in his notes) of a scene from one of Chaplin's Mutual films: *Easy Street*. Vigo makes a cinematic allusion here comparable to a literary quotation from some well-known author. I do not believe that this idea has yet been followed up, except perhaps in *La Règle du Jeu*, where Renoir quotes (also from Chaplin) a scene from *The Count*.[11]

It is time for study hall. The children realize that the head supervisor has searched their desks, and Caussat decides on reprisals. He collects the glue pots and empties them into any nook and cranny the supervisor might search. In the study hall presided over by Huguet, the children smoke, read the newspaper, play cards, and build human pyramids. One pupil even sleeps. Caussat, Bruel, and Colin study their map. Huguet helps a student who is trying to walk on his hands. He himself gives a well-applauded demonstration of how to do it. In this acrobatic position, he draws a caricature of Gas-Snout dressed in a bathing suit. Gas-Snout walks in, the caricature becomes animated, and changes into Napoleon. Huguet is replaced by Dry-Fart; before leaving the study hall, he takes the map the three boys have not yet managed to hide, tears it up, and stuffs the pieces into his pocket.

In this sequence, two things which were to have been tied up later are left in suspension, because the connection was never made. First, Caussat spreading glue all over the desks. The follow-up was to have been the scene hurriedly filmed at ten minutes to midnight on the last day of studio shooting. Vigo had to sacrifice the scene in the editing. It is scarcely missed. The climax for which the scene with the glue pots prepares us is so present in the scene itself that the small demands made on the viewer's imagination are easily satisfied. Perhaps we would even have found the shot of Gas-Snout plunging his hands into the glue superfluous. The success of this scene is due in part to the quality given the dialogue by the method of repetition we have previously mentioned. One does not easily forget Caussat walking among his friends and saying:

> *So he searched?*
> *You'll see. . . . Pass me . . .*
> *your glue pot . . .*
> *. . . your glue pot . . .*
> *your glue pot. . . .*

The other scene left dangling—Huguet tearing up the map—is more crucial to the action. Later on, the children were to have found the map, carefully pieced together again by Huguet, hidden in Caussat's bed. This scene is missing, and Huguet's gesture thus becomes awkwardly gratuitous.

As for the little animated cartoon which is included in the sequence, Vigo wanted it to be in the metamorphic style typical of Emile Cohl's work. The introduction of this cartoon into the sequence does not really create the desired climax to the series of absurdities, which until then had been harmoniously strung together.

Another trick effect occurs at the very beginning of the scene. Caussat is holding a balloon which mysteriously disappears the moment Gas-Snout's face appears in the window, and just as mysteriously reappears the moment he leaves. This scene was to have concluded the "broken windows" sequence which, as we have seen, was never shot. So instead of ending that sequence, it opens another, and is none the worse for it. In the study hall so many extraordinary things take place that one more trick effect is not out of place; besides, it allows Vigo to pay homage in passing to Méliès.

In the courtyard the students are ready to be inspected by the school principal before departing on the excursion under Huguet's supervision. Gas-Snout, hastily separating Bruel from Tabard, makes final preparations. The principal, a small bearded man, arrives and gives the signal for departure, at the same time inviting the head supervisor to accompany him to his office. He addresses a short speech on the approaching celebration to him. In it he refers to Bruel, Colin, and Caussat.

The appearance of the principal is the moment in the film when the satire bites strongest. Just for a moment we have the impression that a child is ridiculing the adult world in borrowed clothing and an enormous false beard. The effect is completed by the thin, high voice which orders, *On your way, Messieurs*, and then invites the head supervisor to accompany him to the office.

In the street Bruel and Tabard come together again, walking side by side. Huguet daydreams and completely forgets about the excursion. The boys take off into a side street, and for a time Huguet walks alone. He buys some cigarettes, greets Dry-Fart, who is perplexed at seeing him alone, and is rejoined at an intersection by the procession of boys.

In his office the principal continues to speak, now of the friendship between Bruel and Tabard and about Huguet's behaviour.

The excursion and the conversation between the two school officials are developed simultaneously, and when the self-possession of Huguet walking happily and freely is followed by the intimidated manner of Gas-Snout in his superior's office, we have a contrast, along with a continuity of movement created by the editing, which Vigo was not able to attain more frequently because of the practical difficulties he had to face.

We are already sufficiently acquainted—having followed it during the shooting—with the scene between Gas-Snout and the principal in the latter's office. In it the principal delivers the first of those little speeches which are his speciality and with which he is so prodigal. As for the excursion, so very inefficiently led by the daydreaming Huguet, it is very well directed by Vigo. The walk is dominated by two events, one poetic and the other comic. The first begins with Huguet's encounter with the young lady, attaining its peak when all the boys, following suit after Huguet, take off their hats to greet her. The comic event begins with her flight and pursuit by the whole retinue. At a street corner, misled by a skirt, Huguet catches up with a priest... the priest becomes embarrassed ... and we laugh. What better way to discredit the priest than to show him escaping in speeded-up motion?

The excursion returns to the school in disorder in the rain, Huguet first, a group of pupils behind him. The principal is in the process of expressing his disapproval to the head supervisor when Bruel and Tabard arrive, sheltering under the same cape. The principal bursts out: *There now, still together! This friendship is getting out of hand. . . . Supervisor, you are right. . . . They must be watched. . . .*

The principal summons Tabard to his office. He is going to give him one of his little sermons, but feels embarrassed. Tabard, slightly uneasy, sits down in front of him. The principal, keeping his lamp trained on the boy, begins:

> *My child, I am almost like your father. . . .*
> *At your age, there are things,*
> *isn't that so? . . .*

The camera moves in a semicircle around Tabard, who doesn't quite understand but nevertheless feels ashamed and hangs his head, shrinking into his chair as the principal's voice continues:

> *. . . things . . .*
> *Bruel is older than you.*
> *Your temperament, your sensibility, his,*
> *isn't that so? . . .*

The principal's voice becomes excited:

> *psychopathic . . .*
> *. . . neuropathic. . . .*

At this point, as Tabard becomes more and more upset, the camera leaves him and, in a shot taken from above, shows the principal suddenly leaping out of his seat like a jack-in-the-box, his beard bristling, his arms waving,

Zéro de Conduite: 'psychopathic . . . neuropathic . . . WHO KNOWS!'

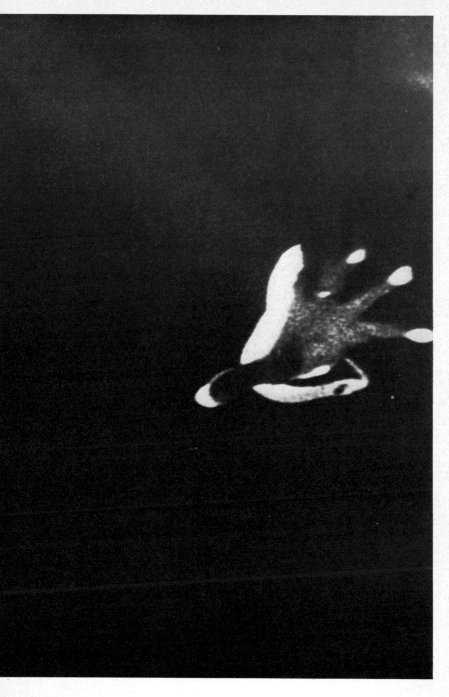

and dramatically crying: *Who knows?* It is with good reason that Tabard, humiliated and furious, looks for a place far from his friend Bruel's desk when he returns to the study hall.

On Sunday Caussat spends the afternoon at his guardian's, playing with the girl. The guardian has his head hidden behind his newspaper. Seated on a chair near the window, Caussat has his eyes blindfolded. The girl, perched on the piano, is hanging the goldfish bowl from a wire. She goes to sit down beside Caussat, takes off the cloth covering his eyes, and motions him to be silent. And they both watch the fish.

Colin spends his Sundays with his mother, the school cook, "Mother Beans." After having had such frequent truck with the principal, Dry-Fart, and Gas-Snout, it is a relief to have this big, worthy woman of the people before us. But here comes Gas-Snout, arriving in his usual manner without making a sound, to look in the saucepan on the stove. The good woman makes some very appropriate observations, unfortunately in the tones of an amateur actress: *Oh, Monsieur supervisor, beans, beans and more beans! I just can't serve these children beans every day!* The head supervisor leaves, naturally, without saying a word. Colin receives the slap really deserved by the supervisor when he enters the kitchen and, seeing the contents of the saucepan, plaintively remarks, *Oh mother, beans again. . . .*

Colin joins Bruel, who renews his efforts on Tabard's behalf. Colin finally agrees to accept Tabard into the conspiracy.

In the versions of the film now available to us, the scene in the refectory that evening starts a few moments before the row breaks out. This was not the case, it seems, in the version presented in 1933. Caussat, having returned from a day at his guardian's, mimed out his imaginary adventures with the girl for his friends, and to overcome their scepticism, he showed them a piece of untwined rope as if it were a lock of her hair.

All that has disappeared. In any case, the whole scene was never included, and I even doubt whether it was ever shot in its entirety. The scene was not to have consisted only of Caussat's mime; we were also to have had a brief glimpse of his inventions. The guardian's chair empty, the little girl made-up like a vamp and playing the closed piano, Caussat moving towards her, she turning and leaning against the piano, Caussat continuing to advance. She seizes one of the fish, and the fearless Caussat, still advancing, opens his mouth and swallows the fish. In the foreground the girl is lying on top of the piano with Caussat leaning over her. He pats her hair and she covers his eyes with a piece of cloth. Suddenly, the guardian reappears in his chair, reading. He feels in his pockets, slowly takes out a pipe, and then, hidden behind his newspaper, menaces Caussat with a pistol. Scissors appear between Caussat's teeth, he grabs them, and cuts a large lock of the girl's hair, making a gesture of salutation. And then, with the scissors raised, he throws himself on the guardian.

It is a pity this fib-telling scene is missing. It would have highlighted the simple, limpid truth: Caussat sitting quietly beside the girl, watching the goldfish bowl in the guardian's old-fashioned dining-room.

Zéro de Conduite: Colin with his mother (*above*) and the riot against the bad food

In the film as it now exists, the children are served their beans in the refectory, and the row begins. The scene, hastily shot from a high angle, as we have seen, so that there would be no need for a set change, develops in a somewhat confused and chaotic manner. The children cry out, *Down with Mother Beans!* Faced with these demonstrations against his mother, Colin hides his face and weeps. Vigo knew what it meant for a child to have a mother or father reviled. Caussat and Bruel bring the demonstrations to a halt.

The next scene, in the chemistry class, had been planned and even shot by Vigo in a much more elaborate manner than the scene as it now stands. Caussat and Colin, in charge of lighting the stove, put a wet rag into it. The teacher entered, followed by a skeleton, a traditional joke. The stove filled the room with smoke, and the teacher, trying to get a chemical experiment to work, thought that the smoke was coming from his test-tube.

The teacher: *What's happening to this experiment? I've been doing it for fifteen years. It's going to make an awful mess!* Getting worried, he asked for a container. Caussat handed him a funnel.

Here the cuts are probably explained by Vigo's self-criticism. The scene seemed contrived and obscured its purpose, which was to establish the personality of the teacher against whom Tabard revolts. Stripped of the smoke and funnel gags, the scene takes on an altogether different density.

Around the stove they are supposed to be lighting, Caussat and Colin talk about letting Tabard into their plot.

COLIN: *Tabard has a hiding-place.*
CAUSSAT: *What hiding-place?*
COLIN: *I don't know.*
CAUSSAT: *Well, if you don't know, then don't bother me with Tabard.*
COLIN: *It was Bruel who wanted to include him.. . .*
CAUSSAT: *Tabard's a sissy.*
COLIN: *Ever since he went to see the principal, I don't know what's wrong with him.*
CAUSSAT: *Well, if you don't know, why bother me with Tabard? Tabard, I tell you, is a sissy.*
Can he do anything?
Can he say anything?

The boys are already in their seats when the teacher, followed by the skeleton dangling from the ceiling of the amphitheatre, enters the classroom. The teacher, armed with his pince-nez, turns towards the students and sarcastically comments: *How very amusing!* He continues in a tired, malicious voice: *But I don't like that at all!* He is a fat, repulsive person. He replaces his jacket with an even dirtier smock. Seated behind his desk, he begins his toilet. He starts by filling his nostrils with an ointment, and finishes by carefully unfolding his handkerchief, his only clean possession, which functions as a receptacle for his spittle. His phlegm is already purring in his throat, but we are spared the actual sight of it, and, as the camera shows us

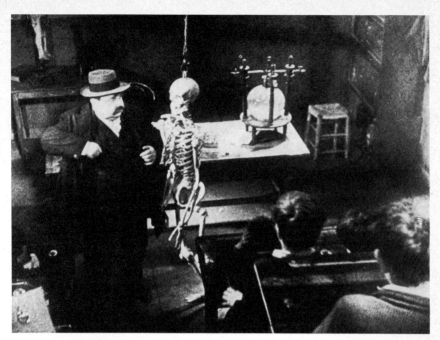

Zéro de Conduite: the chemistry master and Tabard

Tabard behind his desk, worried and separated from the others, only its sound pursues us. The teacher, after having started his lecture, approaches Tabard, caresses his hair, and says with a somewhat ominous tenderness: *Well, my lad, aren't we taking notes this morning?* Tabard starts to write nervously. The teacher, just as he puts his fat, moist, glistening hand on the schoolboy's left hand, says: *That's right, that's very good.* With a sudden brusque gesture, Tabard recoils from him: *Leave me alone!*

The teacher, in a half-conciliatory, half-threatening tone, reacts: *Well, my lad, I only said something nice to you.* And Tabard explodes: *Well, I, I say . . . I say shit on you!*

Later that same day a solemn, tense atmosphere pervades Huguet's study hall period. The door opens, and a full complement of staff enters, with the principal at their head, followed by Gas-Snout, the fat teacher, and Dry-Fart. They all try to appear as serious and dignified as they can. The principal starts the longest of those little speeches which he finds so attractive. He addresses himself to Tabard who stands before him: *My child, the disciplinary council, the disciplinary council has consented, under strong pressure from your overly generous teacher*—the principal turns towards the piglike teacher—*You are generous, Monsieur Viot.* The piglike teacher makes a gesture of modesty, and, as the camera moves from left to right across the room all the way through it, the principal picks up where he left off: *Out of consideration for your family, because of our concern for you, and on the occasion of our beloved commemoration day to be celebrated tomorrow, the disciplinary council has consented to forgive you.* Once the camera has reached the end of the room, Vigo has Kaufman violate one of the basic rules of camera technique: he makes him repeat the same tracking shot, this time from right to left, showing the same field as before. Meanwhile, the principal continues: *But of course you came to me of your own accord, is it not so? to ask me to accept your apology, an apology which would be valueless unless repeated in public in front of all your classmates.* The camera has returned to the principal, who pauses, and then continues, *Well, we're waiting. . . . Say what you have to say. . . .* Another pause. Huguet, disgusted, puts his hat on so as to leave and have no part in Tabard's humiliation. The principal, impatient, insists: *Come now! Say what you have to say!* And once again Tabard bursts out, *Sir, I say . . . shit on you!*

In the next shot we see the dormitory in a complete frenzy. Surrounded by all the other children, Tabard reads a proclamation, of which we are only able to hear fragments because his diction is bad and the quality of the sound worse: *Down with teachers! Down with punishments! Long live revolt! . . . To the rooftops with our flag! We'll bombard them with rotten old books!*

Panicked, in his nightshirt, Dry-Fart hurries over to intervene, but the boys prevent him from doing so. Tabard reads the revolutionary proclamation through to its end, and an incredible shindy begins. The beds are turned upside down, clusters of chamberpots are dragged across the floor, everything the boys can get their hands on is hurled around the dormitory. The boys fight each other with pillows and quilts which burst open. Through a cloud of feathers, Dry-Fart, exhausted, looks for a chair to sit on. The chair is pulled from under him, and he falls over. Jaubert's music sets the tone for the atmosphere of disorder.

At this point in the sequence, two extraordinary things happen: the music and the images change. The images are slowed down; an acrobatic child does a cartwheel, and as his nightshirt momentarily floats free of his body, leaving his penis uncovered, he lands on the chair removed from under Dry-Fart, while the music suddenly assumes a strange texture, as though it were being inhaled. To find a perfect musical equivalent for the slower motion of the images, Jaubert had written a musical theme which was recorded backwards; the sound-loop was reversed during the sound-mixing.

This ghostlike music continues as an accompaniment to the torchlight procession which, still in slow-motion, forms behind the acrobat borne aloft in his chair. The boys in their nightshirts, enveloped in the soft, drifting movement of the feathers, all appear to be seized by a sort of ecstasy. At the tail end of the procession walks a small phantom, a child entangled in the curtains from the supervisor's cubicle.

Once over the initial shock caused by these movements and sounds from another reality, we wonder only at the familiar intimacy of this sublime poetry.

The next morning, fatigue, accomplice of the four . . ., explains a subtitle, as if after all that has transpired any explanation were necessary. What more natural than that Caussat, Tabard, Bruel, and Colin should manage to tie Dry-Fart to his bed with his comforter, that they should then raise the bed into a vertical position, and that they should hang on his sleeping, crucified form, around which a few feathers still drift, twin Chinese lanterns looking like a pair of scales—the scales of blind justice, perhaps? All of this is still so much a part of the world of slow-motion and of the music played backwards (in which nothing is explainable or, conversely, in which everything is clear) that there is no need for clarification.

We then return to the everyday reality of the commemoration day ceremonies—*Our little merrymaking, isn't that so?*, as the principal said—which take place, as Vigo later commented, "on a day appropriately referred to as the day of the Sainte-Barbe" [*i.e.* the Day of the Powder-Magazine].

Perhaps because we have just left the dream world of the torchlight procession and the crucifixion of Dry-Fart, it is undoubtedly a little distressing to see the principal once again, nervously pacing the schoolyard where everything is ready for the ceremonies. He seems even more grotesque than usual, perhaps because we also see a big, strapping fellow drying glasses. In the original prints of the film, we knew that the officials were worried because the four rebellious boys had shut themselves up in the attic and refused to come out. In the prints now available, a certain nervousness still pervades the air. The priest is present, and it is he who welcomes the Distinguished Visitor: *Oh! Monsieur Prefect, what an occasion! Dear God, what an occasion!*

Storck, when he spouts out the few lines given him as the priest, matches

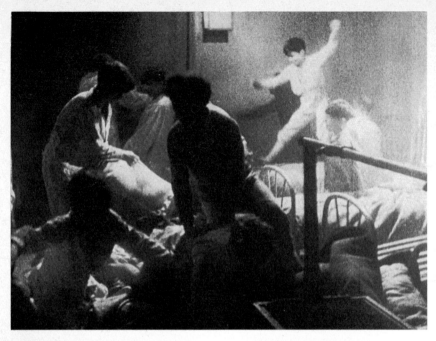

Zéro de Conduite: 'A sort of ecstasy'

Zéro de Conduite: 'the crucifixion of Dry-Fart'

Mother Beans, as played by Mme. Emile, in the amateurishness of his diction. He adds a few words intended for the principal, whose worries are definitely causing his mind to wander: *The Prefect is just sitting down! . . . The Prefect has sat down.*

Soon all of the officials are installed in the first row of the celebrities' stand. The horrible dummies from the Aunt Sally are behind them in the second row, and the two groups seem to go well together. The schoolboys accompanied by Huguet are seated on the sides. In the middle of the yard firemen in their dress uniforms begin their demonstrations. A bearded fireman balances himself with some difficulty on the parallel bars. Why has Gas-Snout gone to prowl around the latrines? We will never know.

Suddenly, the officials and firemen are bombarded with books, old shoes, and stones thrown from the rooftops by the four mutineers. All the students, encouraged by Huguet, join in on the target practice to such effect that the officials and firemen have to take refuge in the attic. Gas-Snout, whose behaviour has by this time become decidedly inscrutable, has a grimacing smile on his face which gives nothing away.

The children have seized the school, and the French tricolour they wave is soon dashed to the ground and replaced by the flag of revolt thrown to them from the roof.

As a whole, this sequence is not really satisfactory. Nevertheless, it has

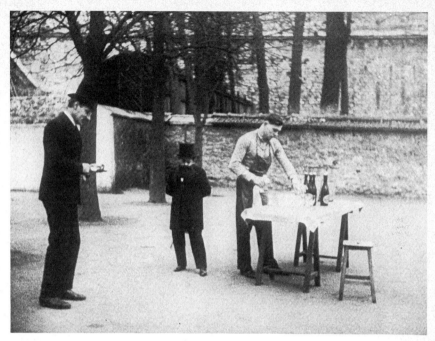

Zéro de Conduite: preparations for commemoration day

its moments: the shot of the fireman on the parallel bars is excellent, and the officials seated in front of the Aunt Sally is an unforgettable image. But when pandemonium breaks out, it is difficult not to think back regretfully to the similar scene in the dormitory.

Caussat, Bruel, Tabard, and Colin leave by the rooftops, singing, sometimes making their way with difficulty on all fours, into the sky, into freedom.

Looking back over the film as a whole, one notes that there are two worlds in *Zéro de Conduite*: on the one hand the world of children and common people, and on the other, the world of adults, of the bourgeois. The casting of the children does not suggest any attempt to stylize them as characters; they represent, on a realistic level, average children in a poor country school. Most of them are skinny, neither handsome nor ugly, and even dirty. These children are like children everywhere. The two adults representing the "people," the cook and the café waiter who wipes the glasses for the celebration, are also realistic, and could be any motherly body or big, hefty fellow. Huguet is not a real adult, since he identifies so completely with the children's world.

With the other characters, we are in a world of puppets, headed by the three manifestations of authority in the school: the principal, the head supervisor (M. Santt, nicknamed Gas-Snout), and supervisor Parrain (nicknamed Dry-Fart). Their grotesqueness is in direct proportion to their importance;

Zéro de Conduite: commemoration day

and they make their appearance in the film in reverse order. First Dry-Fart as he waits at the station for the boys returning from vacation. At once, caught up in his own importance, he gives an impression of obnoxiousness. When Caussat points him out, the disgusted Bruel says, *We won't have any fun again this year. . . . Oh, you think so?* replies Caussat. And he has good reasons for his doubt, since Dry-Fart will end up crucified in his bed, demolished like the others.

Soon after, we are introduced to the head supervisor. From the very moment he appears, Gas-Snout is ridiculous. Only subsequently is an odious dimension added, until he becomes a sinister character, spying on the children, stealing their candy, and never uttering a word.

As we have seen, on the other hand, the principal talks a good deal. Poised at the summit of the school hierarchy, he resumes all the absurdities of his subordinates, and surpasses them all by his pretensions as a well-dressed man, as a leader, and as a dwarf.

Just as he had done for the children, Vigo started from reality to create his adult characters; and to define them clearly as belonging to the world of adults, he did not hesitate to push their mannerisms to the point of caricature. However, to people his world only with members of the school hierarchy was not enough to satisfy Vigo's ultimate aims. He brought in figures of authority far more important than the school: the priest and the prefect.

Zéro de Conduite: 'making their way into the sky, into freedom'

All these men take their place in front of those other puppets, the dummies from the Aunt Sally stall. The firemen, as ridiculous as the rest, make a spectacle of themselves. They are men of the people, but their uniforms place them in the puppet world. One recalls that the silhouette of the railway employee, barely glimpsed at the beginning of the film, had time enough to be unpleasant: it is sad that railway employees should have to wear uniforms. In a sequence in his first outline, not retained subsequently, Vigo had the boys beat huge soldiers in a game of football and make them look ridiculous.

The emotional logic Vigo uses in the creation of these two worlds is almost always relentless. He still had an adult on his hands, one without a uniform: Caussat's guardian, the father of the little girl with whom the boy plays on his occasional outings. In the scenario, in a moment of weakness, Vigo had written: *under the guardian's benevolent eye, Caussat plays in a corner of the dining-room, where everything is old-fashioned, with a delightful girl—the guardian's daughter*. What! A sympathetic adult in a bourgeois dining-room? Impossible! Vigo recollects himself, and hides the guardian's face behind a newspaper. He was only to have emerged from behind the paper in Caussat's story, but since that sequence never occurs, there he remains, hidden for all eternity.

Vigo made exceptions, however, of two bourgeois adults—two women.

The first is Tabard's mother, whom we meet in the railway station. At first we see only her silhouette. Then just as we are about to see her face, it is hidden by a sudden movement of the supervisor. Vigo almost ignores her, barely sketching her in: he did not want to decry her by placing her in the world of puppets. Besides, she was Tabard's mother, and as we know, there is a good deal of Vigo in Tabard. We can see how far Vigo has developed emotionally since *A Propos de Nice*. After the grotesque carnival teeming with women, he now banishes them from the puppet world of *Zéro de Conduite*. He has succeeded in partially overcoming his feelings as a resentful son, and when he allows the mother to tell the supervisor: *Forgive me, Monsieur, but René Tabard will not come to school until tomorrow morning. He is somewhat sad this evening*, we sense that he has forgiven his mother.

It was love that brought Vigo this new balance, and the other woman is, of course, the one who is so engagingly trailed by Huguet and the boys during the excursion, until she is succeeded at a street corner by a worried priest. She cannot but be sympathetic, for she represents a possibility of love.

The guardian hidden behind the newspaper, the watchman passing through the dormitory, perpetually indifferent to the calm or the chaos that reigns there, the vague silhouette of the mother in the station, all of them hover between the two worlds. But Vigo allows the young woman encountered during the excursion to enter the human world of the children, Huguet, the cook, and the café waiter.

This division into two worlds and the conclusion of the film give us all the elements of Vigo's ideology and the social implications of *Zéro de Conduite*. In addition to being a real school with its source in Vigo's childhood memories, the school in *Zéro de Conduite* is also society as seen by the adult Vigo. The division into children and adults inside the school corresponds to the division of society into classes outside: a strong minority imposing its will on a weak majority. The association between the children and their accomplice, Huguet, on the one hand, and the representatives of the people, the cook and the café waiter, on the other, is not suggested through action—which would have been artificial—but through the realistic style in which both are presented, in contrast to the extreme stylization with which adults representing authority are characterized. The victims chosen for the Aunt Sally—the Church, the State, the Uniform—reveal Vigo at grips with traditional anarchist themes. Similarly, the ending (the departure of the four mutineers towards freedom) is an expression of the late nineteenth-century anarchist sentiment which induced so many militants, after attacking society for a time, to leave either individually in search of freedom in Argentina or elsewhere, or collectively in quest of freedom outside society through the creation of "free environments" or communes. The ideology of *Zéro de Conduite* consists of Vigo's fidelity to the political sentiments of another age which remained very close to his heart.

The dialogue in *Zéro de Conduite* has been largely overlooked by critics and has never interested film historians, perhaps because there is so little of it, or because the quality of the sound is so bad. Although Vigo was sometimes forced to work too hastily in writing the dialogue during the actual shooting, he was helped by the fact that he could look for words to suit characters already incarnate before his eyes. He was thus able to free himself from the literary distortion which has always tainted French film dialogue, and to come up with simple, effective lines for his children, and a nicely balanced irony for the principal's speeches.

With regard to the dialogue, the producer's needs were entirely in accord with the director's wishes. Reducing the number of spoken lines reduced the film's cost; while Vigo, for his part, regretted the passing of the silent film, and regarded the "100 per cent talkie" boasted by the publicity posters of the day with a good deal of suspicion. *Zéro de Conduite* is very restrained with its dialogue: only a little over a thousand words are spoken in the film.

In his choice of individual lines Vigo remained haunted by memories of his father's life. A book of reminiscences by Victor Méric, Miguel Almereyda's colleague on *La Guerre Sociale*, had appeared in 1930.[12] In it the author describes the circumstances under which Almereyda had composed a banner headline addressed to the government which stated, in huge letters and without asterisks, "I say shit on you." Vigo determined to have Tabard use that phrase, first to the fat teacher, then to the principal, in order to launch the boys' revolt.

To compensate for the problems caused by the bad quality of the sound and the poor diction of his cast, the children in particular, Vigo had experimented with repetitions: Caussat with his "glue pots," the three children around the supervisor's cubicle speaking of "stomach-aches" or of "going." Although not sensational, the results were good; more than anything else, the method had great possibilities. We will refer again to this approach to dialogue in discussing Vigo's creation of the character of Père Jules, played by Michel Simon, in *L'Atalante*.

Another quality often overlooked in *Zéro de Conduite* is its camera movement. Most of the time Vigo had to content himself with pans. We have seen what he could accomplish with them, notably towards the end of the sequence with the three children around Dry-Fart's bed, when Vigo shifts the camera's field of vision in a controlled and unobtrusive manner, following two of the children to bed, then waiting for the third to get into his. When he has occasion to use a tracking shot, as he does during the principal's speech in the apology sequence in the study hall, Vigo disdains conventional usage and he reveals his mastery.

In Vigo's case, one should add, speaking of the "controlled" manner in which he handles his pans or of his "mastery" of the tracking shot, does not necessarily imply any particular technical expertise. Vigo is often technically awkward. It is his eye, his inspiration, which is sure and which dominates. If he makes "mistakes," more often than not he imposes them on us the way poets do.

Nevertheless, we must not think that the flaws in *Zéro de Conduite* are minor ones. Vigo's intention is not always clearly conveyed to us by the film, which in the last analysis is an unfinished work and has a plot which is often unclear. Yet Vigo had wanted the events in his film to develop in a clear and orderly fashion. While writing his screenplay, he noted that "throughout the film, we will witness a plot closely related to the school's everyday life, and whose rhythm will develop in crescendo, parallel to the preparations for the commemoration-day ceremonies, and to the little scandal which suddenly erupts between the fourth child [Tabard] and the administration."[13]

In the film, as it now exists, there is no easily discernible "crescendo" or even a simple, clear continuity. Vigo's style demands that we see "between the lines." But it should be added that Vigo's problems with his producer's requirements about length have probably given the film that fragmented look which so often baffles audiences. It should also be remembered that the *Zéro de Conduite* which we see today is, in places, even more incomplete than the original 1933 version. Not only are single shots missing, but it seems that at least one complete sequence has disappeared entirely: the scene in the refectory where Caussat mimes out his adventures.

In theory, the sum total of *Zéro de Conduite*'s flaws should have caused the film to be terrible. The criticisms of the editing made by some of Vigo's collaborators before the film was sonorized are quite valid: lack of clarity and almost of action, transitions too brief, lack of rhythm, lack of a prepared script, bad acting. After the sonorization, new faults emerged. In the first place, the sound was very bad. But Vigo had also committed some incredible blunders: at times it is impossible to know which character is speaking.

When one thinks that the end result is a film whose freshness has only increased with the years, it might seem little short of miraculous if we did not already know that this vitality springs from the basic authenticity of the scenario, an authenticity respected throughout the shooting by a director guided by his most personal memories; and also from its basic unity, achieved in the editing by sacrificing clarity to style; and, of course, from the support given by Jaubert's music.

At this point let us stop our discussion of *Zéro de Conduite* and return to the first showing of the film on the evening of April 7, 1933, at 6.15 p.m. at the Cinéma Artistic on the rue de Douai.

Legends about this first showing are rife. At the presentation in 1950 of *Zéro de Conduite* in certain specialized cinemas and film clubs in Paris,[14] it was recounted how the entire French literary and artistic world had been present, and how at the end of the screening all the celebrities, with Claudel and Gide at their head, disliking the film, had left without a word to the director. The only part of all this which is true is that Gide, invited by Aveline, was there and had not liked the film.

The description of the screening written by a member of the audience less than two years afterwards was already an exaggeration: "The bourgeois sentiments of the audience were deeply shocked by the behaviour of the children as shown by Vigo. During the projection the house-lights had to be switched on several times, and the show ended almost in a free fight. In Paris, highbrow audiences have the courage of their convictions."[15]

In fact, nearly all the distributors and cinema managers were shocked, but more by the lack of commercial qualities than for any moral reason. A few comments loudly voiced by younger members of the audience—notably the Prévert brothers and their friends, who heartily applauded the film—drowned out the hisses of the bourgeois element. A good part of the audience consisted of children, the boys in the film and their friends, who immensely enjoyed seeing themselves and their companions on the screen. As for the parents, also present in large numbers, they tenderly followed the images of their progeny. Only one woman subsequently expressed misgivings about having allowed her son "to associate with satyrs" during those weeks.

As for the literary and journalistic celebrities of the time, traces of disapproval can be detected on the part of Georges de la Fouchardière. A reviewer in the satirical weekly *Le Huron*, signing himself as Beelzebub, depicts the old anarchist and pacifist writer as leaving his seat before the end, "raising his hands to the skies in the foyer, his beard bristling and his hat looking rather the worse for wear," and telling the friends around him, "It's lavatory-flushings." After this outburst, la Fouchardière was supposed to have added dreamily: "That boy will go far."

In the same article, the writer speaks of the film in an ironic tone: "Let us first declare to the author's credit that in place of the children's story he was supposed to make he has succeeded in substituting a curious anthology of the thirty-two positions of avant-garde cinema which includes a passing reference to the priest in *L'Age d'Or*, the pillows with their feathers spilling out in *The Gold Rush*, the revolt in the refectory in *The Big House*, and the abortive inauguration in *A Nous la Liberté*, etc."[16]

In the same issue of the weekly, under the by-line "The week's little irritations," we read: "M. Vigo, son of Almereyda, has just launched himself on a cinematic career. He must have taken too much of a run before he jumped. He landed somewhere out in the bushes." The next week, *Le Huron* returned to the fray. In the meantime, *Zéro de Conduite* was supposed to have started its run at the Studio, as support to Jean Benoît-Lévy's *La Maternelle*. This time the journalist did not sign himself Beelzebub, but simply used the initial S. The bantering tone had disappeared as well: "Today, the entire body of film critics will have the breath knocked out of them as they watch Jean Vigo's little joke, *Zéro de Conduite*. We must not exaggerate, however. The film could have been a real cinematic event. What we saw, though, is simply ridiculous, as we have already made clear.

"The time has come when a director will need a good deal more talent to make a good commercial film than to turn out one of those so-called avant-garde pieces which make our backward avant-gardists swoon.

"Luis Buñuel at least had a certain understanding of the cinema, and his work will continue to be cited, perhaps only as an example.

"It may seem strange, however, that Luis Buñuel keeps certain young cherubs of the cinema from sleeping. They swear only by him."

The evening before, in an issue of *Marianne* which announced the presentation of *Zéro de Conduite* and *La Maternelle* at the Studio, Pierre

Ogouz reviewed both films. Of Vigo's film, Ogouz wrote: "An exceptional work which will be hissed and argued over. A film which makes it difficult to understand why a big commercial company should have agreed to distribute it. Angry, violent, destructive, rancorous, it seems replete with all the bitterness the author must have stored up during an unhappy childhood in a boarding-school. Studded with obscenities, noxious and harsh, it pillories vicious, narrow-minded pedagogues, and sings a desperate hymn to liberty. Confusing, bad photography adds to the anguish of the story. A fiery, daring work. M. Jean Vigo is its author: a Céline of the cinema."[17]

The next day the most prestigious cinema weekly, *Pour Vous*, pronounced it: "A rough sketch which was booed by some and vigorously applauded by others. It deserves neither this excessive honour nor this indignation, being less irreverent than it would like to seem, and containing some good ideas. It has the disadvantage of sailing very close to scatology—a source of banality rather than originality—and the advantage of being acted by children and adults who must have had fun doing so."[18]

These extracts indicate the two main critical reactions to the film in 1933. Neither those who praised it nor those who damned it acknowledged anything in *Zéro de Conduite* other than its "avant-gardism" and its harshness. Its poetry was not acknowledged, even less its style. After 1933, the poetry in *Zéro de Conduite* gradually came to be recognized, but not its style until much later.

Le Huron, predicting that *Zéro de Conduite* would take the critics' breath away, was just as mistaken as *Marianne* had been in pronouncing it a work which would be hissed and argued over. In the first place, the planned programming at the Studio, which was to have launched the film on its commercial career, never took place. Certain Catholic circles had reacted vigorously to the private showing, and the censors intervened. After the première of *Zéro de Conduite*, the Catholic weekly, *Choisir*, stressed "its realistic details, its subversive ideas, and its unpleasant effect." One gets the impression that there was some hesitation: all screenings of the film were suspended, but the censors had not yet come to any definite decision.

In its issue of July 2, *Choisir* reproduced an article on the same subject from another Catholic journal, *L'Omnium Cinématographique*: "The work of an obsessed maniac, expressing his troubled thoughts without benefit of art. Eroticism perhaps, but scatology. . . . The film lacks any delicacy of expression, any poetry in its images.

"It is doubtful that the censors will allow this film, which is completely unsuitable for children and will not amuse adults, to be shown."

The editor of *Choisir* sceptically commented on the last paragraph: "Assuming that censorship exists; a real censorship, that is. . . ." What both papers wanted was granted. Shortly afterwards, *Zéro de Conduite* was banned.

In other circles, the censors' intervention was certainly not desired but it was expected, even if the severity of the decision may have caused some surprise. As a caption for a still of the revolt in the dormitory, *Pour Vous* wrote: "A curious still from the film *Zéro de Conduite*, Jean Vigo's satirical sketch which will undoubtedly baffle its audiences if it succeeds in escaping the censor's scissors." The indifferent reception or total silence with which the April 7 screening was greeted by the film weeklies contributed to the fact that the film could be banned without provoking any real public outcry. Yet during the making of the film, these same periodicals had published the usual gossip, news items and articles designed to create a sympathetic attitude towards the film. Elsewhere, we have quoted excerpts from the long report published in *Ciné-Monde* by André Négis, Vigo's colleague from the film club in Nice. Among other things in that report Négis said: "Jean Vigo, a fine blade in a thin scabbard. The symbol of tenacious will. That day, he was so determined! He avoids the contrived as if it were a contagious disease; he looks for truth, he goes after life. When he has created a solid foundation out of both, he embellishes it with his fantasies. '*Fantasy*,' he says, '*is the only interesting thing in life. I would like to push it to the point of zaniness.*' *Zéro de Conduite* will prove that Vigo has begun to realize his dream."[19]

At about the same time, *Pour Vous* published an article by Jean-Georges Auriol: "In a few days we will know whether we were right to believe in this simple, forthright youngster who believes in his work because he does not attempt to cheat and faces his problems squarely."[20]

After the première of the film, *Ciné-Monde* did not print a word, and *Pour Vous* published the disdainful lines already referred to.

Given the violent reaction from certain segments of the Catholic press, it has, of course, often been claimed that *Zéro de Conduite* was banned "under pressure from the clergy."[21] It is not so certain that the clergy had such a decisive influence on the censors.

The president of the Board of Censors supposedly told one of Vigo's friends who had gone to intercede for the film: "We received a note communicating the order to ban *Zéro de Conduite* before my colleagues and I had even been able to see it and judge it impartially."[22] This is highly likely. During the same period that *Zéro de Conduite* was banned, Edmond Sée, president of the Board of Censors, told a journalist: "On all artistic and moral questions our opinion is predominant. . . . But for films which might create disturbances and hinder the maintenance of order, the views of the representatives from the Ministries of the Interior and Foreign Affairs have the force of law. Their veto is in effect without appeal."[23]

There is every reason to believe that, without referring to it directly, Edmond Sée is alluding to the banning of *Zéro de Conduite*. The government therefore felt that public screening of the film might create disturbances and hinder the maintenance of order. Were these fears justified?

It is unarguable that the film's social symbolism was sometimes narrowly interpreted in terms of current political events, and that some reactions, favourable and hostile, were very violent in nature. The day after the première, Damase, a friend of Vigo's, excitedly wrote to him on some pages from a notebook: "I believe I understand your film, it gets through to me. . . . In it I find my own objections against the present rotten government, elected

by a nation of morons, which at this moment is leading us swiftly and surely into decadence. Obviously the school must be turned upside down, and the flag of revolt planted in a place high enough for intelligent people to see. . . .
"I fear that this very beautiful idea will not be understood by, or will frighten, that band of cowards. . . . Last night, they weren't very happy to see the vision of upheaval projected before them; they did not find it constructive. They, old friend, will spew everything they can to obstruct your film, and that must not happen."

Later, during the Stavisky affair, Damase wrote to Vigo from Africa, and again mentioned *Zéro de Conduite*: "This is the moment to show your film; after the latest scandals it would have a much better chance of being understood."

This ardour and this belief in the virtues of *Zéro de Conduite* as an instrument for political agitation might astound a later viewer, sensitive primarily to the film's more permanent qualities, but this state of mind must be taken into account in order to understand why the film was banned. I think that it is possible, even without documentary evidence, to imagine a similar sort of reaction to that of Damase among the establishment and their informers—though directly opposed to his and therefore unfavourable to any release of the film as a threat to public order.

It has often been maintained that the censors clamped down on *Zéro de Conduite* because particular shots—showing an adolescent's penis, or replacing the national ensign by the flag of revolt—were offensive to public morality or patriotism. In that case, a few cuts would have sufficed, and the censors ordered none. They simply, in an act of exceptional severity, banned the entire film; which leads one to suppose that action was being taken against the whole conception of the film.

It would be interesting to know exactly what those responsible for the banning of *Zéro de Conduite* saw in it. At the time there was talk of its "anti-French spirit,"[24] a rather vague phrase. Today, any attempt to determine who was actually responsible for the film's suppression would require an immense amount of arduous investigation and research; and as for discovering what was actually going on in people's minds in 1933. . . .

To conclude this story of the presentation and banning of *Zéro de Conduite*, it only remains to refer to one of the themes of this book: the presence of Almereyda in everything concerning Vigo. To this day, J.-L. Nounez still believes that had the film been credited to someone else, it would not have been banned. Vigo may have been considered a dangerous Communist, and the men in power must certainly have been prejudiced against Almereyda's son.

In a sense, the controversy provoked by the banning of *Zéro de Conduite* launched the film, and through film clubs it started slowly on its career in France. Between 1933 and the war the film-club movement was far from being as important as it had been several years earlier, and even further from the extraordinary proliferation it was to achieve after the war.

However, from 1933 on, *Zéro de Conduite* could be shown quite normally in Brussels, since the French authorities did not then have the power to prevent a film from being exported. The Belgians, who had already attended screenings of *A Propos de Nice* and even of *Taris* with keen interest, were eager to see *Zéro de Conduite*. On April 19, 1933, René Jauniaux of the socialist film centre wrote to Vigo asking for the film, but it was through the Club de l'Ecran that *Zéro de Conduite* arrived in Brussels in October. This club had originally emanated from the ADAC (Amis de l'Art Ciné-matographique), a cooperative whose aim was to distribute Soviet films; but because of the commercial policies of the parent organization, the Club de l'Ecran, headed by André Thirifays, had broken away. Thirifays, however, still continued to give special emphasis to anything Soviet or non-conformist. For the most part the members of the club were recruited from leftist groups, and while remaining an apolitical organization, the Club de l'Ecran had the reputation of being extreme leftist.

So the Club de l'Ecran took the initiative in bringing *Zéro de Conduite* to Brussels, and the ADAC cinema, the Studio du Carrefour, decided to programme it with James Flood and Elliott Nugent's *Life Begins*, starring Loretta Young. Two previews, reserved for club members, took place on October 17 at six and nine o'clock.

Invited by André Thirifays, Vigo came to introduce his film. He had pre-pared five typewritten pages of text, the *Présentation de Zéro de Conduite*[25] already referred to on several occasions. In his speech, Vigo did not hide the fact that he had reservations about his film, though he exaggerated a little so as not to be taken too literally.

While asserting that he was not looking for excuses, Vigo continually insinuated that there were indeed excuses, for he could not tell the audience openly why they would probably find the film badly structured: he would have had to describe in detail his problems with his producers, and par-ticularly with the people from the Gaumont studios, on whom he still had to rely if he was to pursue his career. He therefore sought to excuse himself by creating a certain confusion between the action of the censors and the fact that he had had to cut a thousand feet from the film in the process of editing it. In private conversation with journalists, he probably stressed this interpretation.

In his talk, he stated clearly that his film had been banned in its entirety, but at the same time he made frequent allusions to the most common form of censorship, speaking of people "whose use of the scissors usually ends up making them the real author of a film." He was even crafty enough to state that it would be a lame excuse for him to cry, "The censors mutilated my film! Look: what a disgrace!" He never explains that such a statement would be a lame excuse because the censor had not in fact mutilated *Zéro de Conduite*, and that the film was presented in Brussels complete, exactly as it was when banned in France. No, Vigo is talking of lame excuses in general terms: he refers to censorship by putting it on the same level as the commercialism of distributors, and the stupidity of the general public and producers, handi-caps of which every director is aware when he begins, and which he therefore has no right to use as an excuse afterwards.

After this exordium designed to confuse his listeners, he could enjoy the luxury of declaring himself responsible: "And afterwards what? Will you collect your wages? Will you start another film? Yes? Will you botch it up the way you did the one before? Yes. Then shut up and consider yourself responsible . . . The culprit is here before you, and his accomplices are jointly liable. No one and nothing interfered with our work." Vigo was all the more at ease in making this last statement because he knew no one would believe him.

Reading contemporary press accounts, one sees that Vigo achieved his aims: he won the critics' goodwill.

"*Zéro de Conduite* is a film which was not only banned but annihilated, so to speak, by the French censors. What remains of Jean Vigo's work has become so incoherent that it is difficult even to be sure what he originally intended. . . .

"It could hardly have been otherwise. According to a declaration made to us by the young French film-maker Jean Vigo, the censors cut out one thousand feet in all from the edited film.

"He made the film for a big French film company, and this ultimately forced him to submit completely to the demands of that country's censors. These demands were such that Jean Vigo was forced by his backers to make concession after concession, and so, with one deletion following upon another, the film had one thousand feet amputated from it."[26]

"Of course, the film's merit has been greatly diminished by overindulgence of the French censor's scissors. The development at times seems confusing, apparently because of the censor's intervention. It is therefore impossible to judge the film as a whole."[27]

"Certainly the film suffers from the haste with which it was made . . . from the cuts made by the French censors for reasons as difficult to understand as their insistence on banning the film as it now stands, amputated of one thousand feet out of its total of five thousand."[28]

"It is therefore only fair not to hold Jean Vigo responsible for certain abrupt, even elliptical transitions, which result from cuts made to appease the French censors."[29]

In an interview, Vigo offered another lame excuse. After speaking about the making of *Taris* and of the twenty-four hours he had been given to prepare a script, Vigo added: "As for *Zéro de Conduite*, things were much less simple. I had the theme in my head, and that's all. For reasons beyond my control, as they say, we had to start anyway. While the shooting progressed, I was simultaneously preparing the scenes to be filmed. It is a method I don't recommend to anyone."[30] It is true that Vigo prepared his scenes in detail as the shooting progressed; but as we have seen, he had more than just the theme in his head when shooting began.

These two excuses—censorship and improvisation—have since become legends constantly encountered in articles on Vigo.

The style of the *Présentation de Zéro de Conduite* is reminiscent of the style of the *Présentation d'A Propos de Nice*; it has the same polemical tone, and the same taste for humorous, sometimes apt, images. On censorship: "It would be to despair indeed of the intelligence of the top civil servants, policemen, clerks, and needy, washed-up writers who constitute the Areopagus of a decaying and jesuitical institution, to imagine for an instant that these peaceable but watchful civilians are incapable of seeing beyond the tips of their bayonets. . . ." But most of the time Vigo's attempts at humour as a writer continue to be cold and even heavy-handed.

Politically, Vigo emerges as a "sympathizer" with Communism and the Soviet Union, but as no militant, and someone often exasperated by politics. He denies that he intended to satirize any specific regime or government, and he is undoubtedly sincere. When he speaks of his "unspecified images", however, he goes too far. If the Prefect is not refutation enough, there is the flag lying on the ground which is not just any flag, and we do not need colour to recognize it as the French flag. "What good does it do to caricature this government or that? With a single exception they are all the same.

"I did not intend, like some guide from Cook's Tours leading tourists into the tubercular alleys of poor and picturesque quarters, to take you through a world which must be remade.

"For me, the problem is unfortunately more serious. I was after something greater and purer. Childhood."

Suddenly Vigo's style changes; he becomes personal and full of warmth, and one realizes beyond question that Vigo has become more convincing in love than in hatred:

"Kids on their way back to school, abandoned on an October evening in a schoolyard, somewhere in the provinces, far away from home, yearning for a mother's affection, a father's camaraderie, if the father is not already dead.

"And then I feel myself being overcome by anguish. You are going to see *Zéro de Conduite*, and I am going to see it again with you. I watched it grow up. How puny it seems to me! Not even convalescent. It is like my own child, but no longer my own childhood. I stare at it in vain. My memories are lost within it. Is it really so long ago already? How did I, a grown man, alone, without schoolmates or playmates, dare venture down the paths of *Le Grand Meaulnes*? Inside that train compartment, of course, leaving the school holidays behind in its wake, I recognize two friends on their way back to school. It is there, of course, the dormitory in which I spent eight years as a boarder, with its thirty identical beds. I also recognize Huguet, the junior master we loved so much, his colleague Dry-Fart, and the sullen head supervisor with the crêpe-soled shoes of a ghost. Will the little sleepwalker still haunt my dreams tonight under the glare of the gas night-light? Perhaps I will see him again at the foot of my bed just as he stood there the night before that day in 1919 when Spanish influenza carried him away. Little sleepwalker whose casket was lowered into the recreation yard for the blessing of the priest, who shook his holy water at the devil we were all so afraid of.

"Yes, I know: my friends Caussat, Bruel, Colin the cook's son, and Tabard, whom we called a girl and the administration spied on and tortured, whereas what he really needed was a big brother, since his mother did not love him.

"Answering the roll too, the little girl of those rare Sunday outings. Do you remember how I loved to watch you climb up on the piano and hang the goldfish bowl from a wire which we had strung up, the two of us, our hands touching?

"You used to cover my eyes with your handkerchief, smelling so nicely of your mother's lavender, because I looked at your plump, babyish thighs. And then gently, as one does with the sick, you would remove the festive bandage, and in silence we would both watch the goldfish bowl."

The audience gathered in the Studio du Carrefour barely followed what Vigo said. The auditorium had no stage, so he had been placed on a precarious platform made out of tables so that people in the balcony could see him. The acoustics were bad, the audience was getting restless, and Vigo, stammering and skipping whole paragraphs, finished in less than ten minutes. Throughout his talk, the younger members of the audience continually interrupted him. At first, Vigo was to have addressed both screenings, but after the first one, he decided to leave it at that.

After the two screenings reserved for members of the Club de l'Ecran, *Zéro de Conduite* had a commercial run at the Studio du Carrefour lasting a month, after which the film was shown by film clubs in the principal Belgian cities.

The attitudes revealed by the extracts quoted from the French critics reappear in the Belgian reviews. First and foremost, they react to the harshness of the film: "The audacity, the frankness, even the violence, suggest a powerful temperament. Pamphlets are rare in the cinema . . . *Zéro de Conduite* has the great merit that it is never timid, it never holds back. It is a film which offers us, with no concessions of any kind, the thought, the naked vision of its author. It is a series of episodes juxtaposed with a certain unity of place and purpose, but almost never of action. From one episode to the next the author's rancour, his disgust, increases in a rhythm of bitter progression until it explodes in a despairing cry for freedom. . . . The schoolboys' wretched existence is set into cruel, incisive relief, harsh and violent."[31]

Paul Werris writes: "It is a succession of moments, and even more a swelling, corrosive atmosphere, inhabiting and eating away the school courtyard which it would take only a tiny detail to turn into a prison yard.

"As a matter of fact there is something perpetually, irremediably perverted about the film."[32]

From an anonymous article, probably written by Ludo Patris: "Excessive, violent, at times crude, the plot has furnished material for a succession of images which run through an astonishing gamut of styles from burlesque satire to sordid realism."[33]

Michel A. Mirowitsch, one of the best Belgian critics of the time, wrote in *Documents 33*: "The murderous boredom of a small provincial town, a gloomy and smelly school, pathetic teachers being ragged and reviled, noisy,

Zéro de Conduite: Huguet encourages the revolutionaries

dirty classrooms, greasy refectories, Sundays where desolation and dreariness become palpable, all interwoven with hopeless frustrations and children plotting in the shadows of the schoolyard. . . . A theme full of rancour and pain."[34]

Let us quote two excerpts from the Flemish-speaking press. A centre-leftist newspaper in Brussels: "A truly violent satire, which errs from time to time through the excessiveness of its accusations. The children's psychology is disturbing precisely because of its sometimes bitter frankness."[35] An organ of the Socialist Party: "We are in the presence of a work built on a basis of tenacious hatred and rancour."[36]

If one lists the key words from the articles on *Zéro de Conduite* published in 1933, the results are as follows: hatred, violent, destructive, rancorous, bitter, wretched, coarse, noxious, harsh, despair, anguish, confused, bad, passionate, daring, vicious, subversive, unpleasant, obsessed, troubled, erotic, scatological, excessive, satirical, sordid, exaggerated, insulting, pitiful, relentless, sad, uncouth, provocative, exasperating, cruel, perverse.

This climate of opinion helps to explain a curious phenomenon which was by no means short-lived: the comparisons made between Jean Vigo and Louis-Ferdinand Céline. At first glance one is inclined to deride the critics, seeing in this one of the fraternity's less worthy traits.

It was Pierre Ogouz, writing about *Zéro de Conduite* in *Marianne*, who first referred to Céline. Without attempting to draw any evidence from the works themselves, Ogouz wrote: "A fiery, daring work. M. Jean Vigo is its author; a Céline of the cinema." It seems likely that this comparison was a vague impression occasioned by circumstance: *Voyage au bout de la Nuit* had been published very recently, and the polemic aroused by the failure of Céline's novel to win the Prix Goncourt had not yet abated.

The author of the article in *Carrefour* quotes Ogouz, and "to justify the comparison" attempts a definition which is still very vague: "If the connection must be justified in some way, it lies in their common sensitivity to the atmosphere of a place, and to the moral feeling evoked by a setting, a way of life, a particular regime, or the characters." One's first impulse, despite the years that have elapsed, is to ask: "Which places? Which characters?"

Our socialist reviewer had probably already read the articles in *Marianne* and *Carrefour*, for he is prepared to accept the connection between Vigo and Céline, although he can find little reason for it. He therefore assumes that the scenes he believes were suppressed provided a basis for the comparison. "It isn't difficult to imagine the profoundly sad and harsh environment of the school in some of the cut sequences—a school located, one might say, in the same sad, grey suburb of Paris where the best and most vivid parts of Céline's celebrated novel, *Voyage au bout de la Nuit*, take place."

We would be wrong to shrug and leave it at that, for these allusions to Céline perfectly sum up the basic reaction to *Zéro de Conduite* in 1933. At that time the film affected people almost exclusively because of its "blackness," and if that word doesn't appear in our list, it is simply because it did not become fashionable until much later. We can now see what must have been obvious to everyone at the time: that the references to Céline were a way for the reviewers to summarize their feelings (see the list of words) about the atmosphere of *Zéro de Conduite*.

Not one of the critics we have referred to was sensitive to the element in *Zéro de Conduite* which, more than twenty years later, has become its main attraction: its poetry. Most of them do not even mention it. The three or four who do, deny that the poetry exists, disapprove of it, or denigrate its importance. There is no need to take the denial of the film's poetry in the Catholic weekly *Choisir* too seriously. It would be pointless to expect anything very profound from this article. The film page in this particular issue is mainly devoted to proving that the biggest box-office receipts in 1932 were provided by "wholesome films not offensive to morality," and to denying the story that the Pope's niece was going to launch herself on a career as a film actress.

When the critics refer to the poetic dimension of *Zéro de Conduite* it is, as in *Vooruit*, to see "a sort of poetic absurdity" in the film which strikes the critic as "a laborious and fruitless effort."

Carrefour almost touches on the film's poetic values in referring to "a certain veil of absurdity," or to "the halo of dreamlike delirium." However, the allusion here is mainly to effects considered "surrealistic." The fact remains that of the four sequences referred to in the *Carrefour* article—the principal's entrance, the schoolboys' outing, the nocturnal revolt, and the final rebellion—two are filled with purely poetic qualities. For 1933, coming so close is remarkable.

If the poetic dimension of *Zéro de Conduite* was barely evident to its critics in 1933, they were more sensitive to its social aspect, although they failed to point out the allusions to society in general through the school, and although the words anarchy or anarchism do not appear in our list. Nevertheless, coming from a social democrat, the sentence in *Vooruit* referring to a "certain moral climate owing more to a feeling of revolt than to any really profound social sense," could very well qualify as a rebuke against an anarchist attitude.

As a matter of fact, the cautiousness of the reviewer for *Vooruit* is sometimes rather strange. He says that "the glimpses of life in a French school presented by Vigo are of course rather sensational in nature." However, he then adds that "Vigo clearly did not mean to imply any attack on the official instructional and educational methods used in French state schools and colleges," and then concludes that "his aim was to pillory life as a whole in a boarding school." By blowing hot and cold like this, the writer ends up by giving the odd impression that the question is whether Vigo was for or against secular schools. The trouble taken by the good Belgian Socialist to try to establish that Vigo was not against state education may seem ridiculous to us. But the really amusing thing is that he was not so very far wrong in his worries. For proof, we need only take a leap forward in time. By 1950, certain more open-minded Catholic circles no longer shared the repugnance of their fellow-believers in 1933 for *Zéro de Conduite*. Thus, Father Pichard, writing in the Parisian Catholic weekly *Radio-Cinéma*, attacks the censors for having banned the film and praises it because he sees it as an attack on secular education.[37]

Besides the social-democratic manner of reproaching *Zéro de Conduite* for its anarchism, there is also the Communist and Communist-sympathizing manner. These were the people who, as Michel Mirowitsch wrote, wanted Vigo to be "equally courageous socially." Although the Belgian critic's prejudices prevented him from grasping the social content of *Zéro de Conduite*, he does reveal considerable insight into Vigo's work when he writes: "The general atmosphere is subject to that disgust not unmingled with pleasure which is at the root of certain childhood memories."

One striking thing is that in the articles on Vigo written in 1933 allusions to Almereyda are extremely rare. In fact his name seems to occur only once. Some critics abstained out of delicacy. Others did not associate Jean Vigo with Vigo-Almereyda. The majority, including the Belgians, no longer remembered Almereyda. Later, when *Zéro de Conduite* was presented in France again in 1945, that too would change.

L'Atalante: Juliette (Dita Parlo)

4. L'Atalante

Even before *Zéro de Conduite* was finished, Nounez was considering future productions. An admirer of Georges de la Fouchardière, he had signed a contract in December 1932 with the writer giving him exclusive screen rights to adapt his works, together with exclusive rights to any original scripts he might write. For his films, Nounez preferred subjects he knew something about, like *Affaire Peau de Balle*, in which la Fouchardière wrote about the world of horse racing. It is quite possible that among the reasons which induced Nounez to start producing films—and at least as important to him as the desire to make money—was his desire to try his hand at creating. Among the medium-length films which were to follow *Zéro de Conduite*, he still intended to include his script, *L'Honnête Homme*, a story about an idealistic son's struggle against his father's bourgeois honesty, which he discovers to be hypocritical.

However, Nounez had somewhat modified his plans. He was no longer satisfied with the idea of making three medium-length films as a start, but wanted to begin a full-length feature as soon as he could. The film about prison life was his first choice. Vigo, too, was very attached to this idea of a film based on the experiences of Eugène Dieudonné, the anarchist-militant whom Almereyda had defended in *Le Courrier Européen* in 1913. Having been involved in the Bonnot case (known as the case of the "tragic bandits"), Dieudonné, despite his very probable innocence of the crime of which he had been accused, had been condemned to death because of his refusal to inform on his friends. Moro-Giafferi, his lawyer, had persuaded Poincaré to spare his life in April 1913, and the death sentence was commuted to life imprisonment. About ten years later a reporter, Albert Londres, undertook a major campaign to have Dieudonné pardoned, and he was eventually released.

By the time work started on *Zéro de Conduite*, a meeting had already taken place between Nounez and Vigo on the one hand, and Dieudonné and Julot Dupont, another expert on prisons, on the other. They agreed to base the proposed film on Albert Londres' articles. Dieudonné and Dupont undertook to write a first draft for the script. Dieudonné subsequently agreed to play himself, and the project was moving along well. They thought of offering the principal female role to Gaby Morlay or to Florelle. Vigo wanted to shoot the film in Guiana, but to Nounez that was little more than a fantasy.

Other projects also started to take shape before *Zéro de Conduite* was finished. Vigo was interested in one of Jean Painlevé's scripts, *Le Café du Bon Accueil*, which apparently included some "amazing gags," and in another script by Claude Aveline, *Le Timide qui prend feu*, as well as adaptations of several of Aveline's literary works. Storck proposed his script *Evariste*, and Riéra his *L'Inventeur*, written in collaboration with René Lefèvre. Vigo was also considering an original script of his own, *Le Métro*, the story of a man who worked in a room facing the elevated railway and rode on the railway all day on Sundays so that he could see his room from the outside.

Vigo had persuaded Nounez to forget *L'Affaire Peau de Balle* for the time being in favour of filming a circus story. This was to be an adaptation of one of la Fouchardière's short stories, *Clown par amour*, which Vigo wanted to film with the clown, Bèby, in the leading role. Towards the end of January 1933, Vigo was already telling his friends how he saw "Mère Caca" ["Mother Turd"], one of the characters in the story. Storck was struck by the fact that his conception of her was both burlesque and extremely harsh. Vigo subsequently wrote a complete script for the proposed film.

By the time *Zéro de Conduite* was finished, Nounez had once again changed his plans. Vigo's working schedule for 1933 was more or less as follows: in April, start work on *Evariste*; in June, *Le Métro*; in September, exteriors for the prison film, *Le Bagne*, in Guiana if possible; in October, finish *Evariste*. These plans, however, remained rather vague. Nounez began to look like a "dreamer, disorganized, without much authority."[1]

The première and banning of *Zéro de Conduite* upset all of Nounez's plans. In the business circles he frequented, his friends were starting to reproach him for financing "subversive" activities. Official severity would henceforth be directed against the "dangers" of the film activities of Almereyda's son. There could no longer be any question of making *Le Bagne*.[2] An additional reason may have led Nounez to reconsider the la Fouchardière projects: the writer would probably not have wanted to see his works filmed by the director of *Zéro de Conduite*, a film he hadn't liked.

Besides, the ban had not been good for business, and it was not easy to persuade Gaumont to have anything more to do with Vigo. If Gaumont did not succeed in cutting Vigo right out of Nounez's plans, it was probably thanks entirely to Nounez. He had written to Vigo on April 16: "I think you know something about human nature, for you have suffered a good deal. Don't lose faith in yourself, your film is very good." Nounez had in fact liked *Zéro de Conduite*, although not all of it. He had never, for instance, approved of the idea of having the school principal played by a bearded dwarf. Despite that and other things he was determined to give Vigo another chance.

However, with Gaumont's approval, he intended to take some precautions, and rather serious ones at that, since, to recuperate the capital swallowed up by *Zéro de Conduite*, he was going to have to invest a much larger sum in a feature with well-known stars, songs, etc. These precautions consisted essentially in not allowing Vigo to write an original script again, or even allowing him to select one freely. Nounez felt that what Vigo's imagination—a not very reasonable one according to him—needed was the discipline of an already existing script, and he personally started searching for one.

He had momentarily considered a script by Louis Chavance, inspired by an international congress of hobos which had recently taken place. Chavance was an expert editor who also wrote film scripts, none of which had yet been filmed. However, this idea could only encourage Vigo's non-conformism, and that was probably why the script was dropped. Nounez was finally told about an original script, *L'Atalante*, which had been deposited at the Association des Auteurs de Films by R. de Guichen, a little-known writer whose pen name was Jean Guinée. It was sent to Vigo at the end of July.

The subject of *L'Atalante* was conventional and undistinguished. Jean, the young captain of the Atalante, a motorized barge, marries Juliette, a country girl, and brings her aboard. They live on the barge with the mate— an old sailor called Père Jules—a cabin boy, and a dog. While teaching Juliette to love this simple, monotonous life aboard the barge, Jean also teaches her to hate the shore, symbol of degenerate pleasures. However, while the barge is in port, a young sailor in love with Juliette offers to take her away to the city, tempting her with the pleasures that await her there. Jean chases the tempter away, but Juliette remains haunted by the attractions of the city, and one evening with the cabin boy's help she boards the little local train and leaves. The captain, told what has happened by the remorseful boy, who admits helping her escape, refuses the old sailor's advice to go after his wife. The Atalante leaves for other ports. After spending all her money on innocent pleasures, and tired of being continually propositioned by men, Juliette becomes a waitress in a restaurant owned by a brutal man, where she leads a lonely life. She does not dare go back to the Atalante, and in any case has no idea where it is. One day the barge docks in the area. Père Jules, despite the captain's orders to the contrary, goes off to look for Juliette, vainly searching the streets and cafés of the city. On his return, Père Jules enters a small chapel during evensong. His eyes are drawn to two hands joined in prayer and telling a rosary. The gesture seems familiar; he

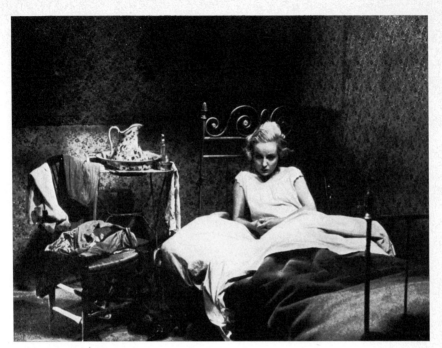

L'Atalante: Juliette in Paris

approaches and discovers Juliette. Jean accepts her return, and life seems to continue as if nothing had happened. But happiness has left the barge.

Vigo must have felt a little discouraged when faced with this story, but since he had no choice, he contented himself with making a few suggestions for the benefit of whoever (probably Jean Guinée himself) was going to develop the scenario into a first draft for the shooting script. And in fact, at least one important change was made. Juliette would not be tempted to go to the city by a young sailor, but by a street pedlar.

Vigo still disliked the project, however. Everything in it centred around the contrast between Jean and Père Jules, the sailors and the shore, the city and the fascination it had for Juliette. As soon as she was on board, she began to envy the air of happiness of the people on shore, swimming, picnicking, enjoying themselves at fairs. And then a street pedlar she meets at a cabaret to which Jean has finally consented to take her tells her about the wonders of the city. The contrast between the sailors' lives and the city was here depicted with incredible heavy-handedness. After a long sales talk, the pedlar made a tour of the room, singing. Finally the spectators took up the chorus of his song. The last two lines, however, were interrupted by noise from a table where four old sailors were playing cards and muttering, *He can keep his city. . . . We're better off with none of that.* One of them then rose and sang the *Chanson des Mariniers*.

The introduction of the pedlar into this rather thin story added some variety, but the character remained crude and clumsy. After trying to seduce Juliette by telling her about dance-halls, cars and fast living, he yells at Jean when the latter sends him packing: *I suppose you think it's fun for her, at her age and as pretty as a picture, living from New Year's Day to New Year's Eve on your stick of wood with you, an old man and a kid. . . . Idiot!*

The other characters were difficult to shape. Jean hates the city. All right: one of the reasons for his hatred is that you have to spend money there, whereas *you must put away for your old age.* At the turning point, when the girl leaves the barge to explore the city, Jean cries out: *When she finds out about the city, she'll come back on her own, Juliette will. . . . And she'll see that it was on the Atalante that she was happy.*

The author never stopped putting his intentions into the mouths of the characters. Here he goes even further and reveals how the future action will develop by predicting things which will actually occur. Jean, of course, turns out to be right when Juliette returns thanks to the efforts of Père Jules. She feels repentant, as predicted. And in the final analysis, when Jean accepts her return, he does so only because desire impels him: *Roughly he pulls her to him and in a harsh voice says, "Undress!" His hands start taking her clothes off.*

Juliette's character is not delineated with any more subtlety. After her first days on board she becomes fascinated by the city, by the desire to enjoy herself there while she is still young. When Jean speaks to her of the need for saving for one's old age, she answers simply by sticking her bust out to show him how young she is, and then looking towards the shore from which come sounds of people having fun. In the cabaret, the pedlar almost succeeds in kissing her; when he comes to see her on the barge, he reminds her that some day her hair will be white, and she will have lost her chance. Overcome at the thought she murmurs: *It's true . . . it's true.* When she asks the cabin boy to get her a train schedule, she pays him to keep his mouth shut. Juliette is full of confidence when she arrives in the city, but she soon spends all her money on a ring, a hat, shoes, a dress, make-up, dancing, films, theatres, the fair, and she has to look for work. A job as a maid of all work is given to a stronger-looking woman who applies at the same time. She could become an extra in the theatre by sleeping with the director, but she slaps him. Finally Juliette becomes a waitress in a restaurant, where she has to scrub the floor on her knees under the owner's watchful eye. She often goes to pray in the little chapel where Père Jules finds her and brings her back on board. When again in the arms of Jean, who is overcome with desire, she has a triumphant expression on her face.

The cabin boy is a depraved youth who tries to peep in on the married couple during their wedding night, and on the meeting between Juliette and the pedlar on the barge. He helps Juliette because he likes her, and does not understand the value of the note she gives him. Then, overcome by remorse when he sees how distressed Jean is by her departure, the boy tells him everything.

Père Jules is perhaps better delineated, but he remains horribly conventional. An old fellow with lots of experience, a bit cynical, brimming with paternal affection for Jean and Juliette, he is of course an enemy to the city and its vices. He teaches the cabin boy, somewhat pompously, about life and human nature. He is, in short, a sort of homespun philosopher full of good intentions and platitudes. Faced by the happiness of Jean and Juliette, all Père Jules can find to mutter is, *What a pleasure to see youth!* He, too, is a little depraved: after discovering the boy trying to spy on the couple through the keyhole and sending him away, he takes his place. When he is wandering the city in search of Juliette, however, he is outraged because people think he is looking for a whore.

Père Jules gives the lad, who does not understand Jean's behaviour, a lesson on pride: *I'll explain it to you. . . . Pride. . . . Wait, let me tell you about it . . . there's a terrific current even though there doesn't seem to be. . . . Pride. . . . How can I explain it. . . . Yes. . . . Sometimes, when you want to do something, you don't do it so the other person won't think you wanted to do it. . . . Then the other person does what you wanted to do but didn't do. And you feel all good inside. 'Cause if you'd done it, well, the other person'd be feeling good. . . . You got it now?*

At the end, after Juliette's return, the cabin boy asks whether they will be happy now. *Perhaps*, Père Jules answers, looking into the distance at the river. When the lad looks puzzled, he continues: *You know, my lad . . . now there's a bit of the shore on board.* And he laughs, looking at his young friend, who does not understand.

That was the story and the characters Vigo was supposed to film. Once he had overcome his initial depression about certain details in the story, Vigo discovered that the author was not disposed to offer any resistance to the changes which always occur during the making of a film. Nounez and his associates had probably cast an eye over the story in its developed form, and there was a chance that their supervision would not be carried so far as to stifle all personal expression when the time came to write the shooting script and then to filming it. Besides, Vigo knew he could rely to a considerable extent on Nounez's sympathetic attitude. He therefore accepted the general outline of the action and the proposed characters, while secretly thinking of them as just a starting point.

The production plan was the same as for *Zéro de Conduite*. Nounez was the producer who took care of the finance, Gaumont furnished the studio facilities, the film stock, and took care of distribution. This time, however, the budget amounted to almost a million francs. For an independent production this was quite a considerable sum. Well-known actors, Michel Simon and Dita Parlo, had accepted the principal parts.

Dita Parlo was a product of the last days of the German silent cinema. She had achieved a notable success in 1928 in Joe May's film *Heimkehr*, starring with Lars Hanson and Gustav Fröhlich. In France she had only been moderately successful, acting in films such as Duvivier's *Au Bonheur des Dames, Rapsodie Hongroise*, and with Mosjoukin in *Manolesco*.

Michel Simon had been acting in films for ten years now. He had to his credit his role in Renoir's *La Chienne*, and his creation on stage and screen of the character Cloclo in *Jean de la Lune*, which had brought him popularity with audiences who continued to enjoy his performances in *Lac aux Dames* and *Miquette et sa Mère*. Although his reputation as an actor was far from what it was to become several years later, Simon was nevertheless already a star in 1933. One of his friends even seems to have been astonished to find him accepting a part in a film to be made by a young man who was practically a beginner. He is said to have replied that he had accepted precisely because it was being directed by Jean Vigo: Simon was sympathetic to this young non-conformist against whom the censors had already vented their spleen.[3] The fact that he had agreed to work under Vigo's direction probably had the immediate effect of overcoming the last resistance offered by Bedoin, Beauvais, and Anglade, that imposing trio of bureaucrats from Gaumont.

The decision to use Michel Simon and Dita Parlo received Vigo's sincere and wholehearted acceptance. Of course, even if it hadn't he would not have been able to do a thing about it. Vigo was, however, free to choose the other actors, and, faithful to his team, he had already hired Jean Dasté and Lefèvre, thus completing the casting for the main roles.

Vigo also kept nearly all the artistic and technical personnel with whom he had worked on *Zéro de Conduite*: Kaufman, Riéra, Berger, Merle, Jaubert, and Goldblatt. Storck had left for Belgium. But because there would be considerably more work involved than there had been on *Zéro de Conduite*, the crew had to be increased: there was no longer any question of having some of his collaborators do several jobs at once. A second assistant cameraman was added, Jean-Paul Alphen; and a continuity boy, Fred Matter. Most important of all, Vigo asked Francis Jourdain and Louis Chavance to help. Jourdain, Almereyda's old friend, would design the sets and interiors. Chavance was to supervise the technical side of editing which had given Vigo so much trouble on *Zéro de Conduite*. Chavance was a good film editor who had worked for Paramount and was therefore familiar with the special problems posed by sound film.

Chavance had been present at the première of *Zéro de Conduite*, he had supported the film, and Vigo had probably seen his name on articles in various French and Belgian magazines, notably the issue of *Sésame* in which Vigo's "Sensitivity of Film Stock" had appeared. In any case, Chavance's lively reputation as an editor had attracted Vigo's attention, and late in the spring of 1933 he wrote and invited him to work on the production. From their very first meeting, Vigo had detected Chavance's anarchist sympathies, and naturally was pleased. He asked his new collaborator to try to be present as much as possible during the actual shooting, which was due to start soon. Since much of the film had to be shot in exteriors, they had to take advantage of the good weather.

With Riéra's help, Vigo had written a detailed shooting script, and Nounez, wanting a polished job, asked Blaise Cendrars to revise Vigo's dialogue. The writer found fault with nothing, so everything was in order in that respect.

Vigo had also taken advantage of the first weeks of summer to take long trips on barges to look for suitable locations and, together with Jean Dasté, to learn how to operate the helm and use the long bargepoles. A few days after first reading the scenario, Vigo—through an intermediary, Eugène Merle—had asked Georges Simenon for information about canals, locks, and the sailors' villages, and Simenon had sent him some facts. He had already chosen the barge for the film, the Louise XVI, owned by the Union des Mines et Industries Annexes; although equipped with a diesel engine, it nevertheless dated from the days when barges were horse-drawn from the tow-paths.

Everything seemed ready for shooting to begin. But although Nounez took a close personal interest in some details of the production, he once again revealed himself to be a poor organizer, and the whole summer slipped by without the production getting under way. September was still a good month for exterior shooting, but when Vigo left to present *Zéro de Conduite* in Brussels at the end of October, nothing had happened yet. It was not until the second week in November that shooting began.

Although there is little detailed information about the shooting of *L'Atalante*, we do know that they began at the beginning. This involved filming the wedding and the newly married couple's departure on the barge. The whole crew was taken to the village of Maurecourt in the Oise, together with Dita Parlo, Michel Simon, Dasté, Lefèvre, and the extras. Of the extras, Fanny Clar and Raphaël Diligent played the bride's parents; René Bleck, the novelist, played the best man; and the rather merry guest who limps was played by the cartoonist, Gen Paul. The other extras were also friends.

It seemed that Vigo was following the original scenario fairly closely. The cast was as follows: Dita Parlo as Juliette; Dasté, Jean; Michel Simon, Père Jules; Lefèvre, the cabin boy. One change seemed unimportant: Vigo replaced the dog—also living on the barge, according to the scenario—by about ten alley cats of the sort Almereyda liked, supplied by a lady from the Society for the Prevention of Cruelty to Animals and transported to the location in a large cage.

While the dog had no particular role to play in Guinée's story, Vigo's cats, on the contrary, invade the entire film, making a powerful contribution to its atmosphere. They become an inseparable part of Père Jules' personality. They hinder the young couple's first embraces, but immediately afterwards cause Juliette's tenderness and desire to surface because they scratch Jean's face so badly that it bleeds. The next morning a cat gives birth to kittens on the marriage bed. The cats are always all over the barge, and they become fascinated witnesses to the miracle of the phonograph. Other cats were to be waiting for Père Jules when the barge came into port, and he was to have stolen yet more cats from citizens—justices of the peace, for instance—who, he maintained, had no right to own cats. Only parts of these sequences with cats on the canal bank were shot, and they were probably never edited.

L'Atalante: the opening sequence

But all this is far into the future. Vigo was shooting the wedding. The dialogue spoken by members of the wedding party remained as written by Guinée; so did the exchange between the cabin boy—*All right! All right!*—and Père Jules as he hurries to make preparations to receive the couple and makes the boy rehearse the words he is to say when he presents the bride with a bouquet of flowers: *Happy days aboard the Atalante.* Vigo, however, carefully made the grotesque and talkative wedding party follow some way behind the dreamy, silent young couple as they make their way towards the barge across fields, round haystacks, and down wooded paths, constantly illuminated by a light which seems to come from within themselves.

The wedding party's arrival on the bank and the departure of the barge are described in the original scenario as follows:

The camera is at the head of the procession as it advances towards the barge. (Sound of voices, an accordion, shouts from members of the procession.) On the barge Père Jules and the boy get up. The boy disappears down the stairs and then reappears with a huge bouquet. He runs down the gangplank just as the procession arrives at the foot of it.

Approaching Juliette, he puts the bouquet into her arms and says, "Happy days aboard the Atalante!" Moved, she leans towards the boy, and kisses him as the procession shouts, "Long live the bride, long live the bride!"

In the meantime, Père Jules approaches Jean, the captain: "Do we leave right away, skipper?" With a slightly distracted look, Jean repeats, "Do we leave?" And then coming back to reality, "Well, you know that company orders are orders, Père Jules." The mate: "Well, then, I'll start up the motor." He goes back up the gangplank.

Shot of the stern in calm water. Sound of people's voices. Suddenly the water becomes turbulent, causing the barge's skiff to rock. Rhythm of the motor.

The couple slowly make their way up the gangplank. Handshakes all round.

The hawsers are dropped and fall into the water; the water splashes on to a few of the women who react with little cries.

The gangplank is hauled aboard.

Shot of the lovers (the camera tipping upwards from the canal bank) on the barge.

Shot of the wedding party (the camera tilting downward from the barge) on the bank.

The Atalante leaves the bank. Père Jules is at the helm.

Hands wave goodbye. Handkerchiefs wave. The embracing couple see the canal bank become smaller and smaller in the distance and then vanish altogether round a curve.

In shooting this sequence, Vigo seemed to be following the script, but in fact he almost systematically undercut the original implications. The reception of the married couple, so meticulously planned by Père Jules, is threatened by an accident which annoys him: the flowers fall into the river. The boy decides to go and look for others in the field, and soon returns with a large bunch of wild flowers, just in time to be able to grab the bouquet which the current has brought close to the bank. From the barge, Père Jules gives instructions, and calls out, *Paper around it, paper around it*, when the boy plants the dripping bouquet in the arms of the bewildered bride and rushes through the welcoming speech. The wedding party has stopped a few yards away, silently standing there.

The differences between Vigo's shooting script and his interpretation of it on the one hand, and the original scenario on the other, are already vast at this stage, and they will continue to grow until Guinée's scenario is virtually lost from sight.

Guinée wrote: *The couple slowly make their way up the gangplank*. Vigo decided that things should not happen that way—there was no gangplank anyway. The bride is hoisted aboard on the cargo mast swung by Père Jules. The mother detaches herself from the silent wedding party and cries out, *Juliette! Juliette!* But she finds herself in the arms of Père Jules, who says, *There's your daughter over there!*, kisses her and gives her the bridal bouquet, snatching it back again just before swinging on board himself.

The barge casts off, the bride alone at the prow, Jean at the helm, shouting goodbyes, waving his arms and throwing his cap into the air. From the receding bank there is no sound, no gesture: the wedding party stands silent, motionless, grim, hostile, and grotesque.

L'Atalante: Jean and Juliette

This ends the introduction. Vigo had planned to include three additional shots. (1) Menacing clouds. (2) Wind and members of the wedding party looking anxiously at the sky as they start to make their way home. (3) Wind and a flock of sheep starting to move. He eliminated these three shots, realizing that any further shots or movement would weaken the impact of the image of the wedding party abandoned on the bank, absurd in their rigidity.

Night falls and life starts aboard the Atalante. Jean joins the bride, standing immobile in white at the front of the barge, caressed by the wind. She yields to his caresses after struggling a little; but a cat brushes past them, and Juliette pulls away and runs off. Jean tries to pursue her, stumbles, and is badly scratched on the face by the cats. He clambers up to look for Juliette, now hiding behind the helm, and lifts her roughly in his arms as Père Jules looks on. But as he carries her to the cabin, she has already softened, and she lovingly caresses her husband's bleeding face.

Thus, from the very beginning, Vigo's Juliette is given a certain ambiguity. Actually, the ambiguity was suggested in Guinée's scenario, where she was snatched from a chapel after her gesture telling her rosary reminds Père Jules of the way she used to knit, and thrown into her husband's arms with a triumphantly seductive look on her face. But because the situations are not properly worked out, the ambiguity of the character in Guinée's script has more the feeling of contradictions cancelling each other out. Vigo was able to create a coherent character, at once a shy country girl, an efficient house-wife, a child making a poetic discovery of the world, a woman troubled by the sensuality of her discoveries, equally attracted by marital fidelity and the fierce pull of eroticism, and yet not unresponsive to the morbid excitements aroused by the sight of blood. When Père Jules demonstrates the efficiency of a *navaja* by cutting the back of his hand till it bleeds, Juliette's expression of horror is preceded by mute fascination and just the suggestion of a vampirish tongue. Jean provides love and the warm presence of another body in bed when he is not forced to remain on deck late to steer the barge. But he cannot satisfy the little curiosities in Juliette's mind. On the contrary, it is she who opens a small window on to the world of marvels for him by teaching him that if you put your head under water with your eyes open, you see the one you love.

Père Jules, mate of the Atalante, proves to have a much richer personality than Jean. An old sailor, he has led a life of adventure in the four corners of the world; his past is not without its secrets, of which he is nevertheless not ashamed, preferring to remember rather than forget them. Père Jules answers the barge company manager who alludes to certain unfortunate events in the past by saying: *If I didn't know, who would? I could even tell you a good one about. . . .*

Although Père Jules is talkative, he is also discreet. When speaking of his past, he always limits himself to allusions which suggest infinitely more than they actually say. After seeing only a quarter of the film, we already know that he has a mania for cats and has filled the barge with them, that he can give a demonstration—with commentary—of Greco-Roman wrestling, that he is fond of complaining, and so on. Then he gives us a first kaleidoscopic glimpse into his past.

Juliette is sitting working at her sewing-machine and Père Jules approaches:

PÈRE JULES: *What are you doing?*
JULIETTE: *I'm using the sewing-machine. Haven't you ever seen a sewing-machine?*

Père Jules' answer is, while muttering *Never seen a sewing-machine!*, to sit down beside Juliette and skilfully finish the seam she has started. Faced with her admiring, *Well, you're a man of many trades!*, Père Jules continues complacently: *Many trades! Oh, these hands! What haven't these hands done? Once even, in a Shanghai back street one evening . . . like this . . . tighter, tighter!* He suits the action to the words by grabbing her by the throat. She pushes him away and wants him to model the dress she has just made so she can hem it. Père Jules is delighted by the idea: *To model it! Oh, it suits me! To model it!* After pretending to be ticklish, Père Jules, using the dress as a prop, embarks on a series of extraordinary exhibitions until the end of the scene. He starts with an Oriental dance, chanting *Travadja la mouquere! Travadja bono!*, or slapping the palm of his hand over his mouth and

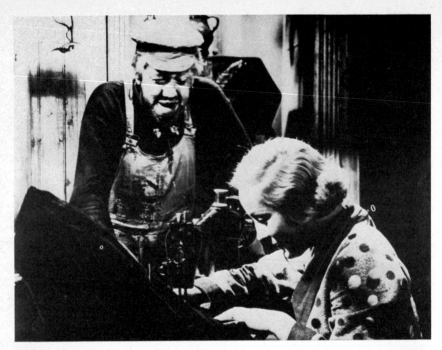

L'Atalante: Père Jules and Juliette

shouting *Hou! Hou! Hou! Hou!* Juliette pricks him with a pin and he takes off into an African dance step. *Oula! Oula! Oulamaoula! Oula!*

JULIETTE: *So you think you're still among the blacks?*
PÈRE JULES: *Blacks? That's not all I've seen.*

And while defending himself against the pin, Père Jules excitedly names a whole string of ports which come gushing from his lips: *Shanghai! Singapore! Yokohama! Melbourne! San Francisco!* Then a pause for reminiscence: *1905, Dorothy! San Sebastián!*

San Sebastián is, of course, in Spain, and Père Jules starts chanting *Olé! Olé!*, using Juliette's dress as a toreador's cape and doing a little Spanish dance. He has begun to get on Juliette's nerves, but backing away out of range from her pin, he slides down into position for a Cossack dance:

> *Vo sadou li da vo gorodie*
> *Vyrasla Petrouchka*
> *Maltchik dievotchkou Tsoloviet*
> *Domaiet igrovchka.*

Juliette angrily snatches the dress away from Père Jules, who stops singing.

JULIETTE: *Get out, then! There's your laundry!*
PÈRE JULES: *Oh! let me catch my breath. I haven't done anything to you. I'm tired!*
JULIETTE: *Are you going or aren't you?*
PÈRE JULES: *Oh, no! No! Absolutely not!*

At this point the cabin boy enters to tell them that they are arriving in Paris, and that the captain needs the mate on deck to help dock the barge. Jules leaves, cursing: *The captain! What captain? Is that what he thinks he is?*

It seems that Vigo's direction of Michel Simon in this scene was as amazing as the scene itself. Explaining all his intentions to Simon, acting out all the movements himself, and speaking all the lines, the director made the actor run through the scene several times until it was perfect. Then the sequence was broken down into separate shots and filmed. The result was sensational. It is perhaps the high spot of their careers for both Vigo as a director and Michel Simon as an actor. Or rather, it is the most spectacular *tour de force* in their respective careers, and the sequence in *L'Atalante* where the continuity and rhythm achieve perfection. In relation to the overall structure, the scene is important because it gives final definition to the character of Père Jules and suggests a certain unease against which Juliette reacts.

Soon after, Juliette takes Père Jules' laundry to his cabin. The weird collection of objects there, and the old man's renewed antics, complete the characterization and increase Juliette's sense of unease.

To fill Père Jules' cabin with its unlikely collection of junk, Vigo made lengthy excursions to the flea market in Saint-Ouen as well as the scrap-metal market on the Boulevard Richard-Lenoir, and also asked friends to contribute. Parry, the photographer, gave him some souvenirs brought back from his recent trip to the Caribbean; Margaritis found a magnificent puppet, a dilapidated orchestra conductor, at the home of an uncle who was a puppet-maker; Merle brought the teeth from some incredible fish; and Painlevé brought a pair of hands pickled in a jar. To this Vigo added some parts from an old phonograph, some lavish oriental fans, photographs taken in Africa, music boxes, shells, etc., and even some old wrought-iron wreaths, which he and his friends had stolen from the Montparnasse cemetery. Vigo went all over Paris looking for one of Calder's mobiles, but he must have eventually realized that, although they were not well known in 1933, the presence of a mobile among an old sailor's mementos would have been out of place.

It is in these surroundings—which he continues to add to whenever a new port offers the chance: buying a set of horseshoes in one place, a record from a hobo called Rasputin in another—that Père Jules lives, sleeps, and putters around, in the company of the cabin boy and a dozen cats.

When she brings Père Jules his laundry, Juliette lingers in the cabin, putting a sea shell to her ear. Père Jules surprises her there, and gives her a guided tour, showing off all his treasures. He starts by making the music boxes play. An alarm clock goes off, but this is not part of the programme. *I'll show you my little man*, he tells her. He starts up the orchestra conductor. *Found him in Caracas during the revolution of eighteen hundred and ninety . . . something!* The tour continues. Juliette is fascinated: *I never thought your cabin would be like this*. Père Jules is flattered. *Talk about shop windows! Well, nothing but good stuff here . . . nothing but good stuff*. They pause in front of some of his treasures. *An elephant's tooth? An anatomical specimen. . . . A hunting horn*, the old man explains. The knife is no knife but a *navaja*, and he demonstrates the sharpness of the Catalonian blade on his skin. Among the photographs there is one of Dorothy, another of a friend whose sole remains are the hands preserved in the bottle. The phonograph doesn't work. *I'll have to work on it*. The Japanese fan is handmade, *all handmade . . . all handmade*. The girl is interested in everything, and the old man undresses to show her his tattoos. On his front, the most remarkable is a woman's head tattooed on his stomach with his navel representing her mouth. On his back, in addition to several nudes, we see the initials for *Mort aux Vaches*, the legendary beggar's battle cry later adopted by the anarchists.

The apparent disorder in Père Jules' behaviour in this situation corresponds to the patient and systematic method of a Don Juan seducer. Yet one also feels that Père Jules is embarrassed to find himself standing nearly naked in front of Juliette, and therefore picks up the accordion not only to play some music but also to hide this embarrassment. Immediately afterwards, however, he admires Juliette's hair, a compliment she returns by trying to part his tangled locks. The sudden entry of Jean, furious at finding his wife there, breaks the heavy spell cast by this revelation of an entirely different world.

The next temptation Juliette finds confronting her seems straight out of a dream: the pedlar she meets in a cabaret. For the cabaret exterior, Vigo had selected the Charentonneau dance-hall in Maisons-Alfort. The interiors were shot on the film's most extensive set. Francis Jourdain found the inspiration

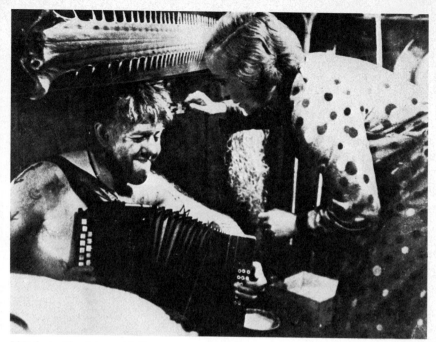

L'Atalante: Père Jules and Juliette

for his set design in his childhood memory of a suburban dance-hall where the dance floor was surrounded by a kind of cage, from behind which the spectators, sitting at tables and looking through the openings, could observe the dancers.

Vigo had not yet succeeded in defining the character of the pedlar. He was still too picturesque, and his sales talk was rather clumsy and uninventive. It was only on the set that he finally caught the right note. Margaritis' charm and agility provided him with first-rate material to work on, and the result was a marvellously appealing, poetic, elusive character, able to play possum when caught out, entirely without rancour and even, at heart, without desire. Despite his persistent pursuit of Juliette, it is really just a game to him.

In the original scenario, his sales talk was a genuine hawker's spiel. It is worth examining in order to watch Vigo at work on one of the occasions where he not only changed the script (that no longer gave him much pause for thought) but also turned his back on reality, not to create poetry for its own sake but to make Juliette's enchantment seem credible. Vigo rejects reality in order to communicate it.

Guinée's pedlar, after his *Good-day, ladies and gentlemen,* walks around the hall glibly enunciating the following speech:

Allow me, ladies and gents, allow me to show you a range of articles of choice

L'Atalante: Jean, Juliette and the pedlar at the cabaret

quality, the very best, the equal of anything offered by a competitor in their impeccable appearance, their irreproachable manufacture, and their very modest price. I'm not offering you sale or bargain goods, nor a collection of second-hand merchandise of the sort you have probably been offered before from time to time. But things made with such up-to-date machinery that every purse can afford a few of these pretty trinkets, these elegant scarves, these magnificent jewels which a husband can give to his wife, a fiancé to his fiancée, a suitor to the object of his desires. It is a gift which always pleases, given on any occasion, a birthday, an anniversary, a christening, or a marriage. And to prove to you, ladies and gentlemen, that my merchandise is of unsurpassable quality, I am going to ask you to take it in your hands when I come among you, and see for yourselves that you've got a real bargain here before you today. A bargain that will only come your way once in a lifetime, and which you cannot let go by without seizing the occasion. Look, gentlemen . . .

And after all that he was to have burst out into a pedlar's song—as if to create a chatterbox it was necessary to have him never stop talking! Margaritis, Vigo's pedlar, greets Jean and Juliette with a speech which is a model of concentrated patter: *How nice of you to come. We were waiting for you to begin the party and serve the dry crackers, arch-dry as the archduchess's very dry pussy.* He says a few more words, does a few conjuring tricks around the room, then—since the distributors had demanded songs in the film— sings *The Pedlar's Complaint.* However, the words are by Goldblatt, the music by Jaubert, and when he sings:

> *I bring joy to the household,*
> *Cures against anger,*
> *I give no sales talk,*
> *I simply say,*
> *That these table knives,*
> *With their rainbow reflection,*
> *Are stainless*
> *Till eternity.*

both music and voice emphasize *till eternity.* Vigo, Goldblatt and Jaubert were mocking the type of song the distributors had in mind.

Each time Juliette stops looking at him, the pedlar stops singing and gently says *Peek-a-boo!* to her in imitation of an old tramp Vigo knew who used to haunt the terrace of a café in Montparnasse, the Dôme.

Soon the player-piano starts up. The pedlar, after having seized Juliette through one of the openings in the cage, much to Jean's astonishment and irritation, leads her into a *Java,* and tells her about Paris amid the crowd of dancers which includes a black soldier with his hands contentedly placed on his partner's buttocks. Jaubert's *Java* was to be used again in *Hôtel du Nord* and *Quai des Brumes,* and each time it makes one yearn for the dance at Vigo's cabaret.

When Jean has finally had enough, he knocks the pedlar down on the dance floor, and takes Juliette away.

But the pedlar has not yet played his game out, and he waits for Jean to leave the barge, then appears, with all the accoutrements of a one-man band on his back, to apologize to Juliette and to say (so he says) a musical farewell, but instead he talks to her about Paris: *I'll take you there on a bicycle, you'll be back in time for roll-call. It's a bargain, it's a deal. A city blazing with fire. The city of light on every floor. Do you want fashions? Window displays. Bicycles, motor-cycles, convertibles for the man about town. It's beautiful. The Champs-Elysées for baby, Les Tuileries for my doll, Notre Dame for Madame. There it all is. I'll carry you away. Once, twice, three times. No takers?*

The reply is a kick in the behind by Jean. Before running away and disappearing forever, the polite pedlar has still time enough for an apology: *Sorry, someone's knocking.* The couple have quarrelled. The pedlar's sales talk on Paris still echoes in Juliette's ears. She decides to embark on the great adventure: to take a suburban train for a flying visit to Paris to do a little window-shopping. The barge was supposed to remain docked for two days, but when Juliette returns several hours later it has already left. As soon as Jean became aware of Juliette's departure he decided, despite Père Jules' objections, to leave immediately for Corbeil. Juliette knows that this is where they usually go, and she only has to return to the station and buy a ticket to Corbeil; but the thin thief decides otherwise. Juliette watches the crowd beating the thief, and a crippled bystander reacting to the spectacle with a fit of hysterics. She does not get her purse back and has to stay in Paris looking for work. Jean, on the Atalante, has become the unhappiest of men.

We have let ourselves be carried away. So much the worse! We will back-track when it proves necessary. For the moment, we are in the middle of the seventh reel and the film consists only of eight. Vigo's approach involves reaching a peak of dramatic tension, and then abruptly resolving it. The logic is there: the separated couple are suffering, Jean cannot stand it any more, Juliette in Paris is unhappy and faithful to her husband. Everything can easily be resolved through the intervention of that good genie, Père Jules. These logistics, however, are only appearance, and artistic reality is altogether different. Jean's crisis is pure poetry; his announcement of his determination to take Juliette back, a miracle. Guinée's script has been lost from sight.

On the Atalante, from which all happiness has fled, Père Jules tries his best to amuse Jean, though without going so far as to stop his outrageous cheating at the game of checkers he has invited the captain to play. Even so, Jean manages to gain the upper hand in one of his rare moments of attention, which leaves the old man with only one alternative—a signal to the cabin boy to throw one of the cats on to the checkerboard. Jean gets up, plunges his head into a bucket of water looking for the image of Juliette, and goes on deck.

Père Jules is at the end of his tether. If only the phonograph would work. He takes the record he bought from Rasputin, absently runs his finger over it,

L'Atalante: Jean, Père Jules and the cabin boy

and the result is accordion music. More interested than amazed by the phenomenon, Père Jules stops running his finger over the record and the music stops. He moves his finger on it again, but for a moment nothing happens, and he hears the boy laughing with the accordion on his knees. Not at all put out, Père Jules immediately takes the offensive: *I've seen more incredible things than records you can play with your finger. Electricity! You know what that is, do you? Electricity? And the radio? Well, then don't give me any lip.*

One shattered miracle does not preclude the success of another. In fact, it is almost as if the failure of the first guarantees the success of the second. Accordingly, an event almost as incredible as playing a record with a finger ensues: Père Jules winds up the phonograph, puts the record on, starts the turntable, puts the needle down, and a waltz, a Jaubert waltz, wells up. The phonograph works! A miracle has happened, hope is reborn, everything becomes credible and possible. Père Jules sends the boy to find the captain. But he has *taken a powder overboard*, as the cabin boy says; Jean is swimming underwater, searching for the image of Juliette, which soon appears to him all in white as on their wedding day, her slow, sweet ghostly movements accompanying the Jaubert waltz which continues to play.

Vigo had finally found a use for what he had learned in the short film *Taris*. Enveloped by music and water, the fairytale vision of Juliette is superimposed on the underwater shots of Jean—his hair waving in the water, his face ravaged by a despair unable to find release in tears because he is already underwater—in a heart-rending dialogue between the two images.

Jean finally comes out of the water, and Père Jules, after drying and dressing him, sends the boy to get the phonograph. Why is the arrival of the two men on the bridge, preceded by the boy carrying the phonograph, so unforgettable? This is not the only time in *L'Atalante*, as we shall see, that a crucial moment remains elusive—a fact that makes the chronicler's task no easier. In any event, Jean is affected by the miracle of the phonograph, and although his only reaction is a wan smile, one is left in no doubt that his will is now set on Juliette's return. And there the sequence ends.

The information we have indicates that the sequences with the phonograph which so miraculously change the nature of events were improvized during the actual shooting. Here, the improvization was not occasioned by some exterior circumstance, some need to overcome a difficulty. The poetic role played by the phonograph came in response to an inner necessity, to an inspiration.

Things had been planned differently. The phonograph was to have started working when Père Jules shook it in a fit of irritation, and at that stage it was just a rather mild gag. When the phonograph was shown off to Jean, the other side of the record, and not Jaubert's miraculous waltz, was to have been played. *It's more cheerful*, Père Jules was to say. The scene did not end with the slight smile on Jean's face, revealing his new resolution, just before his abrupt departure. It was to have continued with Père Jules and the boy dressing up and improvizing a dance in the hope of distracting Jean. The old man and the boy were to have great fun, and then suddenly stop laughing; Jean was gone, and the party a failure. If this scene had been developed along these lines, the miracle of the phonograph would have been the failure.

Some of Vigo's collaborators were not happy about the business of the phonograph actually working. To reassure them, Vigo explained that Père Jules was quite good at fixing things. . . .

A minor discovery probably encouraged Vigo in his purpose. The cats, usually frightened by the lights, the camera and the activities of the crew, behaved in a rather strange way during the phonograph sequences. As soon as the record started playing, they gradually moved closer and closer to the phonograph, sitting around it as if listening attentively to the music. Vigo had no intention of missing a shot like that, and for once work went ahead without trouble from the cats. One of the kittens even nestled inside the loudspeaker, and at that point Vigo must have felt that all resistance to his creativity had ceased. Everything fell into place spontaneously; the idea took shape by itself, offering itself up to his imagination.

Things had reached a point where Vigo needed an encouraging omen. The winter of 1933–4 started unusually early. During the first two weeks, the barge took the crew first into the Oise, along the first section of the canal between the Marne and the Rhine, and then along the Ourcq canal to the barge harbour at La Villette. The work progressed slowly, for the days were

L'Atalante

becoming shorter—so short, in fact, that Vigo preferred waiting for nightfall so that he could simply film in artificial light. But the number of night scenes could not be indefinitely increased. And how could he continue filming scenes which had been started in good weather in a river which was now full of floating ice? The outdoor shooting was already well under way, when Vigo decided to discontinue it temporarily, and move to the studio where an exact replica of the inside of the barge, which he had asked Francis Jourdain to build, awaited them. But whenever the least ray of sunshine seemed imminent, everyone immediately left the studio at La Villette and hurried to the barge docked close by on the Quai de la Loire. All this running back and forth affected the work inside the studio, and most of the time the results were nonexistent. All of the missing exterior transition shots were left until the end so that they could be done at the same time. But when the time came, there was so much snow that the only possible background was the sky; which explains the presence in the film of certain low-angled shots which do not seem to have any precise function. Even among masters, an attempt to get round a problem does not always lead to a creative result.

There was also the problem of Vigo's health. After a week of damp and cold, he was already ill, but there could be no question of a break. So by the time they started work in the studio, Vigo was exhausted. Then, after another fierce battle in the studio, which Vigo somehow found enough energy to fight between bouts of fever and interminable coughing, work had to start again on the exteriors in the snow and ice.

The rather humdrum quality of the exteriors in *L'Atalante* does not prevent some of them from being among the most beautiful outdoor shots in the history of cinema. Usually their virtues are dazzling. For example, the soft, hazy beauty of Juliette in white against the evening mist, or the damp, melancholy greys of the embankment when Juliette returns to find the barge gone. It is not a hidden beauty, but offered to us directly, an integral part of our emotional response. The same holds true for the pure, unsullied landscape of water, sand, and sky explored in depth in Jean's mad race for the sea.

As with that momentous shot when Jean is shown the phonograph, it is difficult to pin down the precise qualities which give the most striking exterior sequence—the barge's arrival in Paris—its extraordinary power. It comes between the two scenes involving Juliette and Père Jules already described in detail: the one in which Père Jules makes himself a one-man entertainment, and the other where he shows Juliette his treasures. Placed between these scenes, both ultimately dominated by a sense of unease, the Atalante's arrival in Paris provides a breath of fresh air.

While Vigo was working on the script, this scene's main function was to show Juliette's discovery of Paris. After Père Jules goes on deck, summoned by the cabin boy to assist in manoeuvring the barge, Juliette picks up the old man's laundry in order to take it to his cabin. She arrives on deck just as the barge comes out of the tunnel and enters the Saint-Martin canal. The entranced Juliette looks all around her.

Her discovery of Paris was to have occurred at this point. A shot of the

L'Atalante: 'some of the most beautiful outdoor shots in the history of cinema'

barge as it rises in the lock was to be followed by a pan upwards taken from the elevator in the Eiffel Tower. The barge would continue rising in the lock as Juliette looked around. Then a panorama of Paris, shot from the top of the Eiffel Tower in one long circular pan.

The idea would probably have produced a unique sense of enchantment. But it was abandoned for economic reasons, and Vigo simply showed the barge manoeuvring in the lock.

The result is no less extraordinary, perhaps because of the editing, or possibly the composition or the direction. Jaubert's triumphant music undoubtedly has a good deal to do with it too. But the reason is unimportant: the images of the barge and the canal bank, as the boy scrambles down the ladder with clumsy haste to grab the hawser and drag the heavy craft, are unforgettable. It may even be that the power of the sequence lies in this evocation of the boy's labours.

So far we have not paid much attention to the cabin boy. He is often present in the film, but without having any particular role to play in the story, since Vigo had not only eliminated the scene revealing his unhealthy curiosity, but also the rather disagreeable part Guinée's script made him play in Juliette's departure. Vigo did retain the idea of making the boy a sort of disciple of Père Jules, but the relationship no longer involves the element of crackerbarrel didacticism implicit in the scenario. Instead, Vigo created a certain identification between them, an identification in both gesture and speech. Thus, when remarking on the birth of the kittens, the boy repeats what Père Jules had said, with the same inflection although he had not heard the old man: *Oh! the darling has had her little ones!*

A number of scenes with the boy which Vigo had planned in his script were either never shot or not included in the versions of the film which were shown. When Père Jules goes out shopping, he takes the boy with him. In some prints, they leave the canal bank with Rasputin, the bearded hobo. These scenes, however, lead nowhere.

They were off to buy provisions and visit an Arab's junk shop. The boy steals oranges from a nearsighted grocer. Père Jules catches him and gives him a lecture. The Arab seizes his chance to retrieve an object from the knapsack left untended by Père Jules. Rasputin looks accusingly at him, but the Arab silences him by giving him another object stolen from Père Jules who, meanwhile, is stealing oranges.

It was not mere chance that Vigo omitted this scene (which is rather reminiscent of René Clair). Aside from the fact that it implied a pessimistic view of human nature not at all in keeping with Vigo's own views, the scene showed the boy in a dubious light. The theft of the oranges was not presented as a reprehensible act, but we have already seen how unexpectedly austere Vigo could be in matters relating to children.

Another scene in which the boy is present throughout—Père Jules' visit to the fortune-teller—had to be completely reworked, partly because of similar scruples. After the consultation, the boy surreptitiously took back the thirty francs Père Jules had paid the fortune-teller. This detail was not all

L'Atalante: Père Jules and the cabin boy

that had to be changed before the scene took the shape it has in the completed film. Vigo was interested in palmistry—at one time he had wanted to make a short film on the subject—and he had developed the scene at some length in his script. It was full of flaws, however: there was too much dialogue, and it dragged; a new character, the fortune-teller's husband, was introduced, and the frightened boy took him for a ghost. The boy, as a matter of fact, remained terrified throughout the consultation.

Vigo changed everything when he came to shoot it. There was no excuse for the fortune-teller's husband, so he was eliminated. The boy is no longer afraid, quite the opposite, since he watches mockingly as the seance proceeds. Vigo turned it into a brief scene, and his distillation of the original dialogue (some three hundred words) is remarkable. He uses about half a dozen shots: the fortune-teller, buxom, fleshy-lipped, greasy-haired, arrayed in bracelets and rings; Père Jules, his worries soon assuaged, and filled with sudden desire. Then about the same number of spoken lines: *I see good news— The cards are running for you—How sensual you are—Oh! those hands!* Père Jules sends the boy outside to wait because the fortune-teller, she says, is going to do *the big one* for him.

Père Jules comes out jubilant. Nothing matters now, since the luck of the cards is with him. He tells the boy to go back alone to the barge and goes into a bar.

Among the out-takes from *L'Atalante* there is a shot which it seems was never used in the film. The boy returns to the bar and looks through the window, and Père Jules comes out and kicks him in the behind. Was it that Vigo did not want to show a child being kicked? (In *Zéro de Conduite*, Colin is slapped by his mother, but one must remember that the head supervisor is responsible.)

The next sequence—Père Jules, drunk, returning to the barge carrying the horn from the phonograph in the bar—contains a continuity lapse in existing prints so obvious that one cannot help but be puzzled by it. In the scene, Juliette is on deck looking at the city lights. Silently Père Jules comes up to her, puts the horn to his mouth, and bellows the Mercier and Millandez song *Paris, Paris, O Infamous and Marvellous City*. Juliette goes below to go to bed, and Jean wakes up just in time to hear the racket Père Jules is making on deck. The captain has to get up, and with some confusion in the sequence of shots, he succeeds with Juliette's help in getting Père Jules to his cabin. Meanwhile there is no sign of the phonograph horn, which has presumably been left somewhere; but when they finally reach the old man's cabin, there it is lying on the bed.

This was not a mistake but a gap in the story. When Jean leaves the cabin to look after Père Jules after putting on his trousers, Juliette is left alone and anxious, while a violent argument develops on deck between the two men. Finally Père Jules picks up the phonograph horn and heads towards his cabin, where he loads an enormous Colt revolver. He goes back on deck with the gun in his pocket, uttering drunken threats. The revolver goes off, making a hole in his pants. Jean takes it and throws it in the water. Juliette, frightened by the noise, rushes up the ladder. Père Jules looks at her, laughs, and then says: *Oh! the captain's lady in her nightshirt!* From that point the action continues as in most of the existing prints.

The missing section would have fallen just at a reel change, and the ends of reels wear out more easily than the rest of a film. In this instance, however, the disappearance of the scene can be attributed to other reasons. If Vigo actually did film the sequence as outlined in the script, he must have realized that it did not fit in with the rest of the film. The argument between Jean and Père Jules, even taking the latter's drunkenness into account, simply goes against the grain of the old man's character and his relationship with Jean. When Jean tells him that if he doesn't like it he can pack his kit and go, Père Jules answers: *My kit, right. I'll pack it and I'll go. But I'm not the only one. You're leaving too, feet first, you hear me, feet first.* And then, cocking his pistol, he mumbles: *And I've never missed! A pity it always has to end this way!*

These scenes with the pistol and the accompanying dialogue would have done more harm to the film than Vigo's apparent oversight with the phonograph horn could possibly have. We do not know whether the scene was shot and then left out, or whether Vigo simply waited for an opportunity which never presented itself of shooting some other version. What we do know, however, is that when Vigo had to choose between unity of style and unity of action, he always unhesitatingly opted for the first.

Although the scene in which Jean confronts the drunken Père Jules is somewhat confusing, it is neatly framed by the old man's mockery of Jean in his undershirt, *Oh! What a good-looking kid!*, and his comment on the *captain's lady in her nightshirt.* The entire scene is dominated by the song which one continues to hear in the background,

> *Paris, Paris, oh infamous*
> *And marvellous city,*
> *Beloved of lovers,*
> *And of thieves*
> *You are the great enchantress. . . .*

sung in a voice which becomes thicker and thicker.

The producers were becoming extremely impatient—as if Vigo and his colleagues were responsible for the delay! The slowing down of the work had caused over-expenditure, and Vigo was being pressured to finish as rapidly as he could. By the third week in January 1934 the sequence in which Juliette is robbed in the station, and several shots of her stay in the city, had still not been filmed. The producers were dubious about giving Vigo the funds he needed for the sequence with the thief; and he was only able to shoot it under conditions of strict economy. He could not count on the studio or on paid extras.

Vigo had obtained permission to use the Gare d'Austerlitz after midnight. A few friends had shown up as extras, but not enough of them. Chavance went off to search for others in the cafés of Montparnasse and Saint-Germain-des-Prés, and he came back with Pierre and Jacques Prévert, Loutchimoukov, and several other members of the "October Group," whom he had found at Les Deux Magots. Dasté, who was enjoying a holiday, was summoned. Goldblatt was chosen to play the hungry thief. The volunteer extras had great fun, and were soon following the lead of the Prévert brothers, deliriously caught up in their parts and trying to involve the policemen on duty, the crew, and the bystanders in the action. Vigo had great difficulty maintaining a semblance of control over his over-enthusiastic friends, and they had to work on until morning.

However, the result proved good: the lynching of the starving thief by a mob of well-fed citizens is oddly reminiscent of the drawings of social themes by pre-1914 anarchist artists such as Steinlen, Grandjouan and Gassier.

To save money, Vigo was forced to adopt a documentary style at times, and in a small way this allowed him to make social comments. Thus, for the images of Juliette looking for work in Paris, he used several very convincing shots of real unemployed workers standing in line in the snow.

It had been agreed that the film would be socially neutral. Vigo, however, did not want to separate the problems of love from the other problems of life; Jean's situation is further menaced by problems with his employers. They treat "good-for-nothings," like the sailor in the company's office who is fired by the manager just before Jean and Père Jules are allowed in, very harshly. The same thing could have happened to Jean had Père Jules not

L'Atalante: Père Jules at the company office

been present. But for an old man who can get a phonograph to work, bringing a company manager round—*Well, I suppose, after all, if that's really so . . .*—is a simple problem.

With the good citizens of Le Havre who gather round the feverish, shivering Jean, and mutter disapprovingly, *Another drunk sailor, it's disgusting*, Père Jules uses a different approach; he frightens them away.

The whole Le Havre sequence is not easy to piece together. The versions extant in 1945–50 include only very small sections of it. A few beautiful shots of the barge arriving, a magnificent shot of Jean's mad rush to the sea: but on the whole very little remains. Among the out-takes are Jean's long walks through the port and a rather strange shot—Jean, probably made thirsty by his fever, licking a huge piece of ice. It is a striking shot, and one is tempted to place it in an ideal reconstitution of *L'Atalante*, but it is not impossible that Vigo himself left it out, considering it rather too outlandish.

We have examined almost the entire film, and are now close to the end. Guinée has disappeared entirely; all the laborious details of Juliette's stay in Paris, including Père Jules' discovery of her telling her beads in a church, have been eliminated.

Vigo wanted to experiment a little during the quest for Juliette. Père Jules was so anxious to find Juliette that he thought he saw her everywhere. A woman on a stool washes a shop window. She half-turns: it is Juliette. He moves closer, and she turns right round: it is not Juliette. Père Jules starts walking on, and hears a beggar-woman asking for charity in Juliette's voice. He approaches her anxiously: it is not Juliette. Vigo was not able to film these scenes, and had to settle for Père Jules walking along the Saint-Martin and Villette canals as he looks for Juliette—a beautiful scene which was cut right down in the prints released.

Père Jules finally finds her and carries her off from the record shop in which she works. Jean, warned by the boy, who has been on the lookout for her return, lathers his face and shaves. Jean and Juliette in a tight embrace roll on the ground together.

The Atalante continues to ride the rivers.

The way in which we have approached the film does not contribute to a clear overall view of it. However, what we have accomplished so far will enable us to examine its structure by summarizing its fourteen episodes in chronological order, at the same time briefly describing the few scenes which have not yet been mentioned. Any precise indication of the total number of shots and how they were distributed in the separate sections is impossible in dealing with a film which can only be reconstituted in the abstract from several different extant versions; but an approximate calculation brings the total to about three hundred separate shots in the film. In the breakdown that follows, these are divided between the fourteen episodes: if one considers each episode separately, the number of shots is probably inaccurate, but overall they do convey the proportions of the film.

I. INTRODUCTION—FORTY-SEVEN SHOTS: The barge. Père Jules and the cabin boy. The wedding. The barge's departure.

II. ELEVEN SHOTS: First night on board. The cats get in Jean and Juliette's way. Jean scratched.

III. TWENTY-EIGHT SHOTS: The next morning. In port. Juliette welcomed aboard by songs, and the start of life aboard. The darling has had her kittens. Juliette starts on her housekeeping tasks: the laundry. Père Jules and the boy go shopping with Rasputin. Plunging heads into water to see a beloved. Jean and Juliette play games. Père Jules gives a demonstration of Greco-Roman wrestling.

IV. TWENTY-SIX SHOTS: The barge on its way at night. Time passes. As on too many evenings Juliette is alone in bed and calls in vain to Jean who is at the helm. Boredom seems to be setting in; the next day they have their first argument, about the radio which Juliette clumsily tries to tune in on Paris. The barge pulls over to the bank because of the fog. Jean looks for Juliette for a long time before finding her sad and dejected on the bridge. Jean, by now irritated, speaks rather brusquely to Père Jules who gets angry and walks off.

V. ELEVEN SHOTS: Dinner, Père Jules arrives late, peace is made. The sewing-machine. Père Jules' exhibitions.

VI. EIGHT SHOTS: Arrival in Paris.

VII. THIRTY SHOTS: Juliette in Père Jules' cabin. Jean arrives and breaks several things. Père Jules has his hair cut by the dog clipper. He is upset to find a broken mirror. (Shots among the out-takes of longshoremen at work.) (Jean, Père Jules and the boy look for Juliette, who is with a woman on one of the neighbouring barges. A few shots among the out-takes.) Jean decides to take Juliette into the city, and she gets ready. Père Jules notices that his charm necklace is broken and decides to consult the fortune-teller. Jean and Juliette have to stay on board.

VIII. EIGHTEEN SHOTS: The fortune-teller. Père Jules returns drunk.

IX. TWENTY-ONE SHOTS: The dance hall. The pedlar comes to the barge.

X. THIRTY-TWO SHOTS: The couple quarrel. Juliette leaves for Paris. The barge leaves. Juliette is robbed at the station.

XI. THIRTY-FIVE SHOTS: The game of checkers. The phonograph. Jean's swim. Jean is shown the phonograph. Intercutting between Jean and Juliette. Their insomnia.

XII. SEVENTEEN SHOTS: In Le Havre. The company office. Père Jules decides to go and look for Juliette.

XIII. SIXTEEN SHOTS: Père Jules' search, he finds her. Jean washes and shaves, Juliette arrives. Conclusion on the barge as it makes its way along the river.

In most of the episodes, the shots of different lengths usually average out. In section V, however, the shots of Père Jules doing his stunts are exceptionally long.

Considering *L'Atalante* as a whole requires a certain effort. This in itself is a pointer, and one can conclude that even before the film was cut, it was not very well proportioned. Often films with very little unity are quite adequately held together by a strong opening and a strong ending. *L'Atalante* has, in fact, a good opening sequence and a good concluding one, but each reaches out towards the other rather hopelessly. This would not constitute a serious problem if the middle held together; but in fact the rapport between one sequence and the next is often extremely weak. But the simple and workmanlike construction Vigo had in mind—and for which he had hired an experienced editor—demanded sequences which could be linked easily together within a coherent whole.

Here Vigo faced an inescapable contradiction. Guinée's mediocre script, with its inconsistent characterizations, did nevertheless possess a certain unity. Vigo had completely reworked the script, but from within. He was able to add a great deal, but he could not create entirely new characters or change the general outline of the action. Yet his personal contribution was such that Guinée's plan had fallen to pieces; so the superb fragments of *L'Atalante* could never be moulded into any real unity.

The overall rhythm of the film therefore suffered greatly. The impression it sometimes gives of being slow paced is not always the result of any conscious style, but stems from the rifts caused by breaks in the continuity.

What rhythm there is, usually comes within a sequence, and very rarely over any larger unit. Exceptions, however, are the beginning of the film up to the first morning aboard, and the section starting with the checkers game and ending with the insomnia scene.

This latter section includes the two passages where Vigo tried to escape one of the limitations imposed on him by the producers. Not only was he to remain socially neutral, but he was not to undertake any formal experimentation. Most of the time he acquiesced in these demands. However, for Jean's swim, he used superimposition underwater. The sequence immediately after Jean is shown the phonograph, in which Vigo makes very effective use of dissolves, is equally striking. The sequence starts with a parallel montage of Jean on the barge and Juliette in Paris: Jean looking at the river-bank, Juliette heading towards a quay; the barge underway, Jean undressing and going to bed, Juliette undressing in her room; Jean in bed, Juliette in bed. Then come the dissolves. Restlessness and desire keep them awake, and the tossings and turnings of a night of insomnia ensue. Little by little, their movements match, the cutting pace quickens, the correspondence between their movements becomes such that the impression of their love enduring becomes inescapable. And the last shot of Jean's suffering face, crushing the pillow with his chin, matches the agonized images of his plunge into the sea.

We have talked a good deal about Vigo's characters, but almost without reference to the actors. Most of them were second-rate, though their bad acting never jeopardized the films: in Vigo's work, the qualities or defects of the cast are not unduly important. His demands on actors varied according to circumstance, but their contribution is never essential.

Two extremes stand out from the middle range of Vigo's actors: Louis Lefèvre is at one end, Michel Simon at the other.

Vigo had learned a good deal about Lefèvre's capacities as an actor, or rather his incapacities, while working on *Zéro de Conduite*, and in *L'Atalante* he simply made good use of Lefèvre's adolescent reserve and natural awkwardness.

With Michel Simon the problem was more complicated. Michel Simon is not only a great character actor, but also a man with enormous personality. Often he does not take direction easily, and on occasion likes to change the lines he is given.

It is not impossible that Michel Simon's bad diction cemented the happy collaboration between Vigo and the actor in creating the character of Père Jules.

While working on *Zéro de Conduite* Vigo had already encountered the problem of actors with bad diction, further aggravated by the bad sound system he was using. The sound in *L'Atalante* was better, but Vigo was still wary: Michel Simon had a good deal of talking to do, and his lines were worth hearing. So he turned his experience with the children in *Zéro de Conduite*—having words or sentences repeated in the conversations or in the course of a monologue—to good account. He gave Père Jules a not uncommon trait: the habit of repeating the other speaker's last few words before replying, as well as saying words more than once. Vigo thus got around the problem of

L'Atalante: 'Plunging heads into water to see a beloved'

Michel Simon's poor diction, and this trait considerably enriched Père Jules' character.

That was not all. By asking the actor to repeat words or phrases from his lines, Vigo was giving him a certain margin of freedom with regard to the lines he had been given to learn. So Michel Simon's natural insubordination was being directed without his realizing it, and whenever the actor followed his instincts, he did precisely what Vigo wanted. Michel Simon had never felt so free, and yet he was under perfect control.

Naturally, this would have been impossible but for Michel Simon's extremely receptive attitude. He liked Vigo, he liked Père Jules, and he liked the cats. He even adopted the kitten which had nestled in the phonograph horn, to the great delight of the lady from the Society for the Prevention of Cruelty to Animals.

At the beginning of February 1934, after four months of uninterrupted effort, during which Vigo worked while sick half the time, the actual shooting was almost finished—only the aerial shots at the end were missing—and a first rough cut had already been made.

The prospect of a vacation before tackling the final cut revived Vigo's spirits. To amuse his friend's mother when invited to lunch by Margaritis, he arrived arm-in-arm with Dasté, both dressed in "women's summer frocks, with bare arms and legs, wearing small hats perched on their heads, one of them apparently in an advanced state of pregnancy."[4]

A few days afterwards Vigo left for Villard-de-Lans with his family and a whole gang of friends: Genya, Margaritis, Chavance, and Alphen. While his friends enjoyed the winter sports, Vigo tried to get back his energy. But the illness had taken hold, and as soon as they returned to Paris, he had to take to his bed.

Kaufman did the aerial shots, and Chavance had to take care of the final cut alone. His task was an easy one, for he and Vigo had already decided on what had to be done, and besides, whenever there was a problem, Chavance could go and discuss it with Vigo, whose condition did not seem to give cause for alarm.

Vigo went out again twice: once to see Chavance's work, the other—the last time—to see the completed film with Nounez and his associates.

Nounez stated that he was quite pleased with the result, and that no cuts were necessary, but his associates were unhappy. They felt that the film was headed for disaster, and that the only way to save it was through massive cuts. However, with the backing of Nounez and under advice from Chavance, Vigo finally agreed—against his better judgment—to only one important change: extensive cuts in the sequence where Père Jules searches for Juliette. According to Chavance, these cuts were designed to lighten the ending, and to this day he is sorry that his advice was accepted.

Beauvais and the other Gaumont employees continued to demand a great many more changes, but finally they had to submit, since Nounez, after all, had provided the finance. It was decided to hold a company preview of the film incorporating the few modifications suggested by Chavance.

The screening took place on April 25, 1934, at ten o'clock in the morning at the Palais Rochechouart. Company representatives, Paris cinema owners and provincial distributors reacted extremely coldly to the film. The people from Gaumont were vindicated, and the pressure on Nounez increased.

Despite the setback of this screening, some possibilities for distribution emerged; but Beauvais rejected them. They probably struck him as not ambitious enough, but it is also conceivable that Beauvais, in agreement with his colleagues at Gaumont, provisionally sabotaged the distribution of *L'Atalante* in order to force Nounez to accept major changes.

Henri Beauvais, the leader of these manoeuvres, was probably no more wicked than the next man, but he was a businessman disturbed to find considerations of an entirely different order getting in the way of what he felt was at that point the best way of producing the expected profits. Nounez must have struck his associates as a businessman occasionally troubled by considerations completely alien to them, someone they had to bring back to "reality" with practical arguments: in other words, sabotaging distribution so that Nounez would be faced with the prospect of a financial catastrophe.

What could Nounez do to convince his more experienced collaborators? Quote the newspaper reactions to the screening? There were very few, for the film had not yet been officially released, and the brief notes and news stories were really little more than company press releases.

Yet, during the few months following the screening at the Palais Roche-chouart, a few articles did appear, including one by Elie Faure. The young intellectual who, together with Léon Blum, had helped to finance Almereyda's trip to the Amsterdam Congress at the turn of the century, had become the foremost art historian and critic of the day, and the first of them in France to appreciate the cinema. Although Elie Faure had written brilliantly about Chaplin, his name was not one familiar to the readers of the film weeklies. When he tried to help the threatened *L'Atalante* by writing an article in *Pour Vous*, the paper had to forestall the probable astonishment of its readers at a style so different from what they were accustomed to by explaining that the author was not only an art historian, but also a philosopher.

"Jean Vigo?" Faure wrote. "One film forgotten, because it was ahead of its time. One film banned, because it was too bitter and subversive. One film not yet released. Why? *A Propos de Nice, Zéro de Conduite, L'Atalante*.

"*L'Atalante*? Humanity. Humanity among the poor. In a sweater and a smock. No dazzling crystal on the tablecloth. Kitchen cloths hanging. Pots. Rough wood bowls. Bread. A bottle of wine. Lights glimmering faintly in the semi-obscurity accentuated by the river mists. The fugitive shadow of Rembrandt, hovering over the rough furniture and wooden partitions, encountering the more artful shadow of Goya: guitars, mangy cats, grotesque carnival masks, stuffed monsters, amputated hands in a jar, that strange odour of exotic poetry every old sailor carries with him beneath the smell of tar and rum, bringing the tang of some bright sea into even the most wretched lair. A clown from the world of slapstick, bearing the panoply of magic, a very demon for those poor devils who have never met temptation before since the boats on canals and rivers do not pass beyond the frontiers of cities. Throughout, I was reminded of those pencils of light thrown out far into the distance by lighthouses from their revolving domes, momentarily picking out from the dark waters a wreck, a body, a knot of seaweed, or a glitter on the surface of the abyss.

"I often thought of Corot, watching these landscapes of water, trees, little houses on peaceful banks, and boats slowly threading their way ahead of a silver wake: the same impeccable composition, the same power invisibly present because so much a master of itself, the same balance of all the elements of a visual drama in the tender embrace of complete acceptance, the same pearly, golden veil translucently masking the sharpness of composition and the firmness of line. And perhaps it was this simplicity of composition, entirely devoid of flourishes or decoration—classical, in a word—that made me appreciate all the more the pleasure of savouring the very spirit of Vigo's work, almost violent, certainly tormented, feverish, brimming with ideas and truculent fantasy, with virulent, even demonic, and yet constantly human romanticism."[5]

Jean Pascal of the *Agence d'Informations Cinématographiques* wrote: "A confused, incoherent, wilfully absurd, long, dull, commercially worthless film, yet it has undeniable qualities: some beautiful, very human scenes here and there are drowned in a mishmash of absurdities and redundancies. Along-

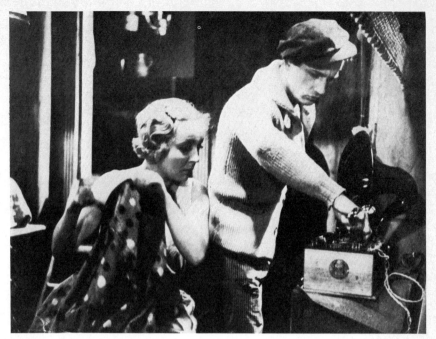

L'Atalante: Jean and Juliette

side some beautiful passages in a very interesting attempt at lyricism, one senses a deliberate reaching out for the ugly and the vulgar."

"Commercially worthless," Beauvais must have echoed triumphantly. What could Nounez say in reply? Quote Elie Faure's article? Surely he did not even try. Refer to Jacques Brunius' very favourable review which had appeared in *Regards*? "There is not a single frame which does not contain something worth seeing and feeling. . . . Vigo's style is completely his own." Beauvais would have answered that the editorial board of *Regards* included Romain Rolland, Gide and Malraux, and that they were not after a Communist *succès d'estime*.

In July *L'Atalante* was selected as one of the French entries[6] in the Venice Biennale. Today, that fact in itself would lend a film prestige. At that time, however, the Venice Festival was not the well-publicized event it has since become, and even film weeklies like *Pour Vous* only gave it a short notice on the back pages.

Other critics, in short articles or comments, had also written favourably of *L'Atalante*: Jean Marguet in *Le Petit Parisien*, Lucien Wahl in *L'Œuvre*, Germaine Decaris in *Les Hommes du Jour*; but with time Nounez's position became increasingly untenable. Sabotaging the distribution had brought the desired results. The million francs Nounez had invested in *L'Atalante* seemed well on their way to following the two hundred thousand francs lost on *Zéro*

L'Atalante: Jean and Juliette on their way to the cabaret

de Conduite. Nounez felt threatened as a businessman, and he capitulated.

The other obstacle no longer counted: a sick young man whose state of health grew worse day by day, and who could no longer participate in the discussions, even from a distance.

In the circumstances, Gaumont could do what they liked with the film. They decided that even if every imaginable cut was made, the film would still not have the ingredients for commercial success; so they decided to inject those ingredients.

In 1934 a song launched by Lys Gauty was enormously popular in France: "Le Chaland qui passe" ("The Passing Barge"), composed by Cesare Andrea Bixio. Since there was a barge in *L'Atalante*, the film was retitled *Le Chaland qui passe*; and to justify the new title, parts of Maurice Jaubert's score were haphazardly lopped out and replaced by Bixio's song. As for cuts, to judge from some of the extant prints of the retitled version, the original was literally hacked to pieces. Only two or three sequences were left intact; the insomnia was completely eliminated, as was the entire scene in which Jean is shown the phonograph. And what remains of Vigo's work is constantly tainted by Bixio's refrain, made all the more repulsively vulgar by its juxtaposition with Jaubert's songs and waltzes.

L'Atalante's metamorphosis into *Le Chaland qui passe* did not, of course, go unnoticed in Paris, and as a result the studio's publicity department was rather hamstrung in its efforts to have some of the song's success rub off on the film. When it opened for its first run at the Colisée in mid-September 1934, the press releases were quite discreet, and contented themselves with pointing out that "A score by Maurice Jaubert and Bixio's celebrated song 'Le Chaland qui passe' provide musical accompaniment for the film's main scenes."[7]

In Marseilles, advertising was easier, and the screening of the film at the Alhambra was accompanied by a press release which began: "Thanks to C. A. Bixio's celebrated melody, so admirably sung by Lys Gauty, *Le Chaland qui passe* . . . will certainly not pass unnoticed! Already that evocative melody can be heard in every street. An equal success is assured for *Le Chaland qui passe* as a film."[8]

In Algiers, even further away from Paris, the press releases unabashedly read: "*Le Chaland qui passe* is a film inspired by the celebrated song so admirably sung by Lys Gauty."[9]

Le Chaland qui passe was a commercial failure. The first run at the Colisée lasted only two weeks. The public for musical films who had been tempted by the promise of the title were disappointed; and those not kept away by Bixio's song were, like the small minority attracted by Vigo's name, puzzled by a film so mutilated as to be incoherent. No amount of misleading advertising could mollify the feelings of deception felt by the Parisian public. At the Colisée, people hissed at every screening. Mostly they wanted to express their displeasure with a film they disliked, but a few, a very few, were condemning the behaviour of the producers.

The critics as a whole were kinder. Fernand Desprès, who read everything relating to his friend's film, wrote to Pierre de Saint-Prix on September 27 that he had "read about twenty very favourable articles." He also mentioned a series of four articles by Lucien Wahl, and said that one by Alexandre Arnoux would be appearing shortly.

The professional critics, although aware of the circumstances (several of them had seen *L'Atalante* in the version approved by Vigo), had difficulty tracing the remnants of the original film—for praise or blame—in the patched-up version they were shown.

Jean Laury, critic for *Le Figaro*, talks about a film that is barely recognizable: "The film is a terribly sad one: from beginning to end everything in it happens under the sign of misfortune . . . M. Vigo likes to draw his inspiration from troubled waters. *Le Chaland qui passe* reminds one of those German productions which were so popular for a time despite their morbidity, or perhaps because of it . . . M. Jean Vigo instinctively deforms everything he shows. If he filmed a ray of sunshine, one would see more of the motes of dust than one would of the light. If he shows us a bowl, it is broken . . . a dog, it limps. He captures a kiss, a smile, an embrace in close-up, but the kiss becomes a bite, the smile turns into a grimace, and the embracing arm sketches a murderous gesture, the hand on a bare neck hesitates between caress and strangulation."[10]

Here, once again, is the tone used by a whole group of critics to describe

Zéro de Conduite. René Jeanne's review makes the same comments that had been made about the earlier film: "M. Vigo has undoubtedly exaggerated the picturesqueness a little too self-indulgently, often in an all too obvious desire to upset or shock the audience. Youth, taste for experiment, faith in the avant-garde, they are all part of *Le Chaland qui passe*."[11]

Verhylle in *Cinoedia* reproaches Vigo for "his exaggerated desire for originality and realism." "Jean Vigo has made something which is neither realistic nor fantastic," Lucien Wahl protested, "but a sort of fantasy rooted in everyday life which may provoke a grinding of teeth but not loss of interest. It may be a film ahead of its time, but it has not had the success it deserves as a worthy descendant of the great primitives of the cinema."[12]

For Antoine, critic of *Le Journal*, the film "gives the impression of being the work of an amateur. . . . The story is awkwardly told and the visual quality one expects from a director is not well presented. One can trace many good intentions, but deprived of craftsmanship and skill, it remains of little interest. Michel Simon works hard to create the character of an eccentric old sailor; his physical presence and his slightly mumbling style of acting help him to present a quaint and colourful figure, but too much time is spent in developing this character who has very little to do with the plot. Hence some rather disconcerting *longueurs* for the spectator."[13]

Jean Marguet of *Le Petit Parisien* had not liked *Zéro de Conduite*. Yet he was enthusiastic about *L'Atalante* in the version shown at the Palais Roche-chouart, and he remained quite partial to *Le Chaland qui passe*. "It is an intelligent film, intellectual in a way that stifles neither sincerity nor emotion. It revolves around a crisis of *ennui* or, to use a phrase which is currently fashionable, a fit of the blues. . . . Everything is simple, yet everything is cinematic. Several moments pass, nothing happens, an atmosphere is created. Dialogue plays only a secondary role. . . . The images in *Le Chaland qui passe* are not avant-garde; they are precious because they bring us something new, that something new we have been so starved of in the cinema."[14]

A review by Alexandre Arnoux, a critic highly regarded at the time, is worth noting: "Jean Vigo's direction has an honesty and conscientiousness one must admit and admire even if one does not entirely share the enthusiasm of some devotees. . . . Meticulous, realistic, lyrical: those are, I think, the characteristics which define his talent, together with a tendency to stress details and to elevate certain objects or secondary characters into symbols. His art, of an exemplary integrity, is not, however, without a certain over-emphasis and a certain dullness: he is after profundity rather than variety. But the daily life on the barge as it glides through landscapes of factories, chimneys and iron bridges is painted by the hand of a master, with a scrupulousness, a disdain for conventional, picturesque or pretty-postcard effects which is enchanting. A healthy attitude and a necessary reaction.

"But let us hope that Jean Vigo can shed a little of that intransigence he uses as armour, that he can acquire some of the elliptical pace which seems to concern him so little at the moment. In any case, here is a young director

L'Atalante

with a splendid and self-evident talent: even his faults and excesses are challenging and refreshing."[15]

The comments in the film magazines were equally favourable. Jean Vidal took the opportunity to lament that the censors had banned "that fine film *Zéro de Conduite*." Since he was in fact one of the editors of *Pour Vous*, this indicates a new stage in the magazine's attitude. About the new film, Vidal writes: ". . . One of those films where the cinema draws closer to poetry than to the novel. Almost nothing happens in *Le Chaland qui passe*, but each shot is evocative, bringing a new feeling with it. An atmosphere of anguish and despair, created very simply, envelops each frame. It is redolent of sincerity and compassion, and perhaps too a sort of muted rebellion. It is not, of course, a film of great spectacular quality. It leaves one with a sense of unease, and at times baffles its audience by its contempt for style and the usual cinematic conventions.

"*Le Chaland qui passe* makes one think of Céline's novel, *Le Voyage au bout de la nuit*. At all events, a sensibility shines through it. And that is rare."[16]

Cinémonde felt that it was "a sensitive, melancholy film, with an atmosphere which both enchants and astonishes, and where the story is subordinated to a harmonious, shifting landscape of fields, water, and sky."[17]

In *Le Courrier Cinématographique*, signed R. F.: "Recently there have been several films on the wandering, vagabond life of bargemen. None of them has reflected their life so intensely, so truthfully, so poetically and so forcefully."

The above is quoted from an issue of *Mon Ciné* where Raymond Berner tried to put things in perspective: "Good God, the film is no masterpiece! But then neither Chaplin, Lubitsch nor Feyder made masterpieces with their third films, or if you like their first major features. And therein lies the problem for the young of today: they have no right to make mistakes. At one time the public, less educated, less difficult to please, was satisfied with approximations; today, gorged on films which are less perfect than they seem, perfect only in their mediocrity, they will no longer put up with a seeming incoherence which is often only the sign of a still maturing talent. *Le Chaland qui passe*, since one must call it by its new name, is a film in which talent literally bursts out throughout—unpredictable, violent, disconcerting. The audience is baffled because they do not find the facile, sweet-smelling environment in which they feel at home. So they hiss, fatuously. . . .

"All they choose to see is the rather obvious clumsiness of certain scenes, and the film's lack of coherence. That these defects exist is beyond question, but are they so serious that the whole film has to be condemned without appeal? The most awkward thing about the film is that the cast seem to be performing their own little acts without bothering about their fellow actors. Hence the rather disturbing lack of unity. With other actors less 'independent' of the director's wishes, and with a little less Germanic romanticism in certain scenes, *Le Chaland qui passe* would still have been *L'Atalante*, and might have been considered a very good film.

"Let's hope that Jean Vigo will soon make another film which will enable him to reveal these same qualities strengthened by experience."[18]

On October 5, 1934, the day after this article was published, and only a few days after the first run of *Le Chaland qui passe* at the Colisée had ended, Jean Vigo died.

Vigo and Dita Parlo on the set of *L'Atalante*

5. Vigo's Death

Some seven months before his death, when Vigo was permanently restricted to his bed, his case had been diagnosed as rheumatic septicaemia. At the time, this was still a terribly exhausting and protracted disease about which medicine could do virtually nothing. Vigo was in such a weakened state that the doctors, fearing a fatal shock, were unwilling to risk serums. Blood transfusions were tried with no results, and while waiting for his organism to manufacture its own antibodies against the disease, his doctors resorted to homoeopathic treatment. For months, Vigo's temperature was 98·6 degrees every morning and about 104 degrees every evening. These jumps in temperature were accompanied by various pains and terrible sweating. In July, stomatitis made his condition even worse, and for two weeks Vigo scarcely ate a thing and became frighteningly thin. His older friends, like Fernand Desprès, wanted to call in Dr. Philippe Neel, Almereyda's doctor, in the hope that, because he knew the family medical history, he might be able to suggest a treatment.

Vigo's spirits never wavered for a moment. He could confide to Fernand Desprès that *L'Atalante* had finished him, but then immediately reveal his determination to live and continue making films. Luce had been sent to stay with friends so that Lydou could dedicate herself entirely to the fight, and Vigo gave her constant encouragement by joking about his sickness. He described the streptococcus as a little fat man in a top hat. Sometimes, he would burst into peals of laughter with Dasté, or make witty comments which delighted Fernand Desprès. He even played practical jokes which required a certain physical effort. One evening, while alone in his room, he was listening to the *Chant du départ* on the radio. In an adjoining room his friends were having a political argument. As the discussion got hotter, the voices got louder. Vigo turned the radio on full blast, without managing to drown out the voices, so he decided to stop the argument by other means. "The door between the two rooms was ajar; suddenly, it opened all the way, and Jean Vigo appeared in his nightshirt, his arm raised, beating out the military march's rhythm. . . . The terrified Lydou couldn't move, and everyone wondered if he had gone mad. . . . Vigo, seeing the effect of his sudden apparition, very silently and repentantly went back to bed, like a punished child, on the arm of his nurse who had hastened over to help him."[1]

By the end of August or the beginning of September, Vigo's friends had given up all hope of seeing him recover. Vigo, already so thin, grew thinner and thinner day by day. Until then he had forced himself to eat a little, but when Fernand Desprès visited him on September 26, he had been unable to take food for several days and his heart was weakening. While the doctor tried to revive him with oil of camphor injections, Jean Painlevé, Claude Aveline and Fernand Desprès waited in silence in the next room. They were finally allowed to see their friend, who was only semi-conscious most of the time, his voice barely a whisper. "Huge rings encircle his eyes. His lips are pale and bloodless. His face is shrunken, like a little child's."[2]

During the next days, he painfully swallowed fruit juices, mineral water or linden tea; but after vomiting up bile, Vigo had become cadaverous, and they were awaiting the end. Then suddenly, on September 30, his temperature, invariably around 104 degrees by ten o'clock in the evening, dropped to normal.

The next day he sat up in bed, arranged his pillow himself, asked for a cup of chocolate, and refused to take it when it arrived because the bowl was only three-quarters full. When Lydou had filled it to the brim, Vigo cut a piece of bread into small bits, and while dunking it into the chocolate, greeted Mme. Margaritis, who had come to visit him. Delightedly, he told her: "It's twenty sous to watch me eat." Lydou, her eyes wide in amazement, was laughing happily. She immediately went out to buy him a bathrobe.

The following day the fever returned, and two days later, a Friday, just before nine o'clock in the evening, Jean Vigo died. Outside the apartment a street musician at the intersection of rue Gazan and Avenue Reille was playing "Le Chaland qui passe". Lydou, lying beside him and holding him in her arms, did not seem to understand. A moment later, she eluded their friends and ran down a long corridor to a room at the end. They caught her just as she was about to jump out of the window.

On Monday, October 8, at 3.30 in the afternoon, Vigo was buried at the Parisian cemetery of Bagneux in a grave next to Miguel Almereyda. Among those present were three women in mourning, recognized only by some of Almereyda's friends as Emily and Vigo's two half-sisters. There were no speeches and no formal condolences. After the sharp rattle of the spadefuls

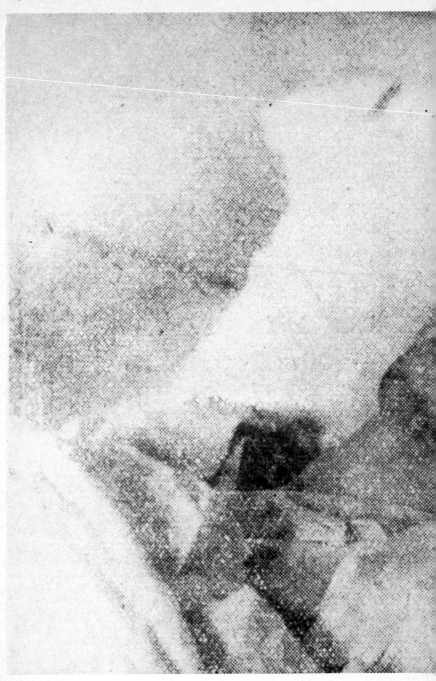

Jean Vigo

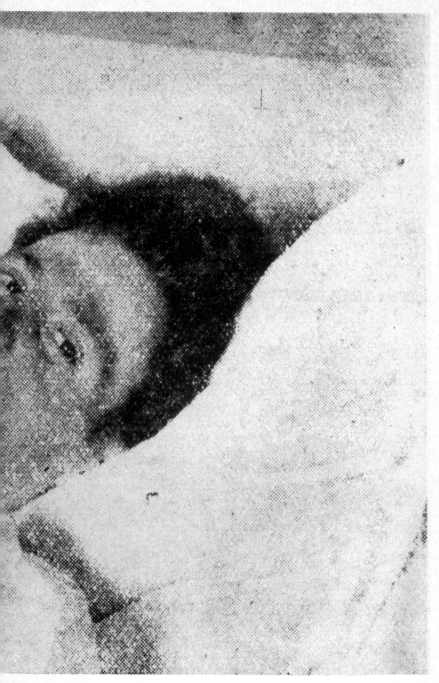

of earth on the oak coffin, the silence was total, and the mourners dispersed rapidly.

Lydou was delirious in a clinic on the rue d'Alésia. She muttered that the Vigos hadn't had any luck that year, and added, in the manner of the principal in *Zéro de Conduite*, "they must be watched." She gave orders. First, she wanted to speak to the streptococcus who was a little fat man in a top hat; she wanted to have a few words with him and then kill him, just a little. Next, *L'Atalante* was to be wrapped around the fat, red producers and set on fire. Urgently, Lydou cried out "Monsieur Jean Vigo! Monsieur Jean Vigo!" several times. Then, softly, "His heart is no longer beating, it's icy cold, making no sound." Lydou asked that she be put in the grave next to Vigo's. "I want to die so I can sleep with him, like I used to."[3]

"Since October 5 I have not been alive," Lydou wrote several months later. "I feel like an object which has been left behind. I am as though petrified. I don't understand. I remain here and the only way I can live through each day is to tell myself that I'll be dead tomorrow. I can't grasp that Jean is no longer alive, that it is all *true*. Sometimes, I think that Jean and Lydou are both dead and that I am Lydou-Jean, both of us in one body. But this feeling occurs only rarely and usually follows a period of extreme suffering, when my organism cannot put up with all the pain and a feeling of unreality results. My world has disintegrated and nothing has any meaning. I think too much and don't cry enough, although it's true that I did cry a great deal during his illness. I fought for his life with all my strength, and I have hardly any left to fight for my own. Worrying about my child keeps me here, but can I continue resisting for long? I really don't know, we'll see. He wanted so much to live, he believed in our life together so much. Do you realize, dear Henri, what has happened to both of us?"[4]

On the evening after the funeral, there was a festival of Michel Simon films at the Salle Adyar, organized by Daniel Maybon, which ended with a screening of *Le Chaland qui passe*. Friends who had gone to the cemetery in the afternoon met again at the cinema in the evening, where Dita Parlo talked about Vigo and his fight for *L'Atalante*.

Since the end of the first run at the Colisée had been followed so closely by Vigo's death, people were still talking about the film, while the obituaries tried to trace his career and assess his work. Jean Marguet, casting aside his former reservations, wrote: "Jean Vigo's death has deprived the French cinema of a director with exceptional personality. . . . *A Propos de Nice* . . . an irony mitigated by the sensitivity which was to reappear in all his films. . . . *Zéro de Conduite*, full of astonishing visual felicities . . . had nothing shocking or subversive about it. . . . *Le Chaland qui passe* . . . which should be restored to its original title of *L'Atalante* . . . a mixture of comedy and tragedy, sweetness and sorrow, and a brutal reality unhurriedly expressed and abruptly pierced by dreamlike perceptions. . . . Although the film was bitterly argued over, at least it could be generally agreed that it brought something new to the cinema. . . . [His death] will sadden those who, through the originality of a film, suddenly discovered the name of Jean Vigo. His career was short, but it will not be forgotten."[5]

Serge Berline wrote: *A Propos de Nice* is a brutal, harsh film, strikingly realistic. . . . *Zéro de Conduite*, a relentless satire on small provincial schools and their strictures, a sort of French answer to *Emil und die Detektive* (at least that is what Jean Vigo told me) . . . a genuine minor masterpiece of cinema . . . considered obscene. . . . *Le Chaland qui passe*, a strange, disquieting work, very beautiful, a bit slow, perfectly reflecting Jean Vigo's anguished spirit. . . . A real film-maker . . . thin, small, hirsute, in the studio he worked frenziedly, was never satisfied. . . . Had he lived, Jean Vigo would undoubtedly have been as renowned as von Stroheim, whose work is strangely similar, but fate did not allow him to give us the full measure of his talent."[6]

"He announced himself several years ago," Georges Charensol wrote, "at the Studio des Ursulines. . . . *A Propos de Nice* . . . already showed an undeniable talent, but it was in *Zéro de Conduite* that this talent was able to express itself fully. . . . The film was never released, but Jean Vigo's friends will undoubtedly set about getting that decision reversed. They will also demand that *Le Chaland qui passe* be given back its original title, for it perfectly evoked that mixture of realism and dream, of comedy and tragedy, which built a Shakespearean atmosphere around the film. It is safe to say that nothing in France since René Clair's first films offered such a sense of originality; an extremely powerful personality revealed itself through these films, which would undoubtedly have risen to join the ranks of the great.

"But destiny decided otherwise."[7]

Frédéric Pottecher wrote that Vigo "was just beginning to reveal his talent, not as a director, but as a poet of living images. His last film, *Le Chaland qui passe*, was widely attacked: a strange film, containing the best and the worst side by side.

"Vigo was above all a poet, a lyric poet. He saw what ordinary mortals could not, and it is not surprising that he was so little understood. But those who were fortunate enough to respond to this thin, soft-spoken young man, with his delicacy of mind and exquisite manners, could appreciate the treasures which his magnificent soul contained, irreplaceable treasures with which Vigo was sometimes able to invest his films. . . .

"The man was charming, very well-read, very perceptive, tender and strong, sensitive and frank; he knew how to get to you, and you felt that everything he said, everything he did, came straight from that soul as pure as a child's, and from that well-tempered heart of a sincere and committed artist."[8]

L'Humanité: "Vigo always fought fiercely against the capitalist cinema. First by getting audiences of workers and intellectuals together to show them Soviet films banned by the censors, then by dealing with problems in his films which the censors and the film magnates refused to have even hinted at.

"An early member of the Association des Ecrivains et Artistes Révolutionnaires, Vigo introduced many young film-makers into the organization who had been won over to the revolutionary cause by his example.

".. . The revolutionary proletariat . . . will recall that Vigo was one of the first film directors to put himself unreservedly on their side and to place his immense talents at their service."[9]

Claude Aveline, in *Pour Vous*, denounced the mutilation suffered by the work of a friend he described as "by turns extremely tough and sensitive, perhaps even excessively so. Always fiercely honest. A special person." Aveline expressed outrage against the interpolated music. "Imagine an orchestra suddenly starting to play 'Speak to Me of Love' in the middle of *Pelléas et Mélisande*."[10]

Pour Vous also published an "open letter to the Chairman of the Board of Film Censors," written by Claude Vermorel, in which, after having ironically catalogued the charges brought against *Zéro de Conduite*, he wrote: "But, Mr. Chairman, Jean Vigo is dead. He will no longer ridicule subprefects, members of the clergy, and school principals. Give us his film."[11] The open letter was an attempt to get a campaign started demanding that the film be released, but it had no effect.

In an unpublished text, written just after *Zéro de Conduite* was finished, Henri Storck wrote that "Vigo left some of his own flesh and blood in the film."[12] After *L'Atalante*, Storck wrote an article in which he accused the cinema of having killed his friend. After recalling the details of Vigo's life, he concluded: "In him, the French cinema has lost an artist of exceptional insight, a film-maker who brought to it a rare faith and enthusiasm, who had something to say and said it, despite the hypocrisy and mediocrity of the Paris film world. His opinions were forthright and sincere. He had long sided with the workers, with the exploited. He refused to be coerced into making the least concession. . . .

"He had an admirable film sense. In France, he was one of the few film-makers capable of humanly and artistically enriching the medium, as René Clair, Grémillon, and Feyder did. He died before he received due recognition, although not without arousing an often fervent admiration for his tiny handful of films."[13]

The obituary published in the Belgian Communist youth organization's paper was not written from a social perspective. The author, signing himself A.M., writes sadly of *Le Chaland qui passe*, seen at the Adyar, of Père Jules and his cabin, that "inventor of dreams" in a "marvellous dream laboratory," and of "Jean Vigo, a tormented soul who leaves us an album bound in black, full of violence, revolt, and tremendous compassion."[14]

As in Brussels with the Club de l'Ecran, audiences in Ghent had been able to follow Vigo's career thanks to the Ghent Film Club, and when Vigo died, the loyal reviewer from the socialist paper *Vooruit*, pending a screening of the fourth and last film, wrote about the other three, which he had liked (*Taris* especially).[15] *Le Chaland qui passe* was not released in Belgium until the middle of 1935.

"Except for some missing fragments and the addition of a popular song," Chr. Delpierre wrote, "Jean Vigo's precious legacy can now be seen by the public. Everything considered, it is better that it should be available for a few weeks to be seen by some perhaps uninformed but at least perfectible spectators, rather than moulder on the shelf in the original version. Some trace of the film, at least, will remain among the rude and the simple-minded.

"For me, it revived a faculty for admiration which had been dormant for years. If Jean Vigo were still alive, there would be cause for happy hope."[16]

The "missing fragments and the addition of a popular song," as well as the change in title, was precisely what the film buffs at the Club de l'Ecran objected to.

André Thirifays, the president of the club, asked friends in Paris to do some research, and soon a prospectus from the club announced the presentation on "October 24, 1935, in the Chamber Music Room of the Palais des Beaux-Arts, of *L'Atalante* in the reconstituted *original* version." After a brief history of how *L'Atalante* had been changed into *Le Chaland qui passe*, the note continued: "*No print of the original version now exists.* With the help of some of Vigo's friends, however, and through its own unflagging efforts, the Club de l'Ecran has been able to assemble all the sections cut out of the first version and to reconstitute the *exact montage* of the original from precise documentary evidence. Only Jaubert's music remains incomplete. With its very limited means, the club cannot permanently preserve this reconstituted version. It will be destroyed after this screening. We therefore invite our members and all true film-lovers not to miss the *unique opportunity to see L'Atalante*, and to come not only in memory of Vigo, but to applaud one of the most remarkable films the cinema has produced."[17]

The promises held out by the prospectus were exaggerated and mostly salesmanship. What was involved here was certainly not an original version reconstituted from documentary evidence. In reality, it was a much more modest undertaking. It had been discovered that Gaumont had preserved a certain number of scenes—between fifteen and twenty—which had been cut out, together with exact references to where they had come in the film. Faced by repeated requests from Thirifays and Storck, the people at Gaumont agreed to let them edit the missing sections into the print which the Club de l'Ecran was going to show. At the same time, they warned that this was something which could not be preserved in that form or repeated, and so as not to have to confront the problem again, they were going to destroy the missing sections. They also maintained that the original negative with Jaubert's music no longer existed. Thirifays asked in vain to be allowed to keep the sections which were to be destroyed, and was forced to send them back to Paris with the copy of the film.

André Thirifays states: "Most of the cuts consisted of fragments of scenes. The reason for these mutilations was simply a desire to shorten the film to the length which, according to these gentlemen, was most suited to commercial exploitation. One scene, however, had been cut out on 'moral' grounds, the scene in which Michel Simon puts a cigarette in his navel."[18]

This extract from a letter from Thirifays plunges us right into the heart of the difficulties involved in attempting to reconstitute *L'Atalante*, even theoretically, having found some at least of the missing shots.

L'Atalante: 'The fugitive shadow of Rembrandt'

Broadly speaking, there were two series of cuts in 1934: one came between the day Vigo viewed the film with Nounez and the first screening at the Palais Rochechouart. These cuts, suggested by Chavance and somewhat grudgingly approved by the director, were aimed at shortening certain scenes. The other, much more extensive amputations (done by whom?) were effected when *L'Atalante* was transformed into *Le Chaland qui passe*. The aim—apart from the musical changes—was still to shorten the film, but this time the film's structure was attacked and modified. The fragments sent to the Club de l'Ecran in 1935 most probably came from the first operation, for it is unlikely that the extensive and haphazard changes undertaken during the second would have resulted in "some fifteen carefully marked fragments, preserved with exact references to where they came in the original."

It is also important to consider the shot of the cigarette in the navel which was supposedly cut out. It is the most famous of all the cuts in *L'Atalante*, and the film has by tradition always been associated with this banned shot. There was even a time when no one seemed to know whose navel had the cigarette in it.

According to some, including Henri Langlois of the Cinémathèque Française, it was Jean in his cabin, in despair over Juliette's absence, who stubbed a cigarette—whether lighted or not was never made clear—in his own navel. However, the majority, including collaborators as close to Vigo as Louis Chavance, opted for Michel Simon's navel; according to them, the shot occurred during Juliette's visit to Père Jules' cabin as he shows her his tattoos. One of these tattoos, it will be remembered—one of the most successful—was a head with a mouth drawn round his navel. Père Jules, so we are told, put a cigarette into the tattooed mouth as a climax to the exhibition of his tattoos.

A still of this "censored shot" was published in 1949 in Paris and later reproduced in London in 1951. Several people then remembered having seen it on the screen. Those who supported Dasté's navel defected to Michel Simon's, and it was agreed that the shot had existed and had been cut out. However, the still in question does not settle matters one way or the other. For it is definitely not a frame enlargement nor a still taken on the set; the plane surface behind Père Jules, probably a reflector, does not exist in the cabin as it appears on the screen.[19]

To return to that so-called reconstituted original print shown in Brussels in 1935: the information given to Thirifays by Gaumont was as a matter of fact untrue, at least in so far as it concerned the destruction of the sound-track with the missing passages of Jaubert's music.

The film was in fact re-released in 1940 with Jaubert's music intact, as well as with its original title and the addition of some missing scenes. Once again it is possible to judge this version only by the prints duplicated from it which were the ones in circulation after the liberation of France and which vary considerably from print to print. This brings us to the most recent attempt at reconstituting the film, made by myself with the help of the Florentine critic Panfilo Colaprete.

This attempt took place in 1950. Research among the original negative out-takes led to a preliminary selection of about thirty of them. We also chose two prints of the 1940 version of *L'Atalante*[20] and a print of *Le Chaland qui passe*. The conditions under which we worked were terrible. We never had access to a Moviola, nor were we able to compare different prints on a synchronizer, so we were obliged to resort to the crude method of repeated screenings. Nevertheless, by combining the three prints and inserting some of the selected out-takes, we ended up with a version less bad than the ones in circulation. We were unable to participate in the technical preparation of the print, which was supervised by the Cinémathèque Française, but on seeing the result, realized that it was not without interest. However, to state that the original version of *L'Atalante* had now been reconstituted—as was done to the Parisian press on the occasion of the Antibes Festival in 1950, or to the meeting of the International Federation of Film Archives at Cambridge in 1951—was, like the earlier declaration in Brussels, an exaggeration. But although reconstituting the original film would now prove extremely difficult, at least some progress had been made, and more is always possible. The fact that a print of the film under the original title existed in London in 1934 is cause for hope to admirers of Jean Vigo.

After this digression concerning attempts to reconstitute the original film, 1934 and London bring us back to the chronological unfolding of our story.

Vigo's work arrived in London in 1934 with the almost simultaneous showing, in the autumn of that year, of *L'Atalante* in a commercial cinema, and of *Zéro de Conduite* at a film club. It is not absolutely certain which version of *L'Atalante* was involved, although references to it in the British press are a good sign: *L'Atalante* rather than *Le Chaland qui passe* is always used as the title. Perhaps Gaumont had doubts about the charms of Bixio's song for a British audience and decided to send them the Palais Rochechouart version.

In addition, the only contemporary English review we have been able to refer to seems less confused (even though the only reservation stems from a misunderstanding[21]) than the French press had been. The author was John Grierson—then in the very middle of his battle for the documentary—and he examines Vigo's style from this bias: "It is an exciting style. At the base of it is a sense of documentary realism which makes the barge a real barge—so exact in its topography that one could find one's way on it blindfold and dead drunk on a windy night. This is important in barges as in all ships, and sea films never seem to realize it." Grierson was also interested in Vigo's fantasy. He sees Père Jules and the street pedlar as two facets of "romance," and concludes: "It is a novel and fascinating way of story-telling, and Vigo is clearly one of the most imaginative young directors in Europe."[22]

Apparently *L'Atalante* was not widely distributed in England in 1934, but it deeply impressed some who saw it. Long afterwards, Roger Manvell wrote: "To see *L'Atalante* again, in spite of its indifferent sound and its

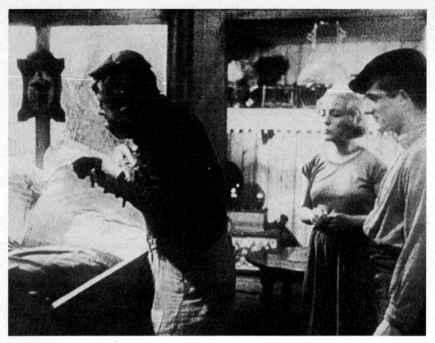

L'Atalante

occasionally rough-and-ready continuity, is to revive the indelible impression it originally made on the imagination."

Zéro de Conduite was shown by the London Film Society in November 1934. The programme note reads: "Although Jean Vigo was never officially admitted to the surréalist ranks, certain sections of the present film, notably the promenade and the scenes in the director's office and the dormitory, are considered in France as being just as much in the surréalist manner as the poems of Eluard and the paintings of Dali."[23]

Alberto Cavalcanti, who inspired if he did not actually write these programme notes, later commented: "The majority of the English critics who saw this film at the Film Society completely misunderstood it and took it for a comedy. The poetry which runs through the film escaped them. . . ."[24]

This poetry had also escaped the French and Belgian critics, and the importance of Cavalcanti's article is that he was the first to recognize it. However, Cavalcanti's affirmation of the poetry in *Zéro de Conduite* is not the only thing worth noting: he was also the first to point out how important the influence of Miguel Almereyda was on Vigo's attitudes and his work. This was the great merit of the Cavalcanti article, despite his many geographical and chronological errors, and his insistence on placing Vigo's style within the surrealist orbit.

Many years were to pass before the English again expressed any interest

L'Atalante

in Jean Vigo's films. Elsewhere, even in France, Vigo was mentioned very infrequently during those last years before the Second World War. During that period, one could live in Paris and be interested in films, yet be almost unaware of Vigo's name or have any opportunity to see his films.

Still, the two histories of the cinema which appeared in French between Vigo's death and the beginning of the war do include a few lines on his work. Like Bardèche and Brasillach, Carl Vincent associates Vigo with Miguel Almereyda and anarchism. The Belgian critic's remarks are more comprehensive, even though they give the impression of being derived from the French book. Both regret Vigo's premature death and the hope it destroyed. As to the films, both histories summarized the commonly accepted views. Vincent, speaking of the "melancholy poetry" of *Zéro de Conduite*, might seem in advance of the critics of his time, were it not for the fact that the expression turns up rather too frequently in his book as an almost automatic formula.

Bardèche and Brasillach in their *Histoire du Cinéma*, published in 1935, wrote: "*A Propos de Nice*, full of a superb cruelty analogous to von Stroheim's, in which Vigo's camera lingers on old harridans, on grotesques, on caricatures of human beings, but also on the graceful beauty of this bay given over to capitalism. *Zéro de Conduite* . . . remarkable gesture of revolt, of sarcastic, humiliated and fun-loving youth . . . heart-rending sincerity, his painful memories. *L'Atalante* . . . it was obvious that he could barely tell a story, and he handles his plot clumsily. . . . But right from the beginning, with the sad caricature of a wedding, one felt the dark tone of tragic buffoonery characteristic of this young man, doomed from the day he was born, who could perhaps have become the Rimbaud or the Céline of the French cinema."

Carl Vincent, in his *Histoire de l'Art Cinématographique*, published in 1939, writes of the "desperate, satirical, cruel, and revolutionary tone of his films. . . . *A Propos de Nice* mingles a romantic evocation . . . with ferocious social caricature. Sarcasm exists side by side with poetry, and human absurdity with a tender love of light. His sharp, brutal vision reveals an acute sense of cinema. *Taris* was merely a short, straightforward documentary on swimming. . . . *Zéro de Conduite* . . . bitter anarchy . . . caustic 'fantasy', full of violence, irony, tenderness, and symbolism. His images revolved around extraordinarily vivid caricatures, painful memories of his childhood humiliations, and a pleasingly melancholy poetry. . . . *L'Atalante* . . . a strange, overpowering atmosphere. Tragedy mingled with farce, 'inner pathos' with caricature. This strange mixture revealed a profound compassion . . . plot awkwardly unfolded. . . . Yet, right from the very beginning—a caricatured wedding party observed with melancholy poetry— Vigo managed to capture his audience. The biting force of the images then broadens out into a deep sensuality and a great visual beauty. Several sequences are endowed with a dramatic power by their extreme bitterness, their appeal to troubled emotions."

The Académie du Film had been founded in 1935 in France, by Germaine Dulac among others. Like its American counterpart it was to award prizes. It did so once. Among the prizes was the "Jean Vigo," to be awarded to "a courageous, even though flawed, work"; in 1939 this was presented to Christian Jaque for his *Les Disparus de Saint-Agil*. That same year, Jean Painlevé had hoped to found a Club des Amis de Jean Vigo, an idea which pleased Lydou, but which never got anywhere. Lydou Jean Vigo (as she now called herself), while caring for her daughter Luce, was busily trying to preserve Vigo's artistic legacy; and, encouraged by her sister Genya who had become an enthusiastic militant, she sometimes worked for Communist-inspired organizations such as the Société des Amis de la Nation Polonaise, created in 1936 around the personality of Paul Langevin. However, all these activities could not fill the great vacuum in her life. On April 24, 1939, the last wish of her delirium was granted. Lydou was buried on the twenty-sixth, and her friends—some of them for the third time—travelled the road that led to Almereyda's grave in the Bagneux cemetery.

In that same year, *L'Atalante* (which version?) was shown at the Basle Festival, and the screening resulted in an article by Siegfried Kracauer, subsequently published in English in both the United States and England.[25] The German critic speaks about all of Vigo's films and compares them to René Clair. According to Kracauer, Vigo has none of "René Clair's wonderful lightness," but surpasses him in his "profound concern with truth."

The first phase in the career of Vigo's work ends during the first months of the German Occupation, with the re-release of *L'Atalante* already mentioned in discussing the different attempts made to reconstruct the original film.

In the meantime, Vigo's films—with the exception of *A Propos de Nice*—had become the property of Henri Beauvais. After the first few weeks of the Occupation, the cinemas reopened their doors. The end of imports from America, the small number of German films available, and the slow resumption of production in France, meant a dearth of films: the market was therefore wide open for reissues. Beauvais, however, wanted to make the revival of Vigo's last film seem like the release of a new film. In this he was encouraged and helped by Dita Parlo, whose name remained associated with the spectacular success of *La Grande Illusion*. In the latter film she played a German peasant girl who hides two French officers during the First World War, one of them Jewish. She becomes the other officer's mistress, an action not quite in keeping with the official ideology of the occupying forces. It may well be that the Franco-German star was faced with the problem of effacing this memory by identifying herself with another film. Dita Parlo felt that *L'Atalante* was a good film which was not likely to jeopardize her career in the new European political situation. It was therefore vital to her that the re-release should be an important event, and having no very high opinion of *Le Chaland qui passe*, Dita Parlo must have felt that the restoration of the original version was a necessary first step.

Beauvais, for his part, had been disappointed commercially by *Le Chaland qui passe*. He hired some unknown person to replace the sections of Jaubert's music which had been removed and to restore the cuts which had been preserved; and, banking on the prestige which the film had acquired among film enthusiasts in spite of everything, he rebaptized it *L'Atalante* and programmed it for the reopening of the Studio des Ursulines on October 30, 1940.

Even if it is not easy to determine exactly what this version contained, prints of it circulating after the Liberation show that it was distinctly better than *Le Chaland qui passe*: among others, the scenes of the lovers' insomnia and the showing of the phonograph to Jean had been reinstated.

Although the results were not as successful as had been hoped, this partial resurrection of *L'Atalante* did not by any means pass unnoticed. The evening before it opened, *L'Œuvre* wrote: "It will be interesting to see how this curious work, which came before its time as far as the general public was concerned, will be received in this cinema by an audience which has been described as the most understanding in the world." Two days later the same paper published a two-column article on the event signed "G.D.," probably the initials of Germaine Decaris. The article was a homage to Vigo and an account of his films, linked to an examination of the problem of censorship as it presented itself at the end of 1940.

G.D. started by saying that Vigo's death had been greeted by the film censors with a sigh of relief, "for Vigo gave offence." There followed a list of his offences. *A Propos de Nice*: "A lampoon crammed with home truths."

Zéro de Conduite: "A nightmare on film, and all the closer to reality for that. The winds of every conceivable freedom blow through this *Zéro*." *L'Atalante*: "Not only gave offence, but frightened. In it, did we not see—this in 1934— lines of unemployed workers, frozen, rubbing their hands together, being watched by the police? It was maintained at the time that nothing in the film was lost, that all the cuts could be restored. . . . Walking behind Vigo's coffin, a tiny handful of us, we were thinking that we would never have any other evidence of his admirable talent and courage. *L'Atalante* can be and must be restored to us, we told ourselves. We have had to wait six years to see it again. The film, now finally restored, and which it is not the business of this article to analyse, offers us proof of the incredible stupidity of 'those good citizens of 1934'."[26]

A few days later the paper's chief critic, Jean Laffray, wrote an article of his own on *L'Atalante* and on censorship: "Jean Vigo was one of their victims, and the Board of Censors, now happily abolished—but is it true that the Vichy regime is planning a new one?—did not hesitate to mutilate his last film, *L'Atalante*. Seeing it now in its original form, one wonders what subversion the censors could possibly have found in it. Yet, remembering who belonged to that Areopagus assembled under the vaulted ceilings of the Palais-Royal, one can hardly be surprised at their flagrant misunderstanding of the film. But that is another story."

These two articles reveal the whole-hearted acceptance of yet another myth: that the censors had mutilated *L'Atalante*. Nino Frank, in an article published in *Les Nouveaux Temps*, brought out the true facts by recalling that the producers had actually been responsible.[27] His article is the most important of those which appeared at the time and remains of real historical interest. Frank tries to give a general assessment of all of Vigo's works with the exception of *Taris*. His article is full of insights which only make the narrowness of his assumptions all the more obvious. The case of Nino Frank is final corroboration that the incomprehension with which Vigo's films met at first cannot be explained by blaming the mediocrity of the critics. Nino Frank is by no means mediocre as a film critic. Besides, he is warmly sympathetic to Vigo and his films, and he attempts—and largely succeeds— in making a personal assessment of both. Frank's article is certainly much better than most of those hitherto published, but he did not escape the narrow bounds which held sway at the time. Like so many critics before— and unfortunately after—him, he describes Vigo's three films as, "Three first steps, three attempts before learning to walk." Despite his real sensitivity to cinematic poetry, Nino Frank sees it only in *L'Atalante*. In *Zéro de Conduite*, he barely suspects its presence. And he asks: "What did Jean Vigo lack to make his first big feature an outstanding film?" One of Frank's answers is: "The dialogue in *L'Atalante* is banal." This leads him into a lengthy discussion of the problems of film writing, and his concluding remarks reveal what he was really after. For he suggests that French cinema, in order to bring about a renewal, should call on the services of Henri Jeanson as screenplay and dialogue writer. The possibility that Frank was doing a favour for a friend should not blind us to a phenomenon which takes us, illuminatingly, right back to the heart of the matter. The fact that critics during this first phase were so insensitive to the quality of Vigo's dialogue has often aroused comment. One tentative explanation was the poor quality of the sound, but now we have a much more substantial one. Critics for whom good film dialogue was exemplified by films such as *Entrée des Artistes, Hôtel du Nord* or *Quai des Brumes*, could not help but reject the dialogue in *Zéro de Conduite* and *L'Atalante* even if, or rather especially if, it had been clearly audible.

In Nino Frank's article, as well as those by G.D. and Jean Laffray, there seems to be an implication that during the Third Republic the climate had been very much less favourable towards Jean Vigo and his work—and indeed towards the French cinema in general—than it was likely to be under the German Occupation. This view, even without counting those who kept an enforced silence and were probably outraged to see Vigo's works being annexed by Marcel Déat's *L'Œuvre* or Jean Luchaire's *Les Nouveaux Temps*, was not a widely held one. The reaction of François Vinneuil, who had made his reputation before the war as film critic for *L'Action Française*, was diametrically opposed to his colleagues from the collaborationist press whom we have cited.

"A few fragments of *L'Atalante* reveal a savage power which would certainly have found better use had Jean Vigo lived. But the film as a whole plods along with infuriating slowness. Made less than five years ago, it looks as archaic and old-fashioned as the avant-garde experiments of the 1920s.

"Its muddled aestheticism and its sordid atmosphere make it more than anything else an example of 'degenerate' art.

"*L'Atalante* may still cause film historians or curiosity seekers to linger a moment. But its public re-release is hardly a major event."[28]

The articles on *L'Atalante* published in the collaborationist press do not necessarily reflect the actual political controversies of the time. In fact, in the article which appeared in *Aujourd'hui*, signed "A. F.," no reference is made to them. The author overflows with admiration for *L'Atalante*, and he himself emerges as one of those spectators he mentions in his article as amazed by "the overabundant richness of the film."[29] *L'Atalante* remained at the Ursulines for three weeks, until November 19, 1940, and was mainly seen by students returning to school for the first time under the Occupation. It seems that the film subsequently had respectable runs in neighbourhood theatres. No information is available on its distribution in the occupied provinces or in Vichy France.

So ends the first phase in the career of Vigo's films. To summarize the prevalent attitudes towards Vigo: people were full of respect for what he could have become; regretted that he was unable to do more than begin his work; and placed a good deal of emphasis on the supposedly avant-garde defects of his films. Apart from France, his films had become more or less known in Belgium, Holland, England, and Switzerland. For several years people were preoccupied with other things or were simply interested in other films; and it was not until 1945 that Vigo's films again set out on their modest and difficult reconquest of an audience.

An Appendix traces the development of this new stage in the critical appraisal and success of his work. Suffice it to say here that in 1945, bringing the wheel full circle, the tendency to associate Vigo with Almereyda had become a habit in the press. Bardèche and Brasillach spoke of "Almereyda's son," and their book, republished during the Occupation and after the Liberation, had become the principal source of reference for most of the new generation of film critics and reviewers. But whereas the mere mention of Almereyda spoke volumes for Bardèche and Brasillach, and for François Vinneuil, all of whom had been associated with *L'Action Française*, the name meant nothing to most of the young journalists who now came across it, and they had to drum up some vague and sketchy information. In other words, each time the names of Almereyda and Vigo were associated after the Liberation—and it happened very frequently—it was always done without much heed to historical truth, Francis Jourdain being the single exception.

Vigo himself had never forgotten his father or his desire to rehabilitate his name. It was to the memory of the young Almereyda of *Le Libertaire* and *La Guerre Sociale* that he was principally attached. All he retained from the *Bonnet Rouge* confusion was Almereyda's pacifism, his defence of Romain Rolland, and the memory of a victim of a cowardly assassination. The only time Vigo's close friends ever saw his face transfigured with hate was on the rare occasions when he spoke of his father's death. Almereyda's influence on Vigo exerted itself on a purely emotional level.

The emotional aspect of Jean de Saint-Prix's influence on Vigo was also important, but here there was also a considerable intellectual influence. During the time he spent reading while at Font-Romeu, Jean de Saint-Prix's works probably took pride of place. He must have had difficulty with Saint-Prix's philosophical writings, but was compensated by the plays, stories, articles and, especially, the collection of letters prefaced by Romain Rolland. (In one of these letters, Jean de Saint-Prix told of meeting Jean Vigo as a child in 1917.) Turning back to Rolland's preface today, it is not difficult to establish a kinship between Jean de Saint-Prix's ideas and Vigo's work. "The revolutionary spirit is and must be only one of the many motivating forces, which, taken together, create within us an impulse towards a new immensity, towards a *vita nuova* based on reality or on dream, which expresses the best in each of us.

"Like art, science, and charity, social revolutions contribute to the deification of our universe, which is the proper role for mankind here on earth."[30]

Vigo re-read the letters several times and reflected deeply on Jean de Saint-Prix's ideas. Afterwards, one must remember, he had little time to read and receive fresh influences.

Vigo was only twelve when he lost his father and when he saw Jean de Saint-Prix for the first and last time. Yet, a living embodiment of both men's ideas existed in Fernand Desprès, who for this reason probably exerted a considerable personal influence on Vigo.

Coupled with Vigo's libertarian spirit was his sympathetic attitude towards the Third International. The fact that the reactionary polemics and confusion of the last years of the war had put the Almereyda of 1917 into the same pigeon-hole as Lenin and Trotsky[31] was not likely to displease Vigo. Jean de Saint-Prix, who had welcomed the Bolshevik Revolution of 1917, joined the Etudiants Socialistes Révolutionnaires, supporters of the Third International, just before his death, early in 1919. As for Fernand Desprès, like many of Almereyda's old friends he had joined the Communist Party when it was founded. All these interacting influences were enough to make Vigo sympathetic to Communism, although not enough to make him a party member. Vigo knew about the party primarily through Fernand Desprès, who, while remaining a party member until his death,[32] never gave up an independence of mind which certainly made his career as a newspaperman on *L'Humanité* more difficult. His attachment to the principles of revolutionary syndicalism, a movement to which he had given so much of himself, made him seem reactionary to the ambitious younger staff members of *L'Humanité* in 1926. Despite the respect due to him because of his exemplary internationalist position during the war, as well as the fact that both Gabriel Péri and Paul Vaillant-Couturier admired him, he was nevertheless not immune from the intrigues which were rife in the party and among the paper's staff. Fernand Desprès complained to his friends about "those doctrinaire discussions during which the expression of any view not conforming to perpetually changing ideological nuances can lead to your being called a *petty bourgeois* or to accusations of being a *left-deviationist.*"[33]

This only increased Fernand Desprès' nostalgia for the movement created during the war. One day, someone in a café walked over to ask him if he had not been a friend of Jean de Saint-Prix, and he remarked immediately afterwards in a letter how proud he had been to be associated in the stranger's mind with "that charming youngster and fearless fighter."[34]

Fernand Desprès did everything he could not to renege on his new faith, and he succeeded: "For you are either for the Russian Revolution or against it. Romain Rolland gives Martinet, Dunois, Istrati, and the other detractors of Red Russia an excellent lesson in political lucidity when he writes that whatever one may think, present-day Russia is *sacred* because she is the Revolution."[35]

Finally Fernand Desprès achieved a certain stability as editor of the paper's coverage of the courts for many years. In that capacity he noted that another tradition of the working-class movement had been abandoned by the Communist Party. Until then, the workers' press had not used sensational crimes and headline stories as bait for its readers. Fernand Desprès used to prepare his copy carefully, make it lively, subtle, social, centred on the class struggle. "It is hardly ever used. They prefer simple news stories to a column on the courts, which is absurd. One could understand it if the paper were *Popu.*"[36]

Fernand Desprès' general state of mind, and the frankness, sometimes touched with melancholy, with which he spoke of his life with his young friends, were not compatible with the work of recruiting future party members. His horizons were much broader than those of a militant. Besides being a witness of a past which had directly affected his own life, Fernand Desprès must have struck Vigo as an exemplar of the traditional revolutionary virtues.

Vigo was sympathetic to Soviet Russia and the Communist movement only insofar as he felt they had inherited some of these virtues. However, there was nothing exclusive about his sympathies, which went also to other leftist movements, ranging from socialism to anarchism. When he drew up the press list for *Zéro de Conduite*, Vigo did not overlook the humblest of those revolutionary sheets, read by a mere handful of people, which always flourish in Paris.

Vigo's independence of mind hardly facilitated political discussions with Communist activists of his generation. Among his immediate friends, the activists were represented by Lydou's sister, Genya, and her companion Marek, with whom Vigo had some spectacular arguments which mutual friends never forgot.

As a sympathizer, Vigo agreed to join the Association des Ecrivains et Artistes Révolutionnaires, founded on December 13, 1932 by Vaillant-Couturier, Barbusse, Léon Moussinac, and Francis Jourdain.

Vigo's last political stance, taken a few days before he was finally confined to bed just before his death, perhaps sums up his political attitudes. It concerned a document which he signed, together with other artists and intellectuals, after the fascist-inspired riots of February 6, 1934.[37] It was an appeal for a united working-class front, addressed chiefly to the following organizations: The Communist Party, The Young Communists' League, the C. G. T. U., the workers' and peasants' federation, the Socialist Party, the S. F. I. O., the Young Socialists, the Young Socialist Guards, the C. G. T., the United Proletariat Party, the Union of Communists, the Anarchists' Union, the Communist League (Trotskyite), the Communist Democratic Circle, etc.

Vigo's last act brings him even closer to the young Almereyda who had worked indefatigably to reconcile and unify all the factions of the revolutionary movement. And this identification between father and son is given the final touch by the presence, alongside Jean Vigo's signature, of two names from the first chapter of this story: Pierre Monatte and Elie Faure. The first was signatory with Almereyda to a revolutionary manifesto in 1902, and the second had subscribed to the expenses of Almereyda's trip to Amsterdam in 1904. The circle thus closes, and the end of this chronicle of the life and works of Eugène Bonaventure de Vigo, known as Miguel Almereyda, and of his son, Jean Vigo, is at hand. The characters did not have happy lives. Almereyda, Vigo and Lydou died young, and are together in the Parisian cemetery of Bagneux. Emily, in the course of the story, became a shadow, having suffered much. The conclusion, however, is not one of despair. Vigo never was able to undertake the rehabilitation of Almereyda. But he was faithful to the better part of his father's life, and the legacy of his stay in this world is some thirteen thousand feet of film which will spread their riches among us for years to come, and a young woman proud to bear the name of Vigo.

Jean Vigo and Lydou in the village of Maurecourt during the filming of *L'Atalante*

Appendix: The Critical Success and Impact of Vigo's Works

The euphoria of the Liberation led to the reissue of *Zéro de Conduite*, and it opened at the Panthéon in November 1945, on the same bill with Malraux's *L'Espoir*.

On November 17, a headline in a sensation-mongering weekly read: "*Banned for twelve years, a dead man's film disappoints its admirers*: Jean Vigo was the son of the notorious Almereyda. . . . He dropped his father's name and made a reputation in avant-garde cinema by filming documentaries. His first feature has been eagerly awaited. Unfortunately the version being shown has been so massively cut that it is difficult to judge."[1]

A few days later the following response resulted: "*Samedi Soir* can be reproached for one thing only: deliberately seeking the sensational in its headlines. And the phrase, 'a dead man's film,' is a disturbing one. Perhaps because we are among Jean Vigo's admirers, we have just seen *Zéro de Conduite*, and *Zéro de Conduite* did not prove so terribly disappointing. Despite the cuts."[2]

On the same day, *L'Ecran Français* spoke of a "Grand première," and added: "Actually, *Zéro de Conduite* was banned after its first screening for rather vague reasons: obscenity, anti-social attitude. In fact, it is quite possible that the motives were less obvious, for Jean Vigo was the son of Almereyda, the Almereyda of *Le Bonnet Rouge*. . . ."

This is already enough to show that the legend of the cuts was still very much current. A few shots may have been missing, and possibly cuts had been made at the beginning of the scene in the refectory, but on the whole, as far as can be determined, the version shown in 1945 was not essentially different from that shown in 1933.

A whole group of sympathetic critics barely managed to hide their disappointment. On the front page of the next issue of *L'Ecran Français*, accompanied by three frame enlargements from the film, Pierre Bost wrote: "The general public is at last being allowed to see that celebrated and yet unknown film, Jean Vigo's *Zéro de Conduite*. The film is now more than ten years old, and was banned by the censors at birth; since that time, admirers of Jean Vigo and of the cinema—who are one and the same, and by the same token enemies of censorship—have surreptitiously screened the film for each other and talked about it endlessly.

"We were right to talk about it. Now everyone can see it. I will not say that the battle has been won. First, because it is too late: Jean Vigo died at the age of twenty-nine after a difficult career, encouraged and aided only by his friends, which is not enough in the cinema. Not won also because it is not easy to judge a ten-year-old film (the print, it seems, is in imperfect condition and incomplete), and above all because we will never know what Jean Vigo would have done next, what skills and what lessons he would have learned from his own victory. But the most moving thing about *Zéro de Conduite*, perhaps better than the film itself, better even than this discovery of a past, is precisely this image of a future which would never be realized."[3]

Didier Daix made no attempt to conceal his disappointment. "*Zéro de Conduite* has finally been released for public showing. It is about time. Much too late, as a matter of fact. The years have gone by, the film has aged, and the dynamite it once contained no longer explodes. No, the hoped-for vindication will not occur. I am not even sure whether it would not have been kinder to the memory of dear, departed Jean Vigo, who died before he was able to complete a body of work of remarkable promise, to have left us with the memories we had of a film which in its time made well-mannered Dame Censorship tremble with indignation.

"Unfortunately, all that remains of what was once an anarchist bomb is an often baffling little sketch, made with an old-fashioned technique which seems almost amateurish, and whose audacities are no longer terribly audacious."[4]

So far we have only quoted those parts of the articles by Pierre Bost and Didier Daix expressing a feeling of sadness and disappointment. Other passages reveal that, despite their feelings, they share in a new attitude towards Vigo's work, a new phase characterized by the fact that critics were no longer responding to only one dimension of *Zéro de Conduite* as they had in 1933.

In 1933 the critics had responded only to the "black" side of the film, and during Vigo's lifetime they were totally insensitive to its poetry, whatever the colour. It was only after 1945 that the poetry in *Zéro de Conduite* began to be evident.

In the first part of his article, Pierre Bost remains true to the tone of 1933 in referring to a film "full of bitterness, harsh in its irony, lucid in its disillusionment." Later on, however, he is sensitive to the new riches revealed by *Zéro de Conduite*: "Don't imagine it is a black film. On the contrary, it is joyous, full of brilliant gags and an incredible, teeming richness of invention which is all too rare in France. . . . A word should also be said about its touch of poetry (a much abused term) which suddenly bursts out, almost disturbingly, during the uprising in the dormitory."

Similarly Didier Daix, after the initial disenchantment already quoted, advises readers to see *Zéro de Conduite* "to discover the spirit, the nonconformity and the poetry with which the heart of this revolutionary film-maker was so full."

For most of the newcomers to love of the cinema, the first revelation of *Zéro de Conduite* was essentially poetic; and the term, never mentioned in the articles of 1933, is used constantly: "Intense poetic force";[5] "a vision both poetic and ferocious";[6] "a poetic sense of humour";[7] "gags, whose intense poetry . . .";[8] "A deliciously poetic satire";[9] "a magnificent poem of childhood. . . . The poetry is Vigo's, the coarseness is in the words themselves, like *Monsieur, can he go?*",[10] etc.

We are far from the impression of vulgarity, excess and despair left by the film twelve years earlier. The comparison with Céline, still found in the Bardèche and Brasillach book, no longer crops up anywhere.

One critic writing in 1945, going to the opposite extreme, even manages to see *Zéro de Conduite* as no more than an amiable fantasy. "Why don't people take things more easily? Why don't they forget about understanding and let themselves be carried into the marvellous world which any director of genius creates for us: a world in which teachers imitate Chaplin and do handstands on one hand on their desks during classes, a world inhabited by people who suddenly walk in slow-motion without being aware of it, a world in which cartoons come to life, in which firemen have beards, and professors wear nightshirts which are too short for them. The real world of cinema [inhabited by] . . . Jean Vigo and René Clair, Méliès, Renoir, and the director of *Monsieur Coccinelle.*"[11]

A reaction to this tendency did not take long to develop. "And these kids wash, play, study, have fights with ordinary, everyday words and gestures; but we are being misled. The real subject of the film is elsewhere, and it is black. We see a schoolboy rag, a teacher tied to his bed, school chums smoking cigars in a hiding-place, and we must hear what Vigo, rightly or wrongly, is crying out all through the film: 'Don't be misled by what we seem to be; we children are terribly alone, you adults are never there, and if you are, it makes things worse. We must therefore consider you as null and void.'"[12]

Here and there, however, the different aspects of *Zéro de Conduite* begin to be described with more precision. The existence of two separate worlds in *Zéro de Conduite* is acknowledged, though without any real understanding of their exact nature or of the boundary between them. For Georges Marigny, there are "two sorts of characters, two clans. On one side, the shirt with the stiff collar, the nicely painted façade with a worm-eaten interior, an arbitrary stupidity: an ill-tempered teacher, a cunning head supervisor, a grotesque principal, and all those Aunt Sally targets at the back of the platform on the school commemoration day.

"On the other side of the barrier erected by the rules, an amiable, lady-killing junior master, a fervent admirer of Chaplin (this is the period of *City Lights*), leads an unforgettable band of children."[13] Another critic writes: "When compared with these precise, tough children, the adults live in a strange fantasy world; which is why, whatever they do, their actions are absurd and inexplicable, their manner unreal, their reproaches and their praise beyond comprehension. The dialogue itself, unabashedly crude between the children, becomes elliptical with the adults."[14]

Even better, the critic who signs himself Captain Blood: "The theme of the film is not in its plot; it is concerned with other things, which explains why the film is so disturbing. Now, there seems to me to be a basically very simple reason for this ambiguity: everything to do with children is presented to us with a realism so extraordinarily stark that it lacerates the screen; everything to do with adults, on the other hand—but nothing else—is constantly distorted by being viewed deliberately but not gratuitously from a special angle. . . . The dialogue itself, astonishingly true with the children, becomes strange and jerky when spoken by the adults."[15] Yet another critic: "A boarding-school gives a child his first experience of the constraints of social life; for him, the world then divides itself into two groups, the teachers and the oppressed. Jean Vigo, the son of an anarchist, naturally finds himself on the side of the oppressed."[16]

"It is true that for Vigo the school is little more than a substitute for society," André Bazin notes.[17] Social satire, Maurice Legay writes, "can be found in Vigo, and it is neither sweet nor sour; it has something strange, disquieting, puzzling about it, which provokes the sort of uneasiness which antagonized the censor."[18] Such was the path taken by the new French film critics in exploring *Zéro de Conduite*.

Another striking thing about the articles written in 1945–6 is the ease with which the critics, unlike those writing in 1933, recognized Vigo's authenticity and the truth with which he bore witness: "These children . . . every one of them in his own way is a little

Vigo."[19] "Vigo is not playing. He has a work to offer us, derived from a vision which may be worthwhile or may not but is authentically his own, and he proceeds to offer it to us. . . . As we watch the boy silently bow his head under the insults showered on his mother, how can one help but recall that Vigo was the son of the Almereyda of *Le Bonnet Rouge*?"[20] "Thus, the loneliness which fills him, he who was the son of an outlaw."[21]

This knowledge of a few facts about Vigo's life is not the only way the critics determined the personal sincerity of Vigo's work. *Zéro de Conduite* has another way of establishing its authenticity, by compelling critics to explore their own childhood memories. "One has to have been a boarder oneself . . . to evaluate the truthfulness with which Vigo has depicted the absurd atmosphere of the 'dump.'"[22] "Jean Vigo has given his scenes from school life an authenticity which is at times hallucinatory; we are faced by the ghosts and shadows of our own childhood."[23] "An astonishing sense of accuracy."[24] "These images from childhood which have wandered into the film from our own memories are unforgettable."[25] "*We* are those children."[26] "The bureaucrats with their stiff collars are playground supervisors to the life."[27] "Those of us who still cherish childhood memories will recognize the truthfulness with which the 'dump' (and all 'dumps' are alike) is depicted in *Zéro de Conduite*."[28] "Neither Angels with Dirty Faces nor Nightingales, his children are terribly true to life."[29] "*Emil und die Detektive* and *Zéro de Conduite*, the charmingly phony and the world as it is, side by side."[30]

The last two quotations reveal a phenomenon which occurs frequently in the reviews: critics feel impelled to compare *Zéro de Conduite* to other films about children, and the latter pale to insignificance beside the truth of Vigo's vision. "We are a long way beyond the sweet little boarders of most films, and the little Germans in *Emil und die Detektive* (a good film, though) seem by comparison rather cute and sentimental."[31] "We are a long way from *Emil und die Detektive, Nous les Gosses* or *La Cage aux Rossignols*. Charming films, all of them, but rather conventional despite their timid attempts at audacity."[32] "But *Zéro de Conduite* has real sincerity; it has nothing in common with *Merlusse, Les Disparus de Saint-Agil* or *La Cage aux Rossignols*."[33] "Take *Les Disparus de Saint-Agil*, for instance. A poetic story told by a good story-teller. The images are quite anonymous; the camera lines them up mechanically, unfolding a story which has children as its object, not its subject. The child's vision never shapes the images; the child is not the creator of the world to be filmed, merely something in it. The images here play a role which is more or less the cinematic equivalent of type in printing."[34] And an enthusiast writes: "This dead man [Vigo] is more alive than the majority of his living colleagues. His ghost marches ahead of them, in the vanguard."[35]

Towards the end of 1945, it was noted that *Zéro de Conduite* was enthusiastically acclaimed at the Panthéon cinema by an audience composed largely of university students.[36] A few years later, in 1950, one reads: "After being banned for fifteen years,[37] *Zéro de Conduite* has finally found its true audience. Jean Vigo's film has not aged; on the contrary, it remains as explosive as it was in 1933."[38]

This last statement is an exaggeration. Nevertheless, between the dates of these last two press reviews, between 1945 and 1950, *Zéro de Conduite* continued to meet obstacles in pursuance of its career. At times one gets the impression that the film had become accepted in France (except by the ecclesiastical censors) by everybody concerned in one way or another with the cinema; but then something crops up to prove that "the dynamite it once contained" is not, as Didier Daix thought, completely defused. In February 1946, for instance, concurrently with the exhibitions commemorating the fiftieth anniversary of the cinema in which Vigo figured prominently,[39] thanks partly to the recent reissue of *Zéro de Conduite*, one could read that in Montpellier, "M. Spitzer, director of the University halls of residence, has prohibited the screening of Jean Vigo's

Zéro de Conduite to his students."[40] During the winter of 1949–50, the University of Paris, with the collaboration of the French Institute at Innsbruck, showed *Zéro de Conduite* to young Austrians, Germans and Italians attending the University colloquia at Saint-Christophe de l'Arlberg, while at the same time in Paris a member of the Chamber of Deputies challenged the government over a decision made by a prefect forbidding the screening of *Zéro de Conduite* in a provincial film society.

After 1946 it was mostly in film societies throughout France that *Zéro de Conduite* pursued its career, as well as in art theatres and at the Musée du Cinéma in Paris. There was nothing triumphal about the film's progress. *Zéro de Conduite* continued to win admirers very slowly, but the main thing was that the process was a continuing one. One reviewer, after attending a showing at a film society, wrote: "I must confess that I don't see anything to get excited about in *Zéro de Conduite*. A divertissement by a soured schoolboy, a satire which is too nasty to be funny." He is probably right when he adds: "And I'm happy not to be alone in thinking so."[41] It is even likely that most of the audience felt as he did. Not infrequently in film societies, where films were often graded after a discussion, the results were similar to those at Boulogne-sur-Mer: "Four points for *Zéro de Conduite*, and a full ten points for *L'Atalante*."[42] Often, too, it was noted that "quite distinct hostility was expressed by the members towards a film in which very few of them did not detect an allegory of society."[43] In Lyons, J. P. Marquet was struck by "a sort of hostility, at times virulent, at times repressed, which greeted two sessions in which Jean Vigo's films were shown."[44] The reasons for this hostility vary, but it happened constantly; which did not, however, prevent the film society from programming the film again the next season—and one realizes that the film had time on its side.

Sometimes misinterpretation lay behind the failure to understand. For example, the organizer of a "Saison d'Histoire du Cinéma" at Casablanca, taking his cue from the Bardèche and Brasillach history, did his best to ascribe common characteristics to the works of Vigo and Rimbaud, thus provoking a vehement reaction from Pierre Rosselot: "It seems rather wilful to try to present this young film-maker as the 'Rimbaud of the cinema.' Being slightly anarchistic and having a taste for poetry does not make a Rimbaud; it takes those fulminating insights of which the poet from the Ardennes had the secret. One must be a poet."[45]

Zéro de Conduite continued on its own only for a few months after it was released. After that *L'Atalante* began to be shown again, then *Taris*, and much more rarely, *A Propos de Nice*. Henceforth, audiences were offered Vigo's work as a whole—with the exception of *A Propos de Nice*—often in a single screening, or at least within the course of a single film-society season.

Considering the place Vigo's work occupies in French film culture and the positive reactions of French film critics after 1945, it is an astonishing fact that foreigners often believe that Jean Vigo has never achieved the recognition he deserves in his native country.

In 1947 an Italian critic wrote that "the French have forgotten him,"[46] and two Americans in 1951 said, "Jean Vigo is probably the least known and most neglected of all the great French directors."[47]

The explanation for these statements is that foreign commentators must have turned for documentation to "establishment" criticism—as manifested by the books and major periodicals which were readily accessible—which scarcely reflected the real reactions of French audiences to Vigo's work. For by now a second stage in the appreciation of Vigo's films was well under way, and "establishment" criticism tends to look like a relic of the first phase. Its practitioners were usually contemporary with Vigo, and this had become a handicap. It is noticeable that, after 1945, the articles expressing an entirely favourable attitude towards Vigo's work are written by young people just discovering him. And there is a significant difference between these generations: for the old critics, Vigo might have been; to the young, he is. A few older people have been able (as one sees in film societies and at the Cinémathèque), to look at the films with new eyes after repeated viewings, but they are almost never film critics or historians.

To understand the disappointment of a modern spectator looking to the proper sources for information or for a good exposition of his feelings about the films, one need only glance at some samples from the "establishment" critics.

Both Bardèche and Brasillach and Vincent, through reprints and translations, remained the sources most often consulted. We have already given some indication of how mildly interested in Vigo they were.

In Georges Charensol's *Panorama du Cinéma*, published early in 1930, Vigo could hardly have been included. But Charensol reprinted his book in 1947 in an "augmented, illustrated version, brought up to date by Lo Duca and Maurice Bessy."[48] Here, therefore, we have the contribution of three critics. It is short and limited to *L'Atalante*: "Its strange atmosphere and its mixture of comic and tragic make it one of the most curious works of the French cinema."

Marcel Lapierre, after mentioning *A Propos de Nice*, and giving a brief résumé of *Zéro de Conduite* and *L'Atalante* which refers to the symbolism of the characters in *L'Atalante*, speaks of Vigo's death and concludes by saying: "With him disappeared one of the great hopes of the French cinema."

Georges Sadoul is a good deal less summary than his colleagues. Sometimes, when he is moved by Vigo's poetry, which, as he says of *Zéro de Conduite*, "exhibits a rare quality in the revolt in the dormitory," Sadoul seems quite modern in his taste. However, the spectator who was an adult in the thirties soon rears his head, revealing that he has not subsequently studied his Vigo very well.[49] About *A Propos de Nice*, Sadoul writes: "The film is dated now by its aestheticism and the naïve sexual symbolism of some of its images and analogies." If, as seems likely, Sadoul is thinking of the chimneys at the end, then it is the observer who is dated in seeing the chimneys as no more than a sexual symbol, thus losing sight of their essential nature as chimneys and their complementary aspect as revolutionary cannons.

Discussing *Zéro de Conduite*, Sadoul gives some information about Vigo which is valid when vague ("Jean Vigo put his memories of his own troubled childhood into *Zéro de Conduite*"), and untrue when more precise ("the anarchist Almereyda, strangled to death by Clemenceau's police," or "young Vigo, shunned by his schoolmates, who called him 'the son of a traitor'").

Sadoul does not limit himself to the social implications of *Zéro de Conduite*. "This tragic childhood explains the bitterness in *Zéro de Conduite*. The film is in effect a transcription of the song the boys sing: *To the pyre with the books, and the teacher with them.* . . . The film is an anarchistic call to children to take over from the adults, but more particularly it represents the almost flayed memories and the dreams of a persecuted child." Sadoul feels that the film was influenced by Chaplin and Buñuel, and detects a surrealist influence in *L'Atalante* as well. "Some sequences are rather overloaded: the 'act' in the dance hall by Margaritis the clown, Michel Simon's antics in his surrealistic den complete with automatons and amputated hands, the sailor swimming underwater in the canal and seeing the face of his vanished wife there. . . .

"Vigo is more affecting when he forgets the literary fashions of 1933 and describes unadorned reality: the canal bank as a touchingly grotesque wedding party wends its way along it, a desolate suburban landscape, life aboard the barge, a shop dealing in phonographs." Sadoul mentions phonographs, but only in reference to a shop. That oversight is less pardonable than the rest of his remarks.

His conclusion is an expression of regret, and here Sadoul rejoins his "establishment" colleagues. "These excellent films, with their roots in the avant-garde documentary, make one deplore the fact that Vigo died at the age of twenty-nine, leaving behind him the promise of films which would have surpassed those of the greatest of his contemporaries."

If we now pass on to the major periodicals, both those specifically concerned with film and the literary magazines which sometimes discussed film at length, it is impossible to find anything in France to compare with the seriousness of research or depth of understanding one sees in Italian or English periodicals of the same period.[50]

The Fédération Française des Ciné-Clubs, the principal medium for the circulation of Vigo's films, devoted an entire issue of its journal, *Ciné-Club*, to a discussion of his work.[51] Even here one is struck by the silence of French critics, not one of whom appears in the Table of Contents, where we find only the names of Vigo's friends: Claude Aveline, Francis Jourdain, Jean Painlevé, Boris Kaufman. The volume does, however, include the first good Vigo filmography.[52] This collection of articles has both the virtues and the vices which go hand in hand with this sort of homage. There is a great deal of useful first-hand information about the man and about the creation of his work; in fact, this issue of *Ciné-Club* was an invaluable guide in undertaking the present task of retracing the lives of Miguel Almereyda and Jean Vigo. Since that journey is now completed, the guide may be left behind and criticized. Jean Painlevé's evaluation of Almereyda in 1917 may be seen under a different light with what has been learned from other sources; Claude Aveline's allusions to the *Action Française* campaign against Almereyda may be filled out in greater detail; the young Vigo's state of mind may be given an interpretation quite different from Francis Jourdain's. But above all, certain rather aphoristic statements no longer make much sense. They emphasize things which no longer seem important to us. For instance, after reading the text Vigo wrote for the "presentation" of *A Propos de Nice*, it is difficult to agree that "in a few minutes it expresses the essential truths about both film and society."[53] A reference to the notion of genius leaves one all the more irresponsive for being accompanied by the traditional expression of regret. "He hoped to create a body of work without compromises. . . . only the foundations exist, but what foundations! They show every sign of genius."[54] The regrets are disarming in this context because they are expressed by friends who could never reconcile themselves to the fact that Vigo's life had been shattered at twenty-nine. How could one expect them not to feel that his work was also broken off in mid-flight?

Boris Kaufman's article also refers to Vigo's genius, but here the regret has roots over and above friendship for Vigo. Kaufman had made films before working with Vigo. During their collaboration he shot other films, and he went on working after his friend's death. He continued an excellent technician in everything he did, but he remained nostalgic for a period in which he felt he had been an instrument intimately involved in the creative process. Recalling his collaboration with Vigo, Kaufman feels that he lost "a cinematographic paradise."

Among the little film magazines which flourished in France after the war, *Raccords* and *Positif* both published articles on Vigo. In the first, Gilles Jacob reacts against the issue of *Ciné-Club* and those friends who had turned Vigo into "a genius who died too soon, before finishing his life's work." Making his position quite clear, Jacob starts off by declaring that he is glad Vigo died young. "Jean Vigo's strength is that his work fits comfortably into a single evening. In that fact, Destiny has amused herself by carefully concealing some formulas for great film-making. Not that one has to dig very deep, but one must dig everywhere. And granting that Vigo is not a genius—purely in order not to debase the word—let us go on to see how Vigo the iconoclast, the rebel, public enemy number one, the anti-conformist, the guillotiner of traditional values, has in less than twenty years become as permanent a national institution as Louis Jouvet; how a revival of *L'Arlésienne* at the Odéon-Comédie Française is no more of a box-office proposition than a programme devoted to this Lilliputian of creation."

One is led to expect a formal demonstration of this argument, and one wonders how the author is going to prove that Vigo's career in film clubs, art cinemas and film museums, the presence of his films at the Biarritz and Antibes Festivals, and a few television airings, could have sufficed to turn him into a "permanent national institution" without that fact ever coming to the attention of the "establishment" critics.

Similarly, when he asks, "What hasn't been said already about the socially committed documentary, about *A Propos de Nice*?" one would like to see his reaction when told, "Very little, and almost always the same things."

But this is not what Gilles Jacob is after. As a matter of fact, his intentions are made quite clear by the title of his article, "Saint-Jean Vigo, Patron des Ciné-Clubs,"[55] which so offended Vigo's young surrealist admirers from *L'Age du Cinéma*. And his epigraph, "M'sieur, can he go? He has a stomach-ache," gives a good idea of the article's general tone. It is not a study, or an essay, or even a polemic. It is more an evocation of Vigo's work by a film-society enthusiast, and one is immediately struck by the author's familiarity with Vigo's work.

Gilles Jacob sees Vigo's films as a whole, and he jumps from film to film with the ease with which, as he says, Vigo crossed the barrier of the sound film, "unselfconsciously, with that miraculous ease usually reserved for those who walk through walls." Jacob admires Jaubert's music, so that one is on the verge of irritation when he states that "the phonograph on the barge only plays the 'Chanson des Mariniers,'" forgetting the waltz and making no mention of the miracle. But reconciliation comes quickly, partly because we do not know what prints he saw, but chiefly because Jacob reveals how moved he was by the miracle that never happened when Père Jules runs his finger over the record.

To describe what he likes about the film, Jacob evokes his own memories: "Vigo handles dialogue like a drum major manipulating his baton: too confidently ever to let it fall. I remember the time, not so long ago, when Sancerre and I used to greet each other with 'M'sieur, can he go? He has a stomach-ache,' or 'How terribly witty!' or 'Well, sir, I say shit on you,' 'You are generous, my dear sir,' 'Glue pot, pass me your glue pot,' all spoken with the exact intonations used by the actors, and which enchanted us just as we had once been charmed by the celebrated song from *A Nous la Liberté*."

Out of all this richness, Jacob selects—and devotes about a tenth of his article to— the sequence between Tabard and the principal in the principal's office. He points out, following Mario Verdone but the first to do so in France, how Vigo loved to show naked flesh. He is the first to note that Vigo was "a marvellous intimist, perhaps the only one in the cinema." Jacob, like so many others before him, is plunged back into his childhood by *Zéro de Conduite*: "Vigo amuses himself too, this time rather more tenderly, by taking a peek at the naked thighs of his sleep-walking dunces, and suddenly revealing —a tired joke, as they say, but they are the first to laugh—the small buttocks of the boys who have finally managed to 'go.' But there is nothing equivocal about such moments; with them, Vigo plunges the spectator back into his own past, trapping his emotions behind the bars of the flashback, in front of a mirror through which no one can ever pass and which simply reflects, with the wrinkles smoothed away, the cherished image of the little theatre the world once was. A world where the only important thing is to amaze one's classmates, where cigars are smoked only because they are forbidden, where little people about to become adolescents have hands which only serve to strike at straw men."

Gilles Jacob's article is a fair sample of the new attitudes held by critics during the second phase in the evaluation of Vigo's work: the tendency to consider it as a finished and coherent whole; the flaws are acknowledged, but seem unimportant; the avant-garde label being too limiting, Vigo is placed squarely among the genuine creators of the French cinema.

But the "establishment" critics weigh heavy in France, and even as late as 1952 one still finds younger critics trying to shake off their influence: "Jean Vigo is an artist, perhaps one of the greatest the French cinema has ever had. Perhaps he had not yet learned to tell a story in *L'Atalante*. But when one thinks of the long process of trial and error before Renoir achieved mastery, one realizes exactly what was lost with Vigo's death. Vigo's films were above all promises of greatness, and his death, by depriving us of their fulfilment, has transformed the films themselves. They are masterpieces in spite of themselves. His films were a preliminary sketch for a portrait of the artist; now they are that portrait, which cannot be completed. It is an evil trick of fate which creates a kind of frustration. To overcome this frustration, perhaps we must become more sensitive to the poetry, that poetry which so often emanates more readily from works which are unfinished, imperfect, but unmistakably genuine, than from something *too* finished."[56]

A year later, *Positif* (which published the above article) devoted a special issue to Jean Vigo.[57] This time it seemed that the cape had finally been rounded.

During the same period, critical opinion abroad had moved ahead. In any case the time has come to leave France—where, in the matter of film culture, the importance given to Vigo in critical writings is not at all commensurate with the size of his audience— to move on to countries where the exact opposite is often true: essays and articles devoted to Vigo arouse a curiosity which remains unsatisfied because screenings are so rare.

This was not the case in Belgium. Vigo had not been forgotten there, and in 1946 Paul Davay wrote: "Who will bring back those palpitating, sloppily made films— amateurish, oh yes, and revolutionary acts to boot, and that's the trouble, isn't it?— called *Zéro de Conduite* and *L'Atalante*. . . ."[58] His wishes were soon granted, for the Belgian Cinémathèque, founded by André Thirifays, included *Zéro de Conduite* and *L'Atalante* among the first films purchased for its archive. After that, these two films, along with *Taris*, periodically made the rounds of the Belgian film societies. These screenings were often preceded by lectures, usually by Henri Storck and André Thirifays. Thirifays continued to publish articles popularizing Vigo's work, while new generations began to discover the films. At the experimental film festival at Knokke-le-Zoute, because no print of *A Propos de Nice* was available, *Taris* was shown so that Vigo would at least be represented. It would seem that no significant articles by younger critics were published in the Belgian periodicals; their source of reference remained the books of Vincent and the French historians.

The English had not forgotten Vigo either. Not sharing the continental taste for general histories of the cinema, the Anglo-Saxons limit themselves to national histories. Any evaluation of what, in the estimation of English critics, Vigo brought to the cinema, has therefore proved impracticable. It is, however, possible to see the importance they grant Vigo in their view of world film-making. The first thing to be noted is that the English critics were not acquainted with either *A Propos de Nice* or *Taris*, but that they had access to a good print of *L'Atalante*.

In the November 1946 edition of his *Film*,[59] Roger Manvell mentions only *Zéro de Conduite* and *L'Atalante*; and one is struck by the importance he ascribes to Vigo's work each time he refers to it. "Film's possibilities have begun to be demonstrated by men like Griffith, Chaplin, Pudovkin, Eisenstein, Lubitsch, Lang, Renoir, Vigo, Rotha, Ford, Welles, and Capra." When referring to the French film at the end of the silent era and during the thirties, the first person he mentions is Vigo. Throughout the book Vigo's works, *L'Atalante* in particular, are continually referred to, whether to evoke the risks any great film artist must take, or to give an example of the proper dramatic use of music in film. Vigo continued to interest Manvell, who repeatedly refers to him in his later books. When he has to illustrate the thesis that technical innovations are artistically valid only when they respond to a profound expressive need, he cites three examples: Griffith, von Stroheim, and Vigo.[60]

Yet, despite all these expressions of high esteem, when it comes to giving a concise and direct judgment of Vigo's work, Manvell often adopts the familiar position of regret for his early death. "He was perhaps the most original and promising of the greater French directors," and "Vigo died with no more than a promise on the screen."[61] But Vigo's work had by no means ceased to preoccupy Manvell. In 1951 he was responsible for the English publication of a long descriptive study on the making of *Zéro de Conduite*,[62] and in the same year he wrote an important article on *L'Atalante* for the Revaluation series in *Sight and Sound*.[63] Manvell emphasized the film's realism and presented it as a precursor of the neo-realism of Visconti's *Ossessione* and of De Sica's *The Bicycle Thief*; he also tried to link Vigo to a form of surrealism. But, having recently had the opportunity to see the film again, Manvell felt slightly surprised: "The main faults of this film are, curiously enough, to a certain extent assets." Obviously renewed contact with Vigo's work was deepening Manvell's critical appraisal.

In Ernest Lindgren's book *The Art of the Film*,[64] *L'Atalante* is also referred to several times as an example or to illustrate a point. Near the end of his book Lindgren indicates what he feels to be Vigo's principal contribution to the cinema: "It might have been supposed, on the evidence of the disastrous experiments which have been made in the past with superimposed angels with wings and haloes, and 'dream balloons' and other gimmicks, that there is at least one kind of experience which lies beyond the film's scope, namely the dream and the vision; but Jean Vigo and others have convincingly demonstrated that by concentrating, once more, on editing, on the relationship of shots in succession, and by replacing the matter-of-fact logic of everyday life with the free associations of the dream state, it is possible to represent that state with a disconcerting vividness."

The interest expressed in Vigo by the English resulted in the publication in 1951 of an issue of the *New Index Series* devoted to his work.[65] The chief interest of this publication resides in its reprinting of several American commentaries.

Vigo's films became known in the United States only after the war. *Zéro de Conduite* was seen first, in 1946, through the efforts of the Museum of Modern Art Film Library. It figured in a programme devoted to the French avant-garde which, after having been shown in New York, toured universities. There was a good deal of interest in *Zéro de Conduite*, particularly among students, and Herman G. Weinberg succeeded in interesting a distributor in Vigo's films. Towards the end of June 1947 *Zéro de Conduite* and *L'Atalante* were released in New York, opening at the Fifth Avenue Playhouse. The films were programmed elsewhere, certainly in Chicago.

Little information was accessible for the purposes of this book as to the reaction of the major American newspaper critics to Vigo's films. George Barbarow in *Politics*[66] quotes the opinion of A. W. in the *New York Times* on *Zéro de Conduite*: "These amorphous scenes, strung together by a vague continuity may be art but they are also pretty chaotic." James Agee, in the *Nation*, refers to "The reviewers who have written so contemptuously of Vigo's work."[67] On the other hand, *Time* magazine speaks of the release of Vigo's films as an event as important as the showing of *The Cabinet of Dr. Caligari* after the First World War.

Hollywood Quarterly published two articles on Vigo: the first, by Siegfried Kracauer, had already been published in Basle in 1940; the second was written by Gyula Zilzer, who had lived in France for some time and had known Vigo.[68] Zilzer's article takes the form of personal reminiscences, but one is shocked to see how closely it is modelled—without acknowledgement—on the Cavalcanti article which had appeared in London in 1935. Like Cavalcanti, Zilzer places Andorra in the Basque country, and states that Vigo had just learned to walk when he was taken to visit his father in prison during the First World War (in other words, when he was already twelve years old). All Zilzer does is modify Cavalcanti's article sufficiently to make it seem personal.

Zilzer not only repeats all of Cavalcanti's errors, he even copies sentences almost word for word.[69] Occasionally he adds new information which is totally untrue. That Jaurès was Vigo's godfather, for instance. Under the circumstances one can hardly take the information he gives about the making of *A Propos de Nice* very seriously.

The other American journals and magazines expressing an interest in Jean Vigo were luckier than *Hollywood Quarterly*, even when their contributions were on a rather low level, as was the case with *Theater Arts*.[70]

Of an altogether different quality are James Agee's articles in the *Nation*,[71] and George Barbarow's, in *Politics*.[72] Like the English, they had not seen *A Propos de Nice* or *Taris*; but, unlike Manvell and Lindgren, when confronted with *Zéro de Conduite* and *L'Atalante*, they were more interested in the first film.

James Agee's articles are perhaps the first to present a coherent overall view of Vigo's work, despite the fact that he had not seen Vigo's first two films, and had seen only bad prints of the other two. The limitations of a magazine article did not allow him to develop his ideas fully. Even so Agee, despite his lack of information about Vigo, cuts to the heart of the matter, often with a surprising insight. For instance he writes: "*Zéro [de Conduite]* seems to have been made, as all the best work has to be, from the inside out; *L'Atalante*, on the whole, is put together from the outside inward." Agee's lack of information and his direct confrontation of the films give his articles a freshness which immediately distinguishes them from European attitudes and conventions. Agee was the first to rebel against the insistence of historians, critics, and institutions on restricting Vigo's work to the narrow limits of the historical avant-garde. "On a foggy day, indeed, or with a prejudiced eye, it would be possible to confuse his work with the general sad run of avant-garde movie work, as several reviewers, including several whom I ordinarily respect, have done. But Vigo was no more a conventional avant-gardist than he was a Hollywood pimp; he was one of the very few real originals who have ever worked on film."

George Barbarow tries to approach the two films mainly by trying to understand the characters. In *L'Atalante*, which he does not rate very highly, only the street pedlar interests him, for he sees him as a sort of further development of Huguet, whom he describes as a self-portrait of Vigo and the central element in *Zéro de Conduite*, a film which he greatly admires. Because of his exclusive interest in the street pedlar, Barbarow remains completely insensitive to the rest of *L'Atalante*. As for *Zéro de Conduite*, the importance he ascribes to Huguet leads him only partially astray. Barbarow is extremely sensitive to the theme of revolt, and he has grasped, even if in a limited way, the existence of two separate worlds in *Zéro de Conduite*. Although one may at times disagree with him profoundly—as when he criticizes the use of slow and speeded-up motion in *Zéro de Conduite*—this does not alter the fact that his basic perceptions make his article one of the milestones in Vigo criticism.

Except for the reactions which resulted from the Fifth Avenue Playhouse run, we have no information on the career of Vigo's films in the United States. We also lack information about Canada and Latin America. But it is probable that, until 1953, few people in any of these countries, except Uruguay, had the opportunity of seeing Vigo's films.

The situation in Asia and in the non-French-speaking African countries in all likelihood was the same.

If we now return to Europe, large areas of the Continent—the Soviet Union, the other Communist nations of Eastern Europe, Greece, Spain, and Portugal—remained totally ignorant of Vigo's work. But we have still not dealt with the country which greeted his work with the most enthusiasm: Italy.

Vigo was practically unknown in Italy until 1946. Pasinetti's *La Storia del Cinema*, the principal Italian reference work for the history of film, does not mention him.

It was the film-maker Luigi Comencini who first tried to stimulate interest in Vigo's work by publishing an article: "The Discovery of a Film-Maker."[73] Comencini had seen *L'Atalante* (probably the *Le Chaland qui passe* version) at the Basle Festival in 1939. The film was a revelation to him, but he had not seen the film since then, and was beginning to doubt his memories when he obtained a print from a cyclist in Geneva who hired out films in his spare time. He viewed it again several times, showed it to his friends, and "the unanimous opinion was that they were confronted with a masterpiece capable of shaking up any notions about cinema the average spectator might have."[74]

Comencini thought he had seen a "fairly complete" version of *L'Atalante*; and in Paris he saw a print of *Zéro de Conduite* which he thought had been "mutilated and revised" by English Puritanism! The print of *L'Atalante* that Comencini saw was probably very mutilated, and it is quite possible that the *Zéro de Conduite* he saw was one of the prints then in circulation which, with the English blameless in the matter, were fairly close to the original. The fact is that Comencini was baffled by *Zéro de Conduite*: "It seems that in the film Vigo became so attached to the ferocity of his satire . . . that he created a work which is undoubtedly inspired but not very convincing."

Zéro de Conduite was soon to continue on its baffling way to Milan. Thirteen years to the day after its Paris presentation, *Zéro de Conduite* was shown to Milanese audiences at the Supercinema Alcione on April 7, 1946, as part of the retrospective festival organized by the Cineteca Italiana to commemorate the fiftieth anniversary of the cinema.[75] The reaction of the public was similar to that of the original Paris audience in 1933. "General scandal," wrote Comencini, "except for a small minority who applauded obstinately. It really is a shame that this brilliant director's masterpiece, *L'Atalante*, a serene and brilliantly structured film, could not have been shown instead of *Zéro de Conduite*, which is a satire of such violence and bitterness that it disconcerts audiences accustomed to a diet of phony escapism. . . . The audience's indignation . . . many of them shouting and hissing. . . . ."[76] One critic comments: "It is both the work of a genius and the work of an amateur . . . . There is no story continuity; he simply tries to create a feeling. This upset a portion of the audience, and they reacted vehemently."[77] Another critic remarks: "The critics seemed embarrassed."[78]

It is clear that not only the public but the more informed critics felt baffled. These critics reacted to the film in very nearly the same way as their French and Belgian colleagues had in 1933. However, the Milanese critics of 1946 knew Vigo's reputation; and although disappointed, they are, nevertheless, cautious. They speak of his genius even while expressing the gravest reservations. "Without wanting to be disrespectful to the memory of a film-maker whose name is often praised by experts, *Zéro de Conduite* looks like a film made by an amateur of genius who had not yet found his own style, and who, because he wanted to say too much, ended up saying it in a muddled way."[79]

The critics regretted the absence of *L'Atalante* from the programme, and were afraid to make an evaluation of Vigo based on *Zéro de Conduite* alone. "The film is so strangely structured, so far removed from all the narrative conventions of the cinema, that a single viewing is not enough."[80]

Rudi Berger's disapproval is unequivocal: "An upsetting experience for many. . . . [Vigo] was a director with an audacious temperament, always exploring new and difficult paths, an authentic avant-garde director; but this effort is not the best introduction to his work for an audience. . . . It was perhaps a mistake to present the film as a satire on schools. For in satire one expects an attack on customs, on a class, on a particular mentality. What we have here is more an abstract fantasy, without any real existence, without roots in any real experience, an arabesque without the slightest credibility. . . . It is an experiment worthy of respect, but one which does not open up any new possibilities for the cinema."[81]

Glauco Viazzi replies in part to Rudi Berger's objections. *"Zéro de Conduite* could almost be considered a surrealist film, with leanings towards Buñuel or Dali, if it were not supported by an intense satirical force and a concrete, even physiological, sense of reality. . . . Vigo has created a world out of his own suffering. . . . Vigo spits in the face of society with the bursting sincerity of an anarchist's protest."[82]

Carlo Doglio, an anarchist, was the first critic in Italy to try to get to the heart of *Zéro de Conduite* and was quite taken with the film's lyricism. In a later article, Doglio wrote of Vigo as the model of what an anarchist film-maker should be.[83]

A print of *Le Chaland qui passe* arrived in Milan at the end of May 1946, and on the twenty-eighth, an evening of Vigo's films, featuring his two principal works, was finally possible. "Undisputed applause greeted Vigo's work this time," Luigi Comencini noted.[84] From this moment, Vigo's films started on their career in Italy.[85] It was not to reach a peak until 1952, when the Italian Federation of Film Societies made all of his films available. The critics continued to write about Vigo, but we have not attempted to follow up on what they had to say. Whatever their interest, however, it is probable that the most important Italian contribution to Vigo criticism was made by Glauco Viazzi. Reference has already been made to his 1946 article in *Costume*, which augurs his later writings. The following year he returned to the subject with a longer study, but one which was still mainly a matter of expressing enthusiasm.[86] "The handful of films he had made at the time of his death placed him in a position of eminence, not only in the French cinema along with René Clair and Jean Renoir, but in all contemporary art. . . . The discovery of a poet is not something which happens every day; the revelation of a 'new' man is something that can leave no one indifferent. . . . This dead man dominated and still dominates French film-making; if the French have forgotten him, that is no reason for us to do the same. Quite the opposite. It is in the name of all those who love film, and above all those who love mankind, that we claim Jean Vigo, placing his films not only among those works which honour mankind, but also among those which have helped to change the world, to make a better, freer, and happier life for all mankind."

Viazzi does not merely dispense words of praise, however. Apart from being the first critic to put Vigo firmly on the same level as René Clair and Renoir, he views the two films he had been able to see as two successive stages of the same ideological and poetic impulse.

An attempt to find common elements in *Zéro de Conduite* and *L'Atalante*; an attempt to clarify the ideological content of the films; a dispute with the Italian anarchists who tried to claim Vigo: these are the themes in Viazzi's article. Two years later they recur in the long article on Vigo he wrote for *Bianco e Nero*.[87]

This is the first really "serious" study of Vigo's work, and that in itself is reason enough to make it worth examining in some detail.

Glauco Viazzi offers a Marxist interpretation of Vigo's life and work, or at least, an interpretation which relies largely on Marxian methodology and terminology. Whether or not he uses this approach properly is something beyond our competence.

It is not easy to summarize Viazzi's ideas, for his article is not very well organized and his verbal exuberance is sometimes excessive. It is also impractical to quote his whole article here; not so much because of its length, or because it seems unfair to ask readers to be as patient as Viazzi expected his to be, as because we would only have to go over the whole article again in order to comment on it. Far better to make the exposition and criticism of the article a single operation.

As a sensitive contemporary of the second stage in the evaluation of Vigo's work, Viazzi opens his essay by attacking the customary expressions of regret for Vigo's premature death. In his view, however, these regrets do not represent a whole period's failure to understand, but an attempt at mythification: the development of this sentimental, commemorative theme is an attempt to stifle the social nature of Vigo's revolt and the internal dialectic of his work. Therefore, to understand why there is so little of significance in the "almost non-existent and very tendentious" material written about Vigo, it is necessary, according to Viazzi, to examine Vigo's relationship to the society in which he lived. Unfortunately, Viazzi is poorly documented, and has only a vague, conventional notion of Vigo's life and personality. After the death of Almereyda, whom Viazzi describes as "an anarchist sentenced to death for high treason," he pictures a Jean Vigo doomed to a life of humiliation, a pariah, morally barred from French society, in particular by the bourgeoisie. Viazzi uses the expression "bourgeoisie" as an entity with which Vigo, alive or dead—and his films—were in constant conflict, as *Zéro de Conduite* had been with the French censors.

Actually, one can hardly account for the incomprehension which greeted Vigo's work in the thirties by ascribing it to the inability of the bourgeoisie—not just in France but in Europe—to forgive Vigo his violence, his satire, and his poetry.[88] The fact of the matter is that the newspaper critics, bourgeois, petty bourgeois, and working-class alike, shared a fundamental failure to understand which had nothing to do with approval or disapproval, and can therefore hardly be ascribed to any ideological basis. During the thirties, Vigo's work was approached by both supporters and detractors in an essentially different way from Viazzi, Agee, or the rest of us now. Until 1940, Vigo's films were not thought of as a key element in the films of the period, whereas it is now very largely in relation to Vigo that the period interests us.

The more one learns the true story of Vigo and his films, the more one sees how conventional and even arbitrary the background to Viazzi's article—the relationship between Vigo and the bourgeoisie of his time—really is. Thus, when Viazzi tries to explain why the snobs of the French haute bourgeoisie, who willingly accepted *Le Sang d'un Poète* or even *L'Age d'Or*, rejected Vigo's films, he is wasting his time. For the situation he imagines (this particular audience confronted with *A Propos de Nice*, *Zéro de Conduite*, and *L'Atalante*) never existed.

Viazzi's quarrel with the anarchists should be stressed; for even though the polemic is conducted in a somewhat superficial manner, it clarifies some of the ideas he develops later. "Vigo was logical in his anarchism, and therefore a non-anarchist in the historical sense of the term. The ideological, utopian, and opportunistic abstraction of the historical anarchists was completely alien to him. His freedom was freedom in the world, in society, in nature, and in things; and precisely because he never detached himself from his circumstances, because on the contrary he incorporated the concrete, profound laws of existence and their dialectical consequence into his thought, he remained part of it and never adopted that complacent, gratuitous, *gauche* irreverence, those pleasures of intellectual exhibitionism, which keep nearly all anarchists from communicating with and loving the world. An anarchist in the historical sense of the term would have ended *Zéro de Conduite* at the moment when the humiliated, threatened schoolboy expresses his anger and dismay by his 'Mr. Principal, I say shit on you.'"

We can now go on to examine the heart of Viazzi's article. Faithful to the dialectical triad, Viazzi sees three basic moments in Vigo's life and art: "bourgeois origins, anarchist revolt, and liberation into proletarian solidarity." There we have it: thesis, antithesis, and synthesis! Viazzi, of course, does not consider these moments as three fixed points, or even as clearly defined in time, but as a continuous movement leading from one stage to the next, and operating simultaneously at several levels. This process, nevertheless, develops in a particular direction, and through its successive stages a linear development emerges which allows Viazzi, broadly speaking, to posit as thesis Vigo as he was moulded by his social origins and upbringing; as antithesis, the Vigo of *Zéro de Conduite*; and as synthesis, the Vigo of *L'Atalante*. Having seen Viazzi draw this line, however, one must immediately efface it in order to allow another aspect of the same process to emerge—this time its operation within each stage. This we shall do (following up with critical arguments later) in order to clarify Viazzi's argument.

Viazzi does not linger long on the first phase, the thesis, Vigo's bourgeois (or petty bourgeois, as he says towards the end of the article) origins. It is not easy to determine the exact social class into which Vigo was born or to which he owed his upbringing. Born of a free union between revolutionary activists in an attic room on the rue Polonceau; another childhood as a "rich boy" in Saint-Cloud with a "successful" father; sudden translation to a provincial photographer's modest home; descent into mediocrity with the school in Millau; then his last adolescent years divided between the boarding-school in Chartres and the Parisian home of his mother and an obscure sports writer; the sanatorium; marriage to the daughter of a Jewish industrialist from Lodz; humble employment in a studio in Nice, and so on. Can one really attempt to reduce all this to formulas like bourgeois or petty bourgeois origins? Does it really help in understanding Vigo? Except for alluding to his father's death, Viazzi does not retrace any of the stages in Vigo's life, and it is difficult to understand what he means when he writes: "In short, Vigo *had* to revolt, considering the entire heritage of his educational and social background." This takes us to the second phase.

The antithesis, the "anarchistic revolt," corresponds in particular to *Zéro de Conduite*.[89] It is a period of analysis of his experience, "exhausting the intellectual and spiritual experiences of a whole culture, getting at its very roots so as to be able to annihilate it with the aid of the positive elements it contains, and thus to create a new one." It is the moment of revolt against the bourgeois and petty bourgeois world by someone who is in many ways still part of it. It is the moment of *Zéro de Conduite*, with its "residue of intellectual pretensions and dross remaining from the excesses of the avant-garde, its blunted, exaggerated deformations, its flights into unreality, into bitter cinematic fantasy." Vigo, he says, was then under the influence of "artistic schools and coteries, technical discoveries and stylistic influences, literary references and artistic indulgences." But at the same time there is a "growing revolt, whose development will result in a defeat of the very concepts upon which Vigo based his narrative."

Vigo, in effect, "continued the process, taking it beyond the completion of revolt." Revolt once achieved, the antithesis exhausted itself and synthesis ensued.

The synthesis is the Vigo of *L'Atalante*. "Everything becomes calm and melts into relaxation." No longer polemical, but "pure lyricism . . . in which the revolt extends itself through the choice of love, through the total exclusion of a world, the bourgeois world, and its replacement by another, the world of the masses and of the proletariat." Once liberated, Vigo can discover the beauty and violence of reality, he can love "workers and peasants, and the soft, grey, silvery landscapes of northern France." Vigo attained "a lyrical and concrete realism." This is the world of "the full and very tender love of Juliette and Jean. . . . In the collective existence on the barge of Jean, Juliette, Père Jules, and the cabin boy, there is neither solitude nor occasion for conflict."

In this way, after having shown Vigo "in the very delicate position of a man of petty bourgeois origins living in a bourgeois society and then withdrawing from it by rebellion," Viazzi tried to establish a dialectical link between *Zéro de Conduite* and *L'Atalante*.

He attempts to impose his schema by repetition of it rather than by making the necessary demonstration of proof. It is safe to say that, even after faithfully following Viazzi in his examination of the internal dialectics of each of the three terms, one remains far from convinced that "*L'Atalante* is born of the internal dialectic of *Zéro de Conduite*".

This search for a dialectical continuity in the body of Vigo's work did not entirely exhaust Viazzi's purpose. To add fuel to his polemic, Viazzi requires of the films a more traditional logic. He dislikes the anarchist ending of *Zéro de Conduite*, so he looks to *L'Atalante* not merely for a dialectical continuation of Vigo's development, but for a logical extension—in a direction he can approve—of the action of *Zéro de Conduite's* characters. "It is no accident that one of the rebellious boys in the first film should reappear as a cabin boy in the second. That is what happens to Vigo's fugitives on the rooftops: they simply go to work." In actual fact, Caussat is transformed into a cabin boy for precisely the same reason that Huguet becomes the captain of a barge, and a fireman becomes, first the bride's father, and then Rasputin: Vigo's loyalty towards members of the team with whom he had worked on *Zéro de Conduite*. There is no sense in seeking further explanations.

The final pages of this book will consist of a critique of Viazzi's article. This course is indicated by the importance of his contribution. Of all the articles considered here, "A proposito di Jean Vigo" is the most remarkable. Hopefully, the present study has succeeded, as a result of fresh research, in approaching Vigo's work more fruitfully than Viazzi. In drawing our conclusions, it is therefore only fair to him to relate them to further criticisms and an extension of his article.

Glauco Viazzi becomes a victim of his own dialectical schema. Instead of considering it as a working hypothesis, likely to be rejected after more extensive research, but nevertheless useful for a time, he thinks of it as definitive. He believes that he has found a magic key allowing him immediate access to an understanding of Vigo and his work. From that moment on, he remains faithful to his schema. He becomes less and less interested in facts, and if need be does not hesitate to twist things his way. This is particularly evident in the case of *L'Atalante*, which Viazzi prefers to *Zéro de Conduite*, synthesis being for him a higher stage than antithesis in the dialectical process. To preserve the harmony and validity of his hypothesis, Viazzi had to maintain that Vigo filmed only what was within himself; and further, that Vigo was in fact most free when he was working on *L'Atalante*. We now know that this was certainly untrue, as James Agee realized even though unaware of the facts. Viazzi was much better informed than Agee was. The Italian critic had been able to read the special issue of *Ciné-Club*,[90] where Claude Aveline's article contained some accurate details of the conditions under which *L'Atalante* was made. But whenever some fact emerges which might upset his schema, Viazzi ignores it. Similarly, he has to remain continually alert to prevent the actuality of *L'Atalante* from destroying the narrow confines within which he tries to enclose Vigo's work.

Viazzi's dialectic requires that *L'Atalante* be "pure song" in which peace and relaxation reign supreme. He knows very well that this is far from evident, for he feels the need of a good deal of explanation, done with an air of boldly refuting any possible objections. He asserts that there is nothing polemical about the film, even in the scenes which lend themselves most easily to such an interpretation: the wedding party, Juliette looking for work, the theft of the handbag, Jean's summons to the company office.

Let us examine the wedding party. After having firmly set the young couple apart, Vigo proceeds to treat the rest of the party without sympathy. Although he is not too hard on Juliette's parents, as the cortège leaves the church Vigo stresses the meanness and vulgarity in both speech and behaviour of these peasants dressed up in their Sunday best. During the walk to the barge, the distance between the silent couple bathed in happiness and light, and the noisy black flock behind them, allows Vigo to indicate exactly where and with whom his sympathy lies, and where his hostility. When they embark, Vigo completes his judgment by leaving the group of peasants on the canal bank, silent, immobile, hostile, and unresponsive to Jean's cheerful farewell.

Viazzi is aware of "the strong sense of caricature about these stiff, ponderous men in black," but when he adds that this sense of caricature is "tempered by sweetness and love," the only basis for this remark lies in the ideological premises of his framework, and not in the sequence itself. For it is a tenet of Viazzi's doctrine that Vigo had a very special love for "the north of France, a region both industrial and rural, and for the men who live and work there," and that everything in Vigo's experience led him "to love the workers and peasants . . . of northern France."

Viazzi is not content just with making Vigo love the peasants from Juliette's village; so as not to disturb *L'Atalante*'s "peaceful song," he must also stifle the few cries of social revolt so important to Vigo and which he did his best to let through in spite of the restrictions imposed on him. Viazzi is well aware of their existence; he refers to the sequences in which they occur, at Le Havre and with Juliette in Paris. But in order to be able to assert that there is nothing polemical in the film, Viazzi simply hurries over the sequences without bothering to examine their key moments. Not a word about the poor, starving thief beaten up behind the railings by a well-fed crowd and carried off by the cops! Not a word about the crippled tramp's fear! Not a word about the good citizens of Le Havre who surround Jean in his despair and whom Père Jules threatens to beat up! Viazzi does refer to the lines of unemployed workers encountered by Juliette, but in another context, using a method of displacement which allows him to understate the social content of the shot. As for the cops keeping an eye on the lines of unemployed outside the factories, Viazzi ignores them.

This by no means exhausts all the distortions Viazzi was forced to make to maintain the framework he had created. Let us consider one final example. From among the possibilities left open to him in *L'Atalante*, Vigo chose to explore his characters in greater psychological depth. This does not suit Viazzi's views, since the barge has to be "a preferential microcosm . . . in which there is not even any subdivision into zones or compartments." As we have already noted, Viazzi goes so far as to assert that "in the collective existence on the barge of Jean, Juliette, Père Jules, and the cabin boy, there is neither solitude nor occasion for conflict." To counter likely objections from readers who had seen *L'Atalante*, Viazzi simply states, in all seriousness, that the violent scene between Jean and Juliette in Père Jules' cabin has nothing to do with the bourgeois notion of jealousy, but belongs to a different reality pertinent to certain aspects of working-class life—precisely which aspects he does not specify.

It is no accident that the only character in whose psychology Viazzi expresses much interest is in fact Jean, and that he carefully avoids delving into the much richer characters of Juliette and Père Jules. This is simply because their richness is inseparable from their complexity, and therefore ambiguity. Viazzi refuses to acknowledge this for fear of contaminating his "working-class society as yet untainted by barbarism."

Yet *A proposito di Jean Vigo* is not just a string of absurdities. Viazzi is better on *Zéro de Conduite* than on *L'Atalante*; he appreciates Vigo's poetry, and the plastic beauty of Kaufman's camerawork under Vigo's direction; and the importance of the article, even though irremediably compromised by Viazzi's ideological mishmash, has already been indicated.

The fact remains that *A Propos de Nice*, *Zéro de Conduite* and *L'Atalante* do indeed correspond to three distinct moments in a continuous creative process. *Taris* belongs through its formal experiments (the movements of a man's head and body under water) which were later used to both poetic and dramatic effect (Jean's dive looking for

Juliette's image under water), but as a creative effort this short film constitutes a paren-thesis in Vigo's work. Actually, *Taris* is the only one of Vigo's films which can still be classified as an avant-garde work, with all the limitations and fustian implied by the term.

His three major films stand resolutely aside from the avant-garde tradition. If, after a direct historical and aesthetic analysis of each film, didactic convenience requires a classification, then suitable terms may be drawn from the traditional styles of our culture. *A Propos de Nice*, as already stated, is essentially the work of a primitive, with its sense of discovery and its naïveté dominant. *Zéro de Conduite*, with its unity of style and the severe restraint of its measure of poetry, seems more and more like a classical work. As for *L'Atalante*, its romanticism has been suspected ever since Elie Faure, and the suggestion seems a valid one. Vigour replacing rigour, individual anarchy replacing social anarchy, ennoblement of animals and of the humblest objects—the key role of the phonograph—without recourse to symbolism, the irrepressible eruption of his poetry: these are the principal characteristics of Vigo's romantic work.

It is evident what makes Vigo's work seem like a perfect, coherent whole. Apart from the experimental parenthesis of *Taris*, his creative development covers three basic styles, one after the other, in chronological succession. But this graduation through three styles would not be enough in itself. It works because the same themes and feelings recur un-changed in the various films. In each of them the same poetry reappears, the same com-passion, the same revolt, the same tendencies.

His poetry, whether it springs from satire as in *A Propos de Nice*, whether it becomes intimate or audacious as in *Zéro de Conduite* (the dormitory, the torchlight procession), whether it overflows as in *L'Atalante*, is always the same poetry. The compassion for the boy whose hands have been mutilated by leprosy or by fire, for the child crying because he cannot defend his mother, or for the downfall of the puppet orchestra conductor, is always the same compassion. As for his social revolt, virulent in *A Propos de Nice*, spread wide in *Zéro de Conduite*, and peeping through here and there in *L'Atalante*, its quality does not change. Vigo's pleasure in the human body, erotic or otherwise, can be seen throughout, and even makes *Taris* burst the bonds of its parenthesis.

Vigo has a position of eminence in the French cinema. The list is brief of French film-makers who have contributed to the art of the film with work of lasting value beyond any ephemeral or historical interest: Méliès, Cohl, Linder, Gance, Clair, Renoir, and Vigo.[91] The list could be even further reduced, and if one were to be unnecessarily ruthless and reduce the number to four, Vigo would still not be eliminated. Vigo's major work, bracketed in time by *Le Million* and *La Règle du Jeu*, dominates the French cinema of the thirties along with the films of Renoir and Clair.

In the course of this book we have seen how film critics and historians rather hap-hazardly claimed the influence of other films on *Zéro de Conduite* and *L'Atalante*. Mostly these claims are vague and made with no effort to justify them: they neither clarify nor help to evaluate. In the case of *Zéro de Conduite*, besides alluding to a sur-realist influence, the critics constantly mention Clair and Chaplin. As far as the latter is concerned, the case apparently rests on Vigo's quotation from *Easy Street* when Huguet does an imitation of Charlie in the schoolyard. One character imitating Chaplin in *Zéro de Conduite* sufficed to convince the critics that Chaplin influenced Vigo. It is interesting to note that not one of them pointed out the nature of this sequence as a quotation. With the possible exception of one scene, René Clair's influence is equally intangible: the slap Colin receives from his mother. This, not merely because children are often slapped by their parents in Clair's films (as in France), but because the scene takes up one of Clair's favourite themes: the venting on someone weaker of the frustration or anger caused by a stronger person. None of this has any great substance; nevertheless it is possible at least to postulate influences on *Zéro de Conduite*. The same is not true of *L'Atalante*.

There remains the problem of the influence of surrealism. Vigo, of course, had been impressed by *Un Chien Andalou*; and without ever actually belonging to the surrealist group, he had been influenced by them, like so many other modern-minded young people of his generation. It can be verified, however, that it is impossible to detect any influence of surrealism as such, or of Buñuel's work, in either *Zéro de Conduite* or *L'Atalante*. The search for films which had a real influence on Vigo's two great films should continue. For the present I have only one suggestion to make. Together with *Un Chien Andalou*, the film which most impressed Vigo was Junghans' *So ist das Leben*. I have never had an opportunity to see the film, but I would be surprised to discover that it had any direct influence on Vigo's work. On the other hand, I would not be surprised at all to find the combined influence of Junghans and Buñuel among the sources from which Vigo's own personal style grew.

As for the influence Vigo may have exerted on other films in his turn, the suggestions made to date have little foundation. Generalizations retain a certain plausibility. Sadoul, for instance, remarks that in the films made between 1935 and 1939 by Feyder, Renoir, Carné, and Duvivier, one can find, among other things, certain lessons learned from Vigo.[92] Well, why not? But it doesn't really get us very far. On the other hand, attempts to be more precise get nowhere at all. For example, Henri Langlois wrote in 1948 that *A Propos de Nice* "greatly influenced recent productions, especially those of the growing young school of Italian documentary."[93]

Perhaps it is pointless to look for Vigo's influence on other film-makers. The virtues of Vigo's films owe very little to problems of technique or language or to acting styles, all of which can be borrowed or imitated. When Eisenstein saw *Intolerance*, he deepened his perception and learned specific techniques which he subsequently used. When De Sica saw *L'Atalante*, he was simply enriched by the experience. And when he displays these riches in his films, everything he may have learned from Vigo has been so thoroughly assimilated that it is quite impossible to trace.

Paris, 1949–1952

Notes and References

1. Miguel Almereyda

1. The Vigos were originally from the Cerdagne. The motto on their coat of arms was: "I protect the weakest."
2. January 27, 1901.
3. *Le Libertaire*, March 9, 1901.
4. Francis Jourdain, "Une Enfance", *Ciné-Club*, Paris, no. 5, February 1949.
5. *Les Lettres Nouvelles*, no. 1, 1953.
6. September 19, 1902.
7. The subscription totalled 1,003 francs 25 centimes. The two largest contributions of 5 francs came from Elie Faure and Léon Blum. "Comptabilité sur la campagne préparatoire du congrès d'Amsterdam." *Le Libertaire*, July 17, 1904.
8. Francis Jourdain.
9. Ibid.
10. April 17, 1907.
11. Victor Serge, *Mémoires d'un Révolutionnaire*. Translation published by Oxford University Press, 1963.
12. Miguel Almereyda, *L'Affaire du Bonnet Rouge*, Lang, Blanchong and Company, Printers, September 1917.
13. Preface to *Mes Crimes*, Ed. de *La Guerre Sociale*, no date (1912).
14. Albert Monniot, *Le Mystère de Fresnes*, Paris, 1919.
15. Daudet's testimony at the Malvy trial, *La Revue des Causes célèbres*.
16. Francis Jourdain.
17. Victor Serge.
18. See especially *Le Bonnet Rouge* of May 16, 1914.
19. Claude Aveline.
20. Louis Dumur, *Les Défaitistes*, Albin Michel, 1923.
21. Quoted by Monniot.
22. *Le Bonnet Rouge*, March 16, 1916.

23. Raymond Poincaré, *Au Service de la France*, vol. 9, Plon, 1932.
24. Jean Martet, *Le Tigre*, Paris, Albin Michel, 1930.
25. Raymond Poincaré.
26. Ibid.
27. Almereyda had met with his associates on July 9, and had presented a report with vouchers accounting for about a million francs from the various subsidies received since August 1914. It was this same report that he presented to Judge Drioux when summoned as a witness in the Duval case. The letter in Almereyda's defence was signed by: Georges Clairet, editor in chief; Maurice Fournié, assistant editor; Henri Dié, desk editor; Arnold Bontemps, sports writer; Marcel Sérano, drama critic; Fanny Clar, Raphaël Diligent, artists; H. P. Gassier, artist; Louis Lévy; Jacques Janin, music critic.
28. B. and P. Dabat, *Souvenirs d'un Directeur de Prison*, Paris, P. Bossuet, 1929.
29. These facts were revealed by the lawyer Paul Morel in a *Mémoire* written for the *Chambre des mises en accusation*.
30. This reconstruction can be found in Monniot's book.
31. Information from Fournier.
32. Letter published in Fournier.
33. Albert Monniot.

2. Jean Vigo

1. Pierre de Saint-Prix, *Lettres* (1917–19), Paris, F. Rieder and Company, 1924.
2. Important sections of this journal appeared in *Positif*, no. 7, May 1953.
3. Georges Caussat and Jacques Bruel, in letters to the author.
4. *Présentation de Zéro de Conduite*, Jean Vigo Archives.
5. Jean Vigo Archives.
6. In the summer of 1924 Vigo spent three weeks with the Mercier family in Tillières.
7. Ten years after his death Almereyda's grave was almost certainly not still tended. It is likely that Vigo wanted to visit it. That he did so is suggested by some notes jotted down for *A Propos de Nice* but never used.
8. *Le Mystère de Fresnes*.
9. The portrayal of Almereyda in Monniot's book probably did not disturb Vigo very much. Ever since he was twelve, he had seen his father's name serve as a target for all sorts of insults. Besides, the knowledge he was beginning to acquire of the *Libertaire* and *Guerre Sociale* period of his father's life must have shown him how inaccurate Monniot's biography of his father was. He probably realized that the rest of the book was not worth much more.
10. Victor Serge, *Mémoires d'un Révolutionnaire*.
11. December 25, 1925.
12. Letter of August 22, 1926.
13. On August 5, 1926.
14. Letter to Mme. de Saint-Prix, August 30, 1926.
15. The conspirators, consisting of poets, sociologists, writers, and musicians, led by a colonel named Macia and the director of a choir, José Fontbernard y Verdaguer, used to meet at the Café du Rocher on the Boulevard Saint-Germain.
16. Letter to Mme. de Saint-Prix, August 30, 1926.
17. Letter of March 8, 1927.
18. Letter to Mme. de Saint-Prix mailed on October 2, 1928, but written in July.
19. Letter of August 16, 1928.
20. Letter of January 19, 1929.
21. Jean Vigo Archives.
22. As late as 1949, Georges Sadoul does this, in his *Histoire d'un Art: Le Cinéma*, Flammarion.
23. Every attempt made by the author to reach Kaufman by letter was unsuccessful.
24. Jean Vigo Archives.
25. Ibid.
26. Ibid.
27. Ibid.
28. Ibid.
29. Most of his superimpositions have deteriorated in the original negative.

30. Alexandra Pecker, in *Comoedia*, November 19, 1933.
31. *Le Soir*, May 24, 1930.
32. *Le Soir*, May 31, 1930, signed F. C.
33. Letter to Pierre de Saint-Prix, June 5, 1930.
34. *L'Echo de Paris*, May 30, 1930.
35. June 5, 1930.
36. Letter cited above.
37. The following films were presented at the screening: *Naissance d'un Illustré* (Pierre Chenal), *Autour de l'Argent* (Jean Dréville), *Histoire de Détective* (Dekeukeleire), *Les Champs-Elysées* (Jean Lodz and Kaufman), *Nogent, Eldorado du Dimanche* (Marcel Carné), *La Nuit Electrique* (Eugène Deslaw), and *La Zone* (Lacombe).
38. In the same issue of *Close Up* of June 1930, Charles E. Stenhouse summarizes the film activities of the month. At the Vieux-Colombier, *La Petite Marchande d'Allumettes* was on the same bill with *Menschen am Sonntag*; the Ursulines was showing *The Terror* with May McAvoy; at the Studio 28, *Un Chien Andalou* continued on its run; the Agriculteurs was showing a re-run of *Lady Windermere's Fan* and *A Woman of Paris*; "L'Œil de Paris" presented *La Souriante Mme. Beudet* and *Finis Terrae*. Still running in Paris were *Jazz, Jenseits der Strasse, La Glace à trois faces, Club 73*, etc. The group L'Effort was preparing a big Méliès evening, and the Tribune Libre du Cinéma, a gala evening of Cavalcanti's films. Jean Painlevé presented his films at the Sorbonne, and Eisenstein, during the lecture he gave there, was not allowed to show *The General Line*, which was shown instead by the Russie Neuve group founded under the auspices of the Soviet Embassy and directed by "M. Autant and Mme. Lara."
39. *Le Soir*, June 21, 1930.
40. Letter of June 21, 1930.
41. *Le Soir*, June 21, 1930.
42. *Histoire d'un Art: Le Cinéma*.
43. June 15, 1930.
44. We were not able to go through all of the contemporary press reports, but did check the results of our research with Fernand Desprès' letters. He tried to read everything written on his friend's film, and always informed Saint-Prix of anything he came across.
45. July 2, 1930.
46. This group, founded a few years earlier by Jean Pascal, editor of *Cinémagazine*, was to exist for some time, and even succeeded in flourishing in the provinces, particularly in Montpellier, where Vigo probably had the opportunity of attending some of their screenings.
47. Letter of August 6, 1930.
48. Fragment of a letter published by Pierre de Saint-Prix in his article "Quelques Lettres inédites de Jean Vigo," *Les Cahiers du Ciné-Club*, Valence-sur-Rhône (no date).
49. Letter of September 3, 1930.
50. Unpublished letter sent to the author.
51. Letter of October 5, 1930.
52. Letter to Pierre de Saint-Prix of October 17, 1930.
53. Letter from Peira Cava of August 31, 1930.
54. *Close Up*, December 1930.
55. Ibid.
56. Marie Seton, in her *Sergei M. Eisenstein* (London, Bodley Head, 1952), states that the only print of this "historic document of nonsense" was lost by Eisenstein himself, "somewhere between La Sarraz, Zürich, Berlin, Paris, and London." A few photographs taken in the course of the shooting remain, together with the hope that one day a reader of these lines. . . .
57. In extant prints the credit sequence has somewhat deteriorated.
58. Letter of May 10, 1931.
59. Letter to Storck, August 30, 1931.
60. Letter to Storck, October 20, 1931.
61. Letter to Storck, November 18, 1931.
62. Letter of February 25, 1932.
63. This talk was repeated by Aveline before the members of the Anatole France Society in February 1939, and published in the April 1939 issue of the society's magazine, *Le Lys Rouge*. In the article, reference is made to the showing at the Nice film club.

64. Reminiscences recounted to the author in June 1950.
65. Storck's journal, note of July 28, 1932.
66. Note in his journal dated November 1, 1932.

3. Zéro de Conduite
1. Miguel Almereyda, "La Petite Roquette," *L'Assiette au Beurre* no. 348, November 30, 1907; drawings by A. Delannoy.
2. André Négis, *Ciné-Monde*, Paris, vol. 6, no. 224, February 2, 1933.
3. *Présentation de Zéro de Conduite.*
4. Letter of March 22, 1950, to the author.
5. *Présentation de Zéro de Conduite.*
6. Scenario for *Zéro de Conduite*. Jean Vigo Archives.
7. For the film he chose a pseudonym: Du Verron.
8. André Négis.
9. Note of January 4, 1933.
10. Joseph Kosma, "Maurice Jaubert," *L'Ecran Français*, Paris, June 19, 1950.
11. In *L'Amour d'une femme*, Grémillon "quotes" the scene with the rolls from *The Gold Rush*. *Ed. note*: Salles Gomes was, of course, writing in 1956, well before the habit of quotation became widespread in the films of Nouvelle Vague directors—most strikingly, perhaps, in Truffaut's *400 Coups*, which quoted heavily from *Zéro de Conduite*.
12. *A Travers la Jungle Politique et Littéraire*, Paris, Librairie Valois.
13. Jean Vigo Archives.
14. Studio Parnasse and Ciné-Club du Quartier Latin.
15. Alberto Cavalcanti in *Cinema Quarterly*, Winter 1934.
16. *Le Huron*, Paris, April 13, 1933.
17. April 19, 1933. In his column Pierre Ogouz also wrote: "Snotty kids, uncombed, noisy, sensitive, and pitiful, men of the day after tomorrow, potential Frenchmen because of their loquaciousness, their malice, their sensitivity, their lack of discipline. . . . We like this film in the same way that its makers like children: with our whole heart." However, he is no longer speaking about *Zéro de Conduite*, but about *La Maternelle*.
18. No. 231, April 20, 1933.
19. No 224, February 2, 1933.
20. No. 222, February 16, 1933.
21. *Le Spectateur Bellevillois*, no. 44, November 3, 1933.
22. *Présentation de Zéro de Conduite.*
23. *Pour Vous*, no. 234, May 11, 1933.
24. *Présentation de Zéro de Conduite.*
25. Original manuscript in the Jean Vigo Archives, in Claude Aveline's possession.
26. *Vooruit*, Ghent, October 27, 1933.
27. *Nieuws van den Dag*, October 27, 1933.
28. *La Libre Belgique*, October 20, 1933.
29. *XXᵉ Siècle*, October 20, 1933.
30. *La Libre Belgique*, October 27, 1933.
31. *Le Carrefour*, periodical of the cinema (Brussels), new series, no. 2, October 17, 1933.
32. *XXᵉ Siècle*, October 20, 1933.
33. *La Libre Belgique*, October 20, 1933, and *National Bruxellois*, October 22, 1933.
34. No. 7, November 1933.
35. *Nieuws van den Dag*, October 27, 1933.
36. *Vooruit*, October 27, 1933.
37. July 16, 1950.

4. L'Atalante
1. Storck's journal, April 1, 1933.
2. In the same issue of *Pour Vous* (April 20, 1933) in which a writer condemned *Zéro de Conduite*, appeared an interview with Mme. Exbrayat, the secretary of the Board of Censors, which was a veritable warning:

THE JOURNALIST:"If *I Am a Fugitive from a Chain Gang* were a French film, the action set in Guiana, do you feel that it would be permitted?"

MME. EXBRAYAT:"Probably not. The representative from the Ministry of Justice would be opposed to its showing."

3. Riéra, in a note to Vigo, tells of the conversation between Michel Simon and himself (*Positif*, no. 7, May 1953):

"Who is this Jean Vigo?"

"You know, in your dressing-room at the theat . . ."

"Oh! Yes, yes . . . very pleasant . . . he must be nice. . . . What has he done?"

"A film banned by the censors."

"Oh! Bravo! I'm delighted."

4. Mme. Margaritis, unpublished text, Gilles Margaritis Archives.

5. "Un cinéaste-né: Jean Vigo, l'auteur de *L'Atalante*," *Pour Vous*, no. 289, May 31, 1934.

6. The French entries were: *Le Grand Jeu, Le Paquebot Tenacity, Le Scandale, La Porteuse de Pain, Jeunesse, Bouboule, Le Roi Nègre, La Croisière Jaune, Amok*, and *L'Atalante*. We have left the titles of the films in the order in which they appeared in the contemporary press. Only the films by Feyder, Duvivier, Lacombe, and Ozep were ultimately shown in Venice.

7. *Le Matin*, September 14, 1934.

8. Clippings from an undated, unidentified newspaper in the Gilles Margaritis Archives.

9. Ibid.

10. "Une suite d'images réalistes en gros plan. Ceci n'est pas un spectacle de famille." *Le Figaro*, September 22, 1934.

11. *Le Petit Journal*, September 21, 1934.

12. *L' Œuvre*, September 21, 1934.

13. *Le Journal*, September 21, 1934.

14. *Le Petit Parisien*, September 21, 1934.

15. *Les Nouvelles Littéraires*, no. 624, September 29, 1934.

16. No. 305, September 1934.

17. No. 309, September 1934.

18. October 4, 1934.

5. Vigo's death

1. Unpublished text by Mme. Margaritis, given to the author by Gilles Margaritis.

2. Letter from Fernand Després to Pierre de Saint-Prix, September 27, 1934.

3. According to Storck's notes, taken on October 7, 1934.

4. Letter to Henri Storck, January 22, 1935.

5. Newspaper clipping given to the author by Gilles Margaritis.

6. "Jean Vigo tel qu'il était." Newspaper article given to the author by Gilles Margaritis.

7. *Intransigeant*, October 8, 1934.

8. *Comoedia*, October 7, 1934.

9. October 7, 1934.

10. *Pour Vous*, October 18, 1934.

11. Ibid., November 22, 1934.

12. "Le jeune cinéma français: Jean Vigo ou l'intelligence au cinéma."

13. *Le Rouge et le Noir*, Brussels, October 17, 1934.

14. *Avant-Garde*, Brussels, October 29, 1934.

15. October 19, 1934.

16. *Les Beaux-Arts*, Brussels, July 26, 1935.

17. Document shown the author by Henri Storck.

18. Letter of September 30, 1950.

19. *Ciné-Club*, no. 5, February 1949; and *New Index Series*, no. 4, British Film Institute, 1951. This is one of the many pictures taken by the photographers Parry and Tabard during filming. One must not forget that a good many of these photographs—such as the series of Dasté naked, or others of Michel Simon comfortably relaxing on a studio sofa, alone or accompanied by beautiful ladies—were not taken for publicity purposes, either as off-sets during filming or as scenes from the film.

20. Numbers 3 and 16 in the numbering used in 1950.
21. "The only possible criticism is that Vigo makes the coming together more sentimental than it need have been. The girl wanders overmuch on desolate bridges looking for the 'Atalante,' when any good proletarian would have had the sense to use the police."
22. *Cinema Quarterly*, Autumn 1934.
23. *Film Society Programme*, London, November 1934.
24. *Cinema Quarterly*, Winter 1935.
25. *National Zeitung*, Basle, February 1, 1940; *Hollywood Quarterly*, April 1947; *New Index Series*.
26. "Le Cinéma mourra-t-il une seconde fois?" *L' Œuvre*, October 31, 1940.
27. November 8, 1940.
28. *Le Petit Parisien*, November 6, 1940.
29. *Aujourd'hui*, November 10, 1940.
30. Jean de Saint-Prix as quoted by Romain Rolland in his preface to the *Lettres* of Jean de Saint-Prix.
31. Romain Rolland himself had shared this feeling. Referring to the imprisonment of the political writer E. D. Morel in London, he wrote on August 15, 1917: "I am convinced that this involves, on the part of all the countries of the Entente, a coordinated plan of accusations and defamations against the leaders of the pacifist movement. After Lenin, Grimm, and Almereyda, the first opportunity was seized to put the grabs on Morel." (*Journal des années de guerre, 1914–1918*, Paris, Albin Michel, 1952.)
32. Fernand Desprès died in Algiers in (?) 1948.
33. Letter to Pierre de Saint-Prix, August 20, 1926.
34. Letter to Pierre de Saint-Prix, February 8, 1927.
35. Letter to Pierre de Saint-Prix, February 3, 1930.
36. Letter to Pierre de Saint-Prix, October 5, 1934.
37. This "call to arms" was issued on the initiative of the surrealists, and was drawn up by André Breton, Paul Eluard, Benjamin Péret, and Louis Chavance. It was reprinted in the Belgian magazine *Documents: 1934*, n.s., no. 1, June 1934.

Appendix

1. *Samedi Soir*, November 17, 1945.
2. *Spectateur*, November 21, 1945.
3. *L'Ecran Français*, no. 22, November 28, 1945.
4. *Nouvelles du Matin*, November 25, 1945.
5. *Cosmos*, November 30, 1945.
6. *Opéra*, November 28, 1945.
7. *Paris-Presse*, November 17, 1945.
8. *Le Messager*, November 22, 1945.
9. *Le Parisien Libéré*, November 23, 1945.
10. *Marseillaise de Seine-et-Oise*, January 19, 1946.
11. *Cosmos* (interim), November 30, 1945.
12. *Spectateur*, December 15, 1945.
13. *Cité Soir*, December 20, 1945.
14. *Spectateur*, December 19, 1945.
15. *Dimanche-Pays*, December 9, 1945.
16. *République du Centre*, Orléans, April 11, 1946.
17. *Le Parisien Libéré*, November 23, 1945.
18. *Patriote de Saint-Etienne*, Loire, April 3, 1946.
19. *Volontés* (Louis Caro), December 5, 1945.
20. *Dimanche-Pays*, December 9, 1945.
21. *Spectateur*, December 19, 1945.
22. *Volontés*, December 5, 1945.
23. *Paris-Cinéma* (Jacques Loew), November 28, 1945.
24. *Opéra*, November 28, 1945.
25. *Gavroche* (P. F. Lacome), December 6, 1945.
26. *Libération-Soir* (A. Diard), December 5, 1945.

27. *Le Messager* (André Tabet), November 22, 1945.
28. *République du Centre*, Orléans, April 11, 1946.
29. *Spectateur*, December 19, 1945.
30. *L'Ecran Français* (Pierre Kast), October 31, 1945.
31. *Voix des Femmes* (Laurence Rousseau), Lyons, March 24, 1946.
32. *Courrier de Paris* (Carlo Rim), December 4, 1945.
33. *Paris-Presse* (Bernard Zimmer), November 17, 1945.
34. *Dimanche-Pays* (Captain Blood), December 9, 1945.
35. *Courrier de Paris* (Carlo Rim), December 4, 1945.
36. *Minerve*, December 7, 1945.
37. The idea of banning had become so closely associated with *Zéro de Conduite* that people often forgot that the ban had been lifted in 1945. Towards the end of 1951 *L'Observateur* and *L'Ecran Français* referred to *Zéro de Conduite* as a banned film.
38. *Franc-Tireur*, March 17, 1950.
39. Notably in the exhibition "Le Cinéma Français, 1895–1945," organized by the Union des Etudiants d'Art and the Ciné-Club Universitaire, and held at the Place de la Sorbonne.
40. *Tigre*, Montpellier, February 8, 1946.
41. *Toutes les Nouvelles de Versailles*, October 28, 1948.
42. *Journal du Pas-de-Calais*, February 11, 1948.
43. *Dauphiné libéré*, Grenoble, March 14, 1950.
44. *Positif*, Lyon, June 1952.
45. *Afrique*, Casablanca, March 10, 1946.
46. Glauco Viazzi, "Omaggio a Jean Vigo," *Rivista Ferrania*, Milan, April 1947.
47. Joseph and Harry Feldman, *Jean Vigo*, New Index Series, no. 4, British Film Institute, London, 1951.
48. Jacques Melot Publishers.
49. Having made this view public, I subsequently received the following rectification from M. Sadoul: "I saw none of Vigo's films in the thirties (during the last years of his life) because I had more or less stopped being interested in the cinema between 1926 and 1934. I must have seen *Nice* and *Zéro de Conduite* in 1938 or 1939 at the Cinémathèque—quite late therefore—but I have a much more vivid memory of seeing them again after 1945, and that determined my attitude much more than my rather vague impressions dating from the end of the thirties." (Letter of June 1, 1953.)
50. *Bianco e Nero*; *Penguin Film Review*.
51. Vol. 2, no. 5, February 1949.
52. By Claude Souef.
53. Claude Aveline.
54. Ibid.
55. *Raccords*, no. 7, 1951.
56. Jean-Paul Marquet, "D'un Duvivier à Jean Vigo," *Positif*, no. 2, June 1952.
57. No. 7, May 1953.
58. *Le Quotidien*, Brussels, April 5, 1946.
59. Penguin Books, Harmondsworth.
60. *Experiment in the Film*, London, The Grey Walls Press (no date).
61. *Film*; *Experiment in the Film*.
62. Henri Storck and P. E. Salles Gomes, "Nought for Behaviour," *Cinema, 1951*, Penguin Books, Harmondsworth.
63. February 1951.
64. London, George Allen & Unwin, 1948.
65. No. 4, compiled by Joseph and Harry Feldman and edited by Herman Weinberg.
66. Winter 1948.
67. July 5, 1947.
68. April 1947, with an introduction by Vladimir Pozner; and Winter 1947.
69. Cavalcanti: "Vigo inherited the strength and energy of these men. He belonged to the vigorous and carefree type of Pyrenean mountains. He had the sense of scale, the feeling for the contrast between great and small, which belongs to those who come from little isolated countries."
Zilzer: "Vigo inherited the strength and energy of his forefathers and the carefreeness of the

mountaineers of the Pyrenees. He had a sense of contrast between great and small, and the feeling of isolation and helpfulness that belongs to those coming from small isolated mountain communities."

70. August 1947.

71. July 5 and 12, 1947; reprinted in the *New Index Series*, no. 4, and in James Agee, *Agee on Film: Reviews and Comments*.

72. Winter 1948: reprinted in the New Index Series, no. 4.

73. *Cinetempo*, "Rassegna settimanale del Cinema," vol. 1, no. 13, December 6, 1945.

74. Ibid.

75. "50 anni di Cinema, 1895–1945. Film festival commemorating the first fifty years of the cinema, under the patronage of the city of Milan, a benefit for the Cineteca Italiana." Super-cinema Alcione, March 27 to April 13, 1946. A screening of *L'Atalante* on the same bill as *Zéro de Conduite* had been announced, but the print did not arrive on time.

76. Article by Luigi Comencini in *Riscatto*, Milan, April 18, 1946.

77. Article by Piero Gadda Conti in *Lunedì del Popolo*, Milan, April 15, 1946.

78. *Film d'Oggi*, May 15, 1946.

79. Article signed D. F. in *La Libertà*, Milan, April 9, 1946.

80. Article signed Vice in *Riscatto*, Milan, April 11, 1946.

81. *L'Italia del Popolo*, Milan, April 9, 1946.

82. "Un festival per il cinquantenario del Cinema," *Costume*, Milan, March–April 1946.

83. The first article was in *La Verità*, Milan, vol. 2, no. 10, April 22, 1946; the second, under the pseudonym of Guido Cenni and called "Un Regista anarchico," was in the first issue of *Gioventù Anarchica*, July 20, 1946. Except for a different title and a new introduction, the second article is exactly the same as that published in *La Verità*.

84. *L'Avanti*, Milan, May 29, 1946.

85. For details, see Panfilo Colaprete, *Jean Vigo*, Florence, ciné-club Controcampo, vol. I, May 1952.

86. "Omaggio a Jean Vigo," *Ferrania*, Milan, vol. 1, no. 4, April 1947.

87. "A Proposito di Jean Vigo," *Bianco e Nero*, vol. 10, no. 3, March 1949.

88. In this exposition of Viazzi's ideas, those parts which are not direct quotations are paraphrases of his words.

89. Viazzi had not seen *A Propos de Nice*, and the brief discussion of it was based on what other critics had said. His impression—on the whole justified—is that the film is part of the same development which led to *Zéro de Conduite* and *L'Atalante*. As for *Taris*, Viazzi was only acquainted with the final sequence, and lack of information kept him from discussing the film. But here again, when he refers to the film as an "intermezzo" in Vigo's development, he comes quite close to the truth.

90. Here we were mistaken. Glauco Viazzi had not yet read that issue of *Ciné-Club* when he wrote his essay. When this material on Viazzi was published in the form of an article, the author of "A Proposito di Jean Vigo" replied by writing "Ancora a proposito di Jean Vigo" (*Rivista del Cinema Italiano*, no. 9, September 1953).

91. No one is included on this list whose work dates from after 1939. Films produced under the Occupation and immediately afterwards up to the present, are not yet distant enough for their permanent value to be determined. The devaluation of Carné's films from the thirties (and even those of Feyder, not to mention Duvivier) is an indication of how prudent one must be. The fact that most of Gance's films, and a good number of Renoir's, are not worth much—with reference to their permanent value—does not alter the fact that directors notable for such peaks as *Napoléon* and *La Règle du Jeu* should be on the list. Moreover, it is not inconceivable that certain film-makers whose names would not be considered for the list have produced a film which merits particular attention: *Angèle*, for instance.

92. *Histoire d'un Art: le Cinéma*, p. 266.

93. New Index Series.

Filmography

A Propos de Nice (1929)
Production Company ⎫
Producer ⎪
Director ⎬ Jean Vigo
Script ⎪
Editor ⎭
Director of Photography   Boris Kaufman
Filmed on location in Nice. First shown in Paris, May 28, 1930.

Taris (1931)
Production Company   Gaumont-Franco-Film-Aubert
Executive Producer   C. Morskoï
Producer ⎫
Director ⎪
Script ⎬ Jean Vigo
Editor ⎭
Assistant Director   Ary Sadoul
Director of Photography   Boris Kaufman
Filmed at the swimming-pool of the Automobile Club de France, and at the G. F. F. A. Studios in Paris.
(Alternative titles: *Jean Taris, champion de natation*; *Taris, roi de l'eau*.)

Zéro de Conduite (1933)
Production Company   Argui-Films
Executive Producer   Jacques-Louis Nounez

Producer	
Director	
Script	Jean Vigo
Editor	

Assistant Directors	Albert Riéra, Henri Storck, Pierre Merle
Director of Photography	Boris Kaufman
Camera Assistant	Louis Berger
Art Directors	Jean Vigo, Henri Storck, Boris Kaufman
Music	Maurice Jaubert
Songs	Maurice Jaubert, Charles Goldblatt
Sound	Royne, Bocquel

Louis Lefèvre (*Caussat*), Gilbert Pluchon (*Colin*), Gérard de Bédarieux (*Tabard*), Constantin Goldstein-Kehler (*Bruel*), Jean Dasté (*Huguet*), Robert Le Flon (*M. Parrain, known as Dry-Fart*), Delphin (*The Principal*), Du Verron [Blanchar] (*M. Santt, known as Gas-Snout*), Léon Larive (*The Chemistry Professor*), Georges Berger (*The Guardian*), Louis de Gonzague-Frick (*The Prefect*), Henri Storck (*The Curé*), Michèle Fayard (*The Guardian's Daughter*), Félix Labisse (*1st Fireman*), Georges Patin (*2nd Fireman*), Raphaël Diligent (*3rd Fireman*), Georges Vakalo (*4th Fireman*), Mme. Emile (*Mother Beans*), Albert Riéra (*Nightwatchman*), Georges Belmer, Natale Bencini, Leonello Bencini, Emile Boulez, Maurice Cariel, Jean-Pierre Dumesnil, Igor Goldfarb, Lucien Lincks, Charles Michiels, Roger Porte, Jacques Poulin, Pierre Regnoux, Ali Ronchy, Georges Rougette, André Thille, Pierre Tridon, Paul Vilhem (*The Boys*).

Filmed at the G. F. F. A. Studios in Paris, and on location at Saint-Cloud and at Belleville-la-Villette railway station, December 24, 1932–January 22, 1933. First shown in Paris, April 7, 1933; banned in France; first public performance in Paris, November 1945.

L'Atalante (1934)

Production Company	Argui-Films
Executive Producer	Jacques-Louis Nounez
Producer	
Director	Jean Vigo
Assistant Directors	Albert Riéra, Charles Goldblatt, Pierre Merle
Script	Jean Vigo, Albert Riéra. Based on an original scenario by Jean Guinée [R. de Guichen]
Director of Photography	Boris Kaufman
Camera Assistants	Louis Berger, Jean-Paul Alphen
Editor	Louis Chavance
Art Director	Francis Jourdain
Music	Maurice Jaubert
Songs	Maurice Jaubert, Charles Goldblatt

Michel Simon (*Père Jules*), Jean Dasté (*Jean*), Dita Parlo (*Juliette*), Gilles Margaritis (*The Pedlar*), Louis Lefèvre (*The Cabin Boy*), Fanny Clar (*Juliette's Mother*), Raphaël Diligent (*Juliette's Father*), Charles Goldblatt (*The Thief*), René Bleck (*The Best Man*), Gen Paul (*Guest with Limp*), Jacques Prévert, Pierre Prévert, Loutchimoukov.

Filmed at the G. F. F. A. Studios in Paris, and on location at Conflans-Saint-Honorine, Maurecourt, Paris, and on various canals, November 15, 1933–end of February 1934. First shown in Paris, April 25, 1934; first public performance (as *Le Chaland qui passe*) September 13, 1934; first public performance of *L'Atalante* in Paris, October 30, 1940.

Vigo's Unrealized Projects

Le Tennis (or *Cochet*) (script by Vigo, Albert Riéra)

Anneaux (script by Henri Poulaille, Serge Choubine)

La Camargue (script by Vigo, Albert Riéra, from an idea by Jacques-Louis Nounez)

Le Bagne (or *L'Evadé du Bagne*) (script by Eugène Dieudonné and Julot Dupont; based on writings by Albert Londres about the Dieudonné affair)

Le Métro (script by Vigo)

Clown par amour (adaptation of a novel by Georges de la Fouchardière)

Lourdes (script by Vigo)

Au Café (script by Vigo)

Lignes de la Main (script by Vigo)

Chauvinisme (script by Vigo)

L'Exécution de Marinèche (script by Claude Aveline, from his own novel *Le Point du Jour*)

Le Timide qui prend feu (script by Claude Aveline)

La Double Mort de Frédéric Belot (adaptation of a novel by Claude Aveline)

Contrebandiers (script by Blaise Cendrars)

La Revanche des Eaux (script by Georges Charensol)

La Boîte à Surprises (script by Paul Gilson)

La Déesse (script by Félix Labisse)

L'Affaire Peau de Balle (adaptation from a novel by Georges de la Fouchardière)

Matinée (script by Léon Lévy, Henri Storck)

L'Honnête Homme (script by Jacques-Louis Nounez)

Café du Bon Accueil (script by Jean Painlevé)

L'Inventeur (script by Albert Riéra, René Lefèvre)

L'Affaire Saint Fiacre (adaptation from a novel by Georges Simenon)

Evariste (script by Henri Storck)

Si on pariait (script by Jules Supervielle)

Le Pensionnat sur le Toit (script by Henri-Pierre Roché)

The world of Almereyda: the police lay siege to Jules Bonnot, the anarchist gang-leader who terrorized France in 1911

251

Index

Index

254

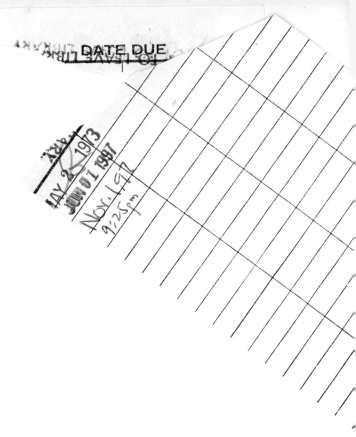